Gorilla Guides
Travel handbooks for the business jungle

RUSSIA

First American edition published in 2009 by
INTERLINK TRAVEL
An imprint of Interlink Publishing Group, Inc.
46 Crosby Street
Northampton, Massachusetts 01060
www.interlinkbooks.com

ISBN: 978-1-56656-776-3

Series originator: Max Scott
Series editor: Christopher Ind
Assistant editor: Charles Powell
Design: Nimbus Design
Photography: © RIA Novosti Photo Library
   www.visualrian.com
Cartography: Amber Sheers
Printing: Oriental Press, UAE

Opposite:
Moscow International Business Centre, better known as
Moscow City, will one day boast the world's second tallest
building. The complex is expected to be complete by 2020.

Russia

The Business Traveller's Handbook

Chris Gilbert

A bronze statue atop St Petersburg's Winter Palace, its surface corroded to malachite green, looks north-west as evening falls across Vasilievsky Island.

A bust of the poet Vladimir Mayakovsky broods at passengers entering the Moscow metro station which bears his name. The system carries more than twice the population of China every year.

Dmitry Medvedev, Russia's president since May 2008, visits the Motherland Calls monument, built in the 1960s to commemorate the Battle of Stalingrad. The monument's sword alone is 100ft long.

Opened in 2008, the Sheremetyevo Express now whisks passengers from the centre of Moscow to the capital's principal airport in just over half an hour.

A priest re-consecrates the spire of the Peter and Paul Cathedral in St Petersburg. The spire is the city's highest point, and will remain so until the completion of Gazprom's new HQ upriver in 2012.

A young pioneer marches along the walls of Moscow's Kremlin. The fortress was originally built as a wooden fortification in 1156.

A generating turbine undergoes balancing at the Silovye Mashiny (Power Machines) plant in St Petersburg.

Acknowledgements

The author would like to express his thanks to Margaret Rowse and Barry Martin at The Russia House, and Gary at O'Grady Air Services for their valuable assistance in preparing the sections on visa requirements and customs procedures.

Chris Gilbert
November 2008

Contents

Foreword

In recent years, the positive development of the Russian economy has attracted the attention of more and more international companies.

The experienced businessman knows how vital thorough preparation is when approaching any potential market. In this regard, the guide you are now holding is undoubtedly of great use. Russia boasts the largest territory of any country in the world, accompanied by a regional variety that is unique. Practically all Russia's regions have their own rich historical traditions of entrepreneurship, something of which we are justly proud.

The Chamber of Commerce and Industry of the Russian Federation has a long history of providing assistance to international companies at every stage of development of their business in Russia. With a network of 173 territorial chambers covering the entire nation, we stand ready to offer help, advice and information to companies of all sizes.

There is no doubt that this business handbook, part of the widely-known Gorilla Guides series, will become an important resource of information for business professionals planning their business strategies in Russia.

I wish you all success in developing your working partnership with this country, may your business and good fortune flourish.

Evgeny Primakov
Academician of the Russian Academy of Sciences
President of the Chamber of Commerce and Industry
of the Russian Federation

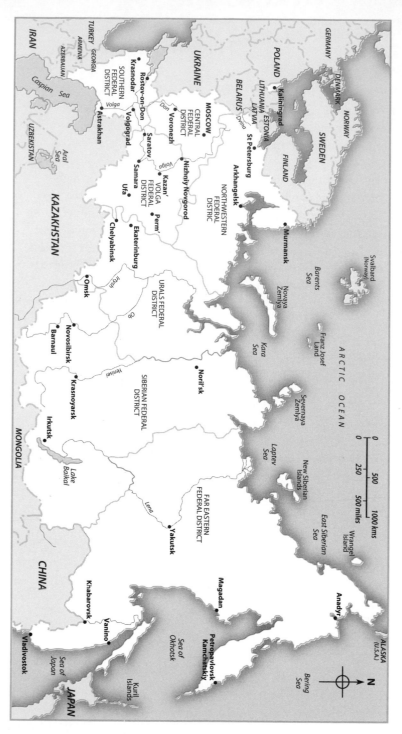

Russia

Russia yesterday and today

Russia yesterday and today

A bird's-eye view of the nation,
its history and the special features
that distinguish it from other countries

A condensed history

The modern country

Overview of a nation
Geography

Occupying a little over 17 million square kilometres, spanning 11 time-zones, and dominating the Eurasian landmass, the Russian Federation is almost unimaginably vast. Around twice the size of Canada, the United States or China, Russia's closest rival in area is the continent of Antarctica. The European Union, even in its recently expanded form, would fit into Russia four times over.

Geographically, Russia is certainly not the homogenous expanse of forest and rolling plains that you might have in your mind's eye when you look at it on the map. Abandoned unprepared in Russia's vast interior, you could find yourself battling heatstroke in the wastes of Central Asia, altitude sickness in the Altai mountains, or (if you were really unfortunate) the world's most fearsome big cat in the primeval forests of Russia's Far East. On the other hand, you could just as easily be paddling in the balmy waters of the Black Sea, strolling through a subtropical tea plantation, or hiking along the shores of Baikal, the world's largest and most ancient freshwater lake.

From west to east, Russia begins in the gently undulating steppe and forest of the East European plain, which stretches between the Baltic and Black Seas, and extends unbroken to the Ural Mountains. To call the Urals "mountains" is a slight exaggeration – the range's loftiest peak, Narodnaya, is comprehensively outdone by even a fairly average Alp at 1,895m. At this point, European Russia doesn't so much end as fizzle out. If you travel in a straight line from Russia's westernmost point along 55° north, by the time you have cleared the Urals you will have covered well over 2,000km, with almost three quarters of Russia's population in your wake, and only two cities lying ahead that are home to more than a million people. You will also still be only around a quarter of the way to Russia's Pacific seaboard, for before you lies the vast Siberian plain, dwarfing even the expanses of European Russia – nearly four fifths of the Russian Federation's territory lies east of the Urals.

From top to bottom, geographically Russia takes the form of a series of horizontal bands. North of the

Russia from west to east

Russia from north to south

tree-line, the landscape is stark tundra – here the soil is permanently frozen to within around a metre of the surface, inhibiting the growth of anything more ambitious than moss or lichen. Next comes the taiga, a belt of coniferous forest stretching clear around the planet through Russia, Canada and Scandinavia. The taiga is Earth's largest biome, or single ecosystem, many times larger than the rainforests, and so broad at times that it touches the northern states of the US and even parts of Kazakhstan.

South of the taiga roll the endless grasslands of the steppe, the most temperate of Russia's climatic zones, and by far the most developed and populated. Yet even here the Russian concept of "temperate" will come as a shock to those of us used to gentler climes: for the most part, far from the mollifying influence of the sea, the steppe experiences hot, arid summers and cold – sometimes brutally cold – winters.

Latitude For comparison, consider this: Moscow lies south of Edinburgh, a city itself not known for its balmy winters, by less than a quarter of one degree. When did you last hear about people battling along Princes Street through temperatures of -35°C and lower? And the deeper you travel into Russia's interior, the more extreme the conditions you will find: Irkutsk, in southern Siberia, is on the same latitude as Amsterdam and London, yet regularly records January temperatures of -45°C. If, as I hope, you become a regular visitor to Russia, you may well encounter this kind of temperature, but don't panic, or put this book back on the shelf if you have read this far, casting around either side for a less risky destination, like maybe Qatar, or Rwanda. In a later chapter there will be advice on how to cope with what the Russians call a Real Winter, and if you are flicking through this section in your local bookstore in Ottawa or Minneapolis – relax, you're going to feel right at home.

At the southern edge of the steppe, Russia reaches the shores of the Black Sea. This is the Krasnodar Krai, home to the afore-mentioned tea plantations, and to the former apparatchiks' playground of Sochi, host city of the 2014 Winter Olympics. Krasnodar Krai stretches to the

1

western edge of the Caucasus, the mountain barrier separating Europe from Asia. A league apart from the Urals, the Russian Caucasus boasts Europe's highest peak, Mount Elbrus, standing nearly a full kilometre higher than Mont Blanc at just over 5,600m. One of the most dramatically beautiful regions on earth, the Caucasus is probably best known as an area of bitter memories, territorial dispute and simmering political and ethnic tension.

Moving east, you will come to the Caspian Sea, the planet's largest landlocked body of water. More a lake than a true sea, the Caspian's salinity is less than one third of that of the world's oceans, 90% of its inflow is made up by the Volga and Ural rivers on its northern shore, and its only outlet is by evaporation. So shallow in some of its northernmost reaches that you can still see the sea-bed just a couple of metres beneath your feet when you are many miles out from the shore, it is the Caspian's hidden depths which have brought it to the fore in recent years. Beneath its bed lie some of the world's largest deposits of oil and natural gas, recently estimated at anywhere between 17 and 49 billion barrels, and a staggering 232 *trillion* cubic feet respectively. Only a small fraction of these reserves lie within Russian territory, but the Caspian as a whole will remain a key part of the global energy equation for many years to come.

The Caspian Sea

On your eastward journey from the Caspian you will be forced north again into the steppe, skirting the borders first of Kazakhstan, then Mongolia, and finally China as you sweep back down into the Primorsky Krai, which curls like an end-bracket around Manchuria. An area of immense natural diversity, the Primorsky Krai makes up less than one per cent of Russia's total area, yet contains more than half of the bird species of the entire former USSR, as well as the largest living big cat, the Amur (or Siberian) tiger.

A particularly determined traveller can now continue north for many more thousands of kilometres with the Sea of Japan to the east and the vastness of Siberia to the west. Just across the horizon is the island of Sakhalin, a former penal colony nearly equalling Britain in length.

1

Anton Chekhov spent time here when he was still working as a doctor, writing to a friend on his return, "I was in hell, represented by Sakhalin, and in heaven, that is on the island of Ceylon." Today Sakhalin is better known as a place of seemingly endless, if hard-to-get-at, mineral wealth, with recent estimates putting its reserves of oil and gas at around 7 billion barrels and 80 trillion cubic feet respectively. Further north, the Sea of Japan gives way to the Sea of Okhotsk, where if you follow the shore all the way you will reach the Bering Straits, where Siberia and the former Russian territory of Alaska face each other across just under a hundred kilometres of frigid water.

The great rivers

Moving back inland, both the European and Asian portions of Russia are drained by some of the world's mightiest rivers. West of the Urals, the largest of them all is the Volga, the longest river in Europe, almost as long as the Rhine and Danube combined. On its meandering 3,700km journey from the Valdai Hills north-west of Moscow to its mouth at Astrakhan, the Volga drains an area slightly smaller than Mongolia, discharging 8,000 tonnes of water into the Caspian Sea each second. Yet even the Volga pales in comparison to the river systems that lay further east. The Irtysh, the Ob, the Yenisei, and the Lena are all larger still, in terms of the volume of water they bear if not distance alone. The Yenisei, the world's fifth longest river, bears the rainfall of a fifth of Siberia – four times as great as that borne by the Nile – north to the Kara Sea in the Arctic. Yet by a fateful twist of geography, all four of Siberia's great rivers flow north, to the Arctic Ocean, meaning that, unlike elsewhere in the world where river systems have historically opened up land for settlement, these giants wind much of their lonely courses through areas wholly unmolested by human activity – voluntary activity, at least.

The beginnings of Russia

Earliest history

West of the Urals, the river systems of European Russia were much more of a catalyst to the expansion of human activity. Linked together by portages, they formed one of the most important trading routes of early Europe, linking Byzantium with Scandinavia – "the way from the Varangians to the Greeks". A territory with this kind of built-in infrastructure was bound to be colonised quickly: the ethnic forebears of modern Russians first made their mark around the 6th and 7th centuries AD, but they were no more the first to arrive on the scene than were the Anglo Saxons in England.

Russia's original settlers arrived as part of the mass human expansion across Europe from the Middle East, which began around 7000 BC. Beginning in the first millennium BC, a whole series of tribes, among them Sarmatians, Huns, Goths, Avars and Khazars, followed the trail blazed by the first distinct ethnic group to arrive, the Scythians. Nomadic herdsmen originally of Iranian descent, the Scythians are mentioned in the historical accounts of Herodotus and Arran, and throughout Antiquity much of southern Russia and Ukraine was known as Scythia. In point of fact, the Scythians were quickly supplanted by their ethnic cousins, the Sarmatians, but such was their impact that the name was applied to any inhabitants of the steppe-lands between the Black Sea and the Caspian. Even the Huns were termed Scythians by Byzantium's emissary to Attila, Priscus, centuries after they had quit the stage.

Early settlers

With the passing centuries, the transition from a hunter-gatherer existence to an agricultural way of life handed advantage to more sedentary peoples, and the Slavs emerged to dominate the lands east of the Danube. The Slavs are traditionally divided into three groups: the Western Slavs are the Czechs, the Poles and the Slovaks; the Southern Slavs are the Serbs, the Croats, the Slovenians, the Macedonians, and the Bulgarians; the people of Russia, Belarus and Ukraine are, ethno-linguistically speaking at least, the Eastern Slavs. Whence the Slavs emerged onto the stage of history remains a matter of conjecture. We tend to expect a convenient diagram with arrows showing how and when people arrived in a given part of the world, and where they came from. The reality is that it is almost impossible to reconstruct the arrival of ethnic groups unless they make a lot of pottery and drop it in handily placed middens for archaeologists to find later. What we can say about the ancestors of modern Russians is that, at some point early on in the second half of the first millennium AD, they were there, and there to stay.

The rise of the Slavs

Kiev Rus'

Located along a key trading route, and with immense animal, mineral and vegetable riches at their disposal, any early Russians not tilling the land were buying and selling anything they could lay their hands on: furs, honey, timber, flax. What the early Slavs lacked was political cohesion, leaving their rich lands open to attack from outside. For the early part of their existence they were under the rule of the Khazars, a Turkic people who had converted to Judaism. The "Khazar conquest" was not accompanied by the brutality of Attila who came before, or Genghis Khan who was to come after – as long as the Slavs paid regular tribute, they were pretty much left in peace. Nevertheless, the fragmented nature of the Eastern Slav lands hindered further development: their settlements were spread out in small trading posts and towns, variously estimated at anywhere between 300 and 600. To the Varangian traders in the north, the area was known as *gaardaríki*, the "kingdom of the towns".

The Kingdom of the Towns

Towns – yes, but no king. Incessant strife prevailed as disparate fiefdoms attempted to seize territory from one another. According to the Primary Chronicle, the Eastern Slav's first written account of their own history, the solution came in the form of an appeal to the Varangians, to bring order and "rule as princes" over them. Readily accepting, in 862 Rurik, chieftain of the Rus' group of Varangians, seized Novgorod, one of Russia's oldest surviving cities (although the name literally translates as "New Town"). Following Rurik's death in 879, his successor Oleg continued the campaign south along the trading route, taking Kiev in 882 and making it his new capital. Kiev Rus', the precursor to the modern Russian state, was on the map.

Rurik

As with the Norman Conquest of England a couple of hundred years later, the conquerors were soon culturally absorbed by the more numerous vanquished, and Oleg's successor, Igor, was to give his first son, born in 942, a Slav name – Svyatoslav. Still a true Viking by inclination, if not by name, on ascending to the Kiev throne Svyatoslav immediately applied himself to the task of further conquest and expansion, leaving domestic matters to his mother. Having finally thrown off the Khazar yoke, he came to grief only on his return to Kiev, when his forces were overwhelmed by nomadic Pecheneg tribesmen at the Dnieper cataracts. His skull was reputedly made into a drinking cup for a Pecheneg prince.

Svyatoslav's death sparked off a period of internecine bloodletting back in Kiev, with his illegitimate son Vladimir ultimately victorious. Vladimir I's priority was to unify the state, and he began by putting out to tender for a state religion. Having examined proposals from Jewish, Muslim and Christian delegations, he settled on Orthodox Christianity, no doubt with an eye to the impact his decision would have on trading relations with Byzantium. The reign of Vladimir the Great, as he was to become known, marked the end of the early, pagan period of development of the Eastern Slavs. His son, Yaroslav the Wise, was determined to make Kiev into a Slav Constantinople, and met with some success: a German chronicler of the time wrote of Kiev that it was "the fairest jewel in all the Greek [*sic*] world".

Vladimir the Great

However, all the churches in the world – and Kiev at this point had around 400 – could not make up for the deep-set fissures in the fabric of the state, and Yaroslav's death in 1054 led to yet further successional strife. By the end of the 11th century, Kievan Rus' had fragmented into twelve separate principalities, and the next century brought little improvement. In 1169, Andrei Bogolyubsky sacked Kiev and transferred the capital to Vladimir, 150 miles east of Moscow. But Vladimir's self-appointed status lent it no more influence over the rest of the state than had Kiev's – just as 300 years before, Rus' lay in disorder, supine in the face of an invader. And the next chieftain wasn't the kind to wait for an invitation.

The Tatar-Mongol Yoke

It was said that the smell of burning reached you even before the sound of thundering hooves. Genghis Khan's hordes, "soldiers of the Antichrist come to reap the last dreadful harvest" in the words of a contemporary chronicler, swept across Europe in a horse-mounted blitzkrieg which abated only when it reached Poland. As with the Khazars, the Horde ruled by exacting tribute, although they were much more hands-on than their Turkic predecessors should anyone get behind with the payments. Russia was to lie under the Tatar-Mongol Yoke for nearly two and a half centuries, and the vassal princes were just as brutal with their subjects as were their Mongol masters. The influence of this period can still be found in the modern Russian language: *poshlina* ("toll"), *tovary* ("goods"), even *den'gi* ("money") are all of Tatar origin, as are many of the most commonly used Russian swear-words.

The rise of Muscovy

Muscovy

Of all the Russian principalities, the Horde's favourite must surely have been Moscow. A provincial town situated on an unremarkable river, and less than a hundred years old, Moscow was more assiduous than any in collecting and paying both tribute and homage to its rulers from the east. Moscow's princes even fought on the side of the Mongols in suppressing their neighbours, and in return the city gradually gained more freedom and power. The principality of Muscovy, as it became known, was happy to prosper, and to bide its time.

Ivan the Great

Muscovy princes came and went, some even attempting to throw off the dominance of the Mongols. Most notable among these was Grand Prince Dmitry Donskoy, who scored a first victory over the occupiers at the Battle of Kulikovo in 1380. But it was to Dmitry's great grandson, Ivan III (Ivan the Great) that the opportunity fell exactly a century later to break the stranglehold once and for all. Having already made himself unpopular with the Golden Horde for withholding tribute, in a fit of rage Ivan put several of its envoys to death, and trampled on a portrait of Ahmed Khan, the horde's leader. This was an unforgivable slight: determined to teach the impudent prince a lesson, the Khan immediately marched on Moscow, encountering, much to his chagrin, a well-equipped army waiting for him on the west bank of the River Ugra, 150 miles south west of the city. What happened next was one of military history's great non-events: as the two armies stared at each other from opposite banks, the Ugra began to freeze – a clash of arms appeared inevitable. With that, both armies simultaneously turned and fled. The reasons soon became clear – both sides were worried about attack from other

1

forces to their rear, but the spell had been broken. The Mongols were not invincible, and more importantly for the future, Muscovy had emerged as the dominant force in the Russian lands.

Ivan the Terrible

Ivan was just three when his father died, and during his minority, with his mother as regent, he observed at first hand the corruption and intrigue that surrounded the court. By the time of his coronation as tsar in 1547 (Ivan was the first to use this title, taken from the Latin "Caesar") he had already fostered an intense distrust and hatred of the boyars. Before he could deal with them, however, he had first to quell the final pockets of Tatar-Mongol influence at the south eastern edge of his dominions. In 1552, the Khanate of Kazan' fell to Ivan's troops, Astrakhan four years later. The Crimean Tatars proved more resilient, laying siege to Moscow twenty years later, and forcing Ivan to briefly relocate his government to Yaroslavl. In a brutal campaign, they were finally driven back to the peninsular, where they were left to their own devices, by now a spent force. Their conquest was completed some 200 years later by Catherine the Great, who simply placed posters around Crimea welcoming them as her subjects.

The yoke is lifted

The descendants of Genghis Khan now largely out of the picture, Ivan turned his attention to the boyars. His pursuit was relentless, alternately whittling away at their privileges and increasing the level of duty they owed to the state. At the same time, Ivan established and actively promoted a separate landed class, the *pomeshchiki*, who were granted privileges in return for service. Ivan thus created a *de facto* service state, with each level of society owing a debt of service to the level above. Ivan's repression of the boyars was not restricted to legislative manoeuvrings, however: he also created Russia's first internal state security force, the *oprichniki*, a black-clad army which unleashed a reign of terror throughout the realm, including the sacking of Novgorod in 1570 with the deaths of 60,000.

Notorious for his ruthlessness and cruelty at home, Ivan was keen to make friends elsewhere. Muscovy remained cut off from trade with the rest of Europe by hostile neighbours (Sweden, Livonia and Poland-Lithuania), and in 1553 a potential solution presented itself. It took the form of a group of shipwrecked English merchants led by Richard Chancellor, who had seen their attempt to find a northern passage to the markets of the east founder, literally, when their fleet made inadvertent landfall near Archangelsk. Making the best of things, they unloaded the goods from the one vessel left afloat (the aptly named *Bona Fortuna*) and set off for Moscow, for no reason other than that it was the nearest major city. Ivan welcomed Chancellor with open arms, beginning a close English-Russian trade relationship which was to last throughout his reign, culminating even in the tsar's proposal of marriage to Queen Elizabeth.

The Birth of Anglo Russian Trade

Another way to establish a trade route, of course, was by force, and several attempts were made to break through to the Baltic Sea during Ivan's reign. His campaigns were ultimately fruitless, however – in 1582, he was forced to concede defeat, with nothing to show for decades of war. That same year, Ivan's attempts to create a monarchic power structure in Russia were also undone when he killed his eldest son in a fit of rage. Although Ivan's death two years later did not instantly trigger a succession crisis, his younger son Fyodor was simply not fit to rule. Weak in both body and in mind, the new Tsar, whose main hobby was bell-ringing, was no match for a scheming gentry eager to reassert their power now that their nemesis was gone. It was an ignominious end to the 700-year dynasty of Rurik. Fyodor was hurriedly replaced by his uncle Nikitin Romanov, but the latter died in 1586, to be replaced in turn by Fyodor's brother-in-law, Boris Godunov.

The end of the Rurik Dynasty

The Time of Troubles

Godunov continued Ivan's promotion of the *pomeshchiki* at the expense of the boyars, and pressed on to extend Russia's frontiers. He even met with some success in re-taking the territory surrendered to the Swedes and Livonians, but these were to be his only victories. Godunov's regency marked the beginning of the Time of Troubles, a period of famine, invasion, and even a series of pretenders to the throne. All of the latter claimed to be Dmitry, Ivan the Terrible's son by his seventh wife, who had in fact been murdered in 1591 at the age of only nine, with the widely suspected involvement of Godunov himself. The circumstances surrounding the boy's death were so vague that many were ready to believe in this miraculous resurrection of the Rurik line, and three pretenders appeared between 1605 and 1612, although they met with little success. The first "Dmitry", whose true origin was never established, came to a particularly spectacular end when his erstwhile supporters, the boyars, turned on him. His charred remains were loaded into a cannon and fired towards Poland, whence he had led his liberating army.

The False Dmitries

The Beginnings of the Romanov Dynasty

The question of who would rule Russia was finally solved in 1613, when the Zemsky Sobor, a feudal parliament originally created by Ivan the Terrible, gathered to elect the next tsar. Their choice fell on Mikhail Romanov, a compromise candidate whose family had managed to alienate relatively few people during the Troubles. Inheriting a country ravaged by famine, war and poverty, his only consolation was that the boyars had intrigued among themselves to such an extent over the preceding decades that they had ceased to be a cohesive threat.

Peasant rebellions

Much more danger was to come from those who worked the land, rather than owned it. The epic suffering which Russia's peasantry had endured for centuries found its outlet in a series of uprisings over the next centuries, beginning with those of the Don Cossacks Stenka Razin in 1670 and Pugachev just over 100 years later and, it could be argued, culminating in the Bolshevik Revolution of 1917. Still Russia remained politically, economically and culturally backward, and it was Mikhail's great grandson Peter, crowned tsar when he was still only ten years old, who was to dedicate his entire reign to building a modern nation state.

Russia under Peter the Great

Peter the Great, like Ivan the Terrible before him, had ample opportunity in his youth to witness the chaos of the Russian court during a succession crisis. Sidelined during the brief reign of his half-brother Fyodor, Peter returned to the Kremlin in 1682 to find it in revolt, and observed (calmly, it is said) the deaths of many of his family at the hands of the *streltsy*, an elite part-time army created during the reign of Ivan the Terrible. Under the cobbled-together regency of his half-sister Natalia, Peter spent his teenage years away from the Kremlin, and embarked on a grand tour of Europe once power was fully his in 1696. The first tsar ever to travel beyond his own borders, Peter's eighteen month journey took him to Latvia, Germany, Holland, and even England, where he stayed for four months, much of it spent in Deptford near the Royal Docks, where the spectacle of a powerful, modern navy left a deep impression.

Peter's Grand Tour

Peter's voyage of discovery was cut short by worrying news from home: the *streltsy* were again in revolt. This time, however, he would not be returning as a 10-year-old boy, but as an autocrat bent on revenge. In the autumn of 1698, around 1,200 rebels were executed, some reputedly by Peter himself, and many more were publicly flogged, broken on the wheel or roasted over a slow fire. With dissent crushed at home, Peter again turned his gaze on the outside world, and in particular on the open sea. Where his predecessors had failed, Peter finally secured a foothold in the Baltic, cemented in 1703 by the city that he was to make his capital – St Petersburg. The route to the sea was by no means a smooth one, however: the Great Northern War against King Charles XII of Sweden would last over two decades, with massive losses on both sides, and indeed, would ultimately spell the end of the Swedish Empire. 2009 marks the 300th anniversary of the pivotal victory over Charles' troops at Poltava, seen by many as the moment of Russia's emergence at the top table of military powers.

Peter's reign also saw the beginnings of Russia's advances south into the Caucasus and east into the Central Asian khanates, which would in time bring his new empire into conflict with Turkey, Persia and, later still, Britain. At home, he was just as determined to modernize, taking a similarly direct approach both to centralizing power and to dragging Russia out of the middle ages. One of Peter's better known measures was to prohibit beards at court, but he did not restrict himself to such trivialities. Wars are expensive, as are new cities and navies, and many sections of Russian society were to bear the financial burden. Church income was confiscated, and taxes were imposed on coffins, bee-keeping, knife-grinding, the sale of salt, even the weddings of non-Russian tribesmen.

When this was not enough, Peter imposed a direct poll tax to replenish state coffers. Forced labour was routinely used, not only in the construction of the new capital, but also in the newly-built factories in the Urals, and control was maintained by a secret police and a far-reaching system of informants. If that rings any bells among students of more recent Russian history, it should come as no surprise: "When Peter the Great was confronted with the more advanced countries of the West, and feverishly went about building factories and mills to supply his army... it was an extraordinary attempt to jump out of the framework of backwardness," observed Josef Stalin just over two centuries later.

Poll tax

It will not surprise those of you who have read this far that Peter failed to leave a clear descendant. His first son Alexei, under suspicion of treason against his father, had died during interrogation in 1718, and all the tsarevich's direct descendants were also excluded from succession. In 1722, Peter claimed by decree the right to name his own successor, but when the time came three years later, he was too racked with pain, not to mention crazed by syphilis, to speak. Over the next decade and a half until the accession of Peter's daughter by his second wife, Elizabeth, four rulers would occupy the Russian throne.

The rise of the Russian Empire

Elizabeth ruled for twenty years, and had inherited not only her father's physique, but also his vision of Russia's destiny as a great world power. Much of the pomp and grandeur of St Petersburg today can trace its roots back to her reign. What she lacked in attentiveness to domestic affairs – documents routinely waited months for her signature – she more than made up for as a statesman, displaying exceptional acumen in uniting anti-Prussian forces during the Seven Years' War. Elizabeth was perhaps the first of Russia's rulers to truly practise the art of self-interested diplomacy ahead of (sometimes in parallel with) all-out war. Only her death in 1762 prevented the collapse of the Prussian empire: Russian troops had occupied Berlin and Frederick II was already contemplating suicide when Elizabeth succumbed to ill-health, in what became known as the Miracle of the House of Brandenburg. Peter III, Elizabeth's nephew, mentally immature and famously pro-Prussian, lasted just six months before being arrested by his own personal guards regiment and murdered. His wife and successor, Catherine, never prosecuted those responsible and it is widely believed that she had authorised his death.

Born Sophia Augusta Frederica, a minor German princess, Catherine the Great took her more familiar name when she converted to Orthodoxy at the age of 15. Such was Catherine's zeal to be accepted in the Russian court that she nearly died of pneumonia just a few months before her conversion as a result of walking barefoot round the palace at night reciting her Russian lessons. Catherine never entirely lost her German accent, and was regarded by many at court as a foreign-born usurper, but if her provenance was in doubt, her expansionist instincts were not. "I came to Russia a poor girl. Russia has endowed me richly, but I have paid her back with Azov, the Crimea and the Ukraine." Partition of Poland with Austria and Prussia added 36,000 square miles to Catherine's western dominions, after which she went on the offensive against Turkey. Declaring war in 1768, within two years the Russian navy had decimated the Turkish fleet in the Black Sea. The peace agreement reached in 1774 brought Russia important territorial gains, including freedom to sail through the Bosphorus and the Dardanelles – now Russia had two routes to the open sea. Combined with the accretion of agricultural land to the south, the effect of this on Russia's balance of payments is hard to overstate – exports of grain alone had increased by 1,200% by the end of the 18th century.

At court, Catherine continued to build on Elizabeth's legacy, and not only by taking progressively younger lovers. St Petersburg blossomed into one of Europe's

Catherine the Great

great capitals, not only architecturally, but as a centre of culture and intellect. Seeing herself as an enlightened despot, Catherine trod a careful, and not always successful, course between autocratic ruler and modern thinker. Sometimes she betrayed a wilful naivety in her concept of how her subjects really lived, once stating to Voltaire, "no single peasant in Russia could not eat chicken whenever he pleased." Not long after, Pugachev was at the head of a 30,000 strong army burning his way through the lower Volga. When the rebel leader was finally captured, he was brought in a cage to Moscow, where he was executed and his body publicly dismembered – history does not record what Catherine said to Voltaire at that point. Indeed, Catherine soon had to hurriedly reduce French influence in Russian society after the storming of the Bastille, putting all French-speaking foreigners in the capital under police supervision, and impounding a newly-produced Russian translation of the French writer's works. In Russia, the French went from *de rigeur* to anathema at the drop of a guillotine blade.

Catherine suffered a fatal stroke at the age of 67, and was succeeded by her son Paul. An erratic, controversial character, Paul remained on the throne for slightly less than four and a half years before being beaten, strangled and trampled to death in his bedchamber by his own guards in early 1801. The more ghoulish among you can still visit the scene of Paul's assassination at the Mikhailov Palace (also known as the Engineer's Castle) in St Petersburg. Alexander I, who may or may not have had a hand in his father's death, succeeded Paul at the time of Napoleon's military ascendancy in Europe, and six years into his reign his forces were defeated by the French at the Battle of Friedland, south east of present day Kaliningrad. Napoleon did not press his advantage, preferring instead to invite the tsar into an alliance against the British.

Alexander I

In this way, Russia was spared any territorial losses, but the alliance made at the Treaty of Tiflis (now Tbilisi, the capital of Georgia) was not to last long. Just five years later, Napoleon turned an army of 400,000 men against Moscow, setting off a chain of events that would remove any lingering doubts as to Russia's place in the league

1

of military powers. Marching his troops against an apparently non-existent enemy, Napoleon arrived on the outskirts of Moscow just as the winter of 1812 was drawing in. More than two millennia previously, the Persian Emperor Darius the Great had narrowly escaped a similar trap set by the Scythians, but Napoleon confidently pressed his troops on to the gates of the city.

Moscow was deserted. Not only that – it was on fire. With the defenders having razed their own city, and unable to billet his troops and commandeer stores to continue the campaign, Napoleon was left with no option but to turn back. What began as a retreat quickly degenerated into a rout: the Russian troops suddenly emerged out of the forests and materialised on the plains, initially to harry, then to slaughter the Grand Armée as it struggled home through the snows. The scale of the disaster is perhaps best summed up by a monument which still stands today in the Lithuanian capital Vilnius, through which Napoleon passed in both directions. It bears two plaques: on the side facing the West, it reads "Napoleon Bonaparte passed this way in 1812 with 400,000 men", while the opposite side reads "Napoleon Bonaparte passed this way in 1812 with 9,000 men." The Grand Armée was pursued all the way back to Paris by the jubilant Russian troops. The French word "bistro" dates back to this time, when the victorious but hungry Russians burst into the French houses, demanding food *bystro* – "fast".

The defeat of the Grand Armée

Russia's reinforced status as a world power threw its social problems at home into sharp relief when compared with its peers: just as Britain was gearing up for the Industrial Revolution, Russia was still a neo-feudal state. The intellectual elite were becoming increasingly vocal about Russia's social backwardness, finding their outlet not only in the great body of literature unleashed on the world in the 19th century, but in more direct action such as the Decembrist Revolt of 1825, an abortive *coup d'etat* which originally envisaged the assassination of Alexander during a troop review in southern Russia. In the event, Alexander inconveniently died of typhus before he could be done away with, although rumours abounded that he had merely gone to ground, haunted by his inability to reform Russia and, it is said, guilt over his father's

The Decembrists

murder. According to this version of events, Alexander emerges later as Fyodor Kuzmich, a Siberian hermit of regal bearing with an impressive knowledge of life at court in St Petersburg.

Alexander's youngest brother, Nicholas, acceded to the throne in 1825, not troubled in the slightest by any pangs of social conscience. He brutally put down the Decembrists following their hastily cobbled-together attack on him in St Petersburg as he took the oath of allegiance from his troops. Those of the conspirators who weren't hanged were exiled to Siberia – the novelist Fyodor Dostoevsky was among the latter. The revolt left Nicholas with a deep conviction that reform spelt trouble, and under his rule the Russian state became ever more reactionary. Censorship was tightened, and the state became increasingly intrusive and bureaucratic, prompting even Nicholas himself to despair "I do not rule Russia; ten thousand clerks do."

Dostoevsky

Continuing Russia's forward foreign policy, Nicholas extended his Central Asian dominions, and crushed any dissent closer to home, coming into direct conflict withBritain, France and the Ottoman Empire in the Crimean War, which lasted from 1853 to 1856. Nicholas did not live to see Russia's defeat, dying in February 1855. Some say he poisoned himself in despair at the fate of his forces.

Crimean War

Nicholas was succeeded by his eldest son, Alexander. Where Russia's victory over Napoleon thirty years earlier had concentrated minds, her abject defeat in Crimea showed that action was now needed to modernise the state and avert social collapse, and Alexander II saw that the penalties of further inaction far outweighed the risks of reform. At a gathering of Moscow nobles just weeks after Russia's defeat, he said: "…the existing order of serfdom cannot remain unchanged. It is better to abolish serfdom from above than to wait for the time when it will begin to abolish itself from below."

Alexander's task was all but impossible – the 1861 legislation to emancipate the serfs, as an attempt to reconcile the interests of the landowners and the workers, benefited no one. Over the course of the year

1

no fewer than 499 outbreaks of rioting were put down by troops. The lid on a centuries-old pressure cooker of unrest was beginning to tremble, and Alexander's attempts to diffuse the situation were not having the desired effect. During his 26 year reign, Alexander introduced a number of other reforms to the penal code, local government and the armed forces, but none of this was to bring him popularity. Alexander has the unfortunate distinction of being the European leader with the most attempts made on his life – in 1866, 1879 and 1880 a series of revolutionaries and students lobbed bombs or fired revolvers at the hapless tsar, before Ignacy Hryniewiecki, a Belarusian-born revolutionary with the unlikely party codename of *Kotik* ("Kitten") threw the fatal device which exploded at Alexander's feet on March 13th 1881. Today the Church of the Saviour on Spilt Blood, inspired by St Basil's Cathedral on Moscow's Red Square, marks the spot where he fell.

Again the pendulum swung back to repression: if the revolutionaries thought that the death of the tsar at the hands of his people would be the spark to ignite revolt throughout the land, they were mistaken. The Russia of Alexander III would go beyond even the autocratic regime of Nicholas. The fact that one of the conspirators was Jewish set off a series of pogroms (from the Russian, meaning "riot") in the spring and summer of 1881, with Kiev seeing some of the worst outrages. Konstantin Pobedonostsev, one of Alexander's advisers and a hitherto liberal-leaning thinker, proclaimed that "one third of the Jews must die, one third emigrate, and one third assimilate."

Alexander III

This wave of nationalism and repression provided the background for Russia's emergence as a world industrial power. By the end of the century, Russia had moved up to fourth place in the world in iron production. Investment increased hugely, the major European powers now queuing up to pump money into the emerging market – by 1900 it is estimated that almost half the investment capital for Russian companies was coming from abroad. Pressures in the countryside drove the expansion of the urban working class, with a total of over two million by the turn of the century having exchanged the poverty of the fields for the squalor of the factory-towns. The strain on Russia's social fabric was becoming steadily more intense.

Alexander III, unlike his father, died of natural causes, although he didn't live to see his fiftieth birthday. Not that his life passed without threat: in 1887 the tsarist police uncovered an assassination plot by the terrorist group People's Will, who had also been behind the third unsuccessful attempt on Alexander II. Among the conspirators tried and hanged for treason was Alexander Ulyanov, elder brother and inspiration to one Vladimir Ulyanov. According to his own accounts, it was this event that set the 17-year old Vladimir, better known as Lenin, on the path to radicalism.

It was Nicholas II, who together with his father had witnessed at first hand the assassination of Alexander II, who was to finally reap the whirlwind. In this broad overview of a thousand years of Russian history, it would be impossible to go into any detail on what led to the series of uprisings which culminated in the Bolshevik Revolution of 1917, suffice it to say that the court of Nicholas was under siege almost from the day of his coronation in 1896. A year earlier, Lenin had helped to form the catchily-named St Petersburg Union of Struggle for the Liberation of the Working Class, which would make its presence felt with a series of strikes in the capital for the remainder of the decade. In Europe, revolutionaries were debating how to foment revolt in Russia, while a series of poor harvests in 1897, 1898 and 1901 fuelled the fires of peasant discontent. The tsar's desperate hope that a successful naval campaign against Japan in the Pacific in 1904 would divert the energies and attention of the population also backfired. The relatively inexperienced Japanese navy comprehensively humiliated the Russian forces, spreading depression and dissent still further.

The Last Tsar

On Sunday, 22nd January 1905, striking workers gathered in front of the Winter Palace in St Petersburg to petition the tsar for better conditions. The crowd was large (around 150,000), but peaceful and unarmed – some were even bearing portraits of Nicholas. The tsar was not in residence, but the imperial guard were still ranged in front of the palace. No one knows who gave

Bloody Sunday

1

the order to shoot, but once the first cracks of gunfire were heard, in the ensuing panic the army fired volley after volley into the terrified crowd. When the square fell silent again around 1,000 people lay dead, with many thousands more wounded.

Bloody Sunday, as it became known, outraged all levels of Russian society, from peasants to doctors. Nicholas's response was to offer the people a consultative assembly, a Duma, but with the mood of the time this was far too little, far too late. In the Black Sea, there was mutiny on the battleship *Potemkin* (named, ironically, after one of Catherine the Great's lovers), and throughout the countryside store-houses were raided, estates set ablaze, and land-registers destroyed. The momentum of 1905 now appeared unstoppable. And yet, the regime somehow remained intact. In October, a constitutional manifesto was produced which guaranteed a limited set of civil liberties and the provision of a degree of elected representation, and a St Petersburg Soviet (Council) was formed to champion the interests of the workers. This, for now, appeared enough to diffuse the situation.

The 1905 Revolt

Although mutiny, strikes and wholesale arson continued throughout 1906, across such a vast territory no cohesion could be achieved – at least, nothing to threaten the seat of power. The St Petersburg Soviet was but a short-lived experiment: after it had appealed to workers not to pay their taxes, the leaders were arrested and the body dissolved. Leon Trotsky, who had at one time been co-chairman of the Soviet, proclaimed with characteristic irony "La Révolution est morte, vive la Révolution." The Duma did indeed sit in 1906, but was hurriedly adjourned with the help of armed troops when it became clear that no consensus would ever be achieved between factions who were, politically speaking, light-years apart. Demoralised, but still showing remarkable resilience, the old regime limped on. It would take events elsewhere in Europe to finally deliver the *coup de grace*.

As brutal as the wars of the 19th century had been, the modern weaponry of the First World War delivered carnage on an unprecedented level. Russian casualties were almost unimaginable – just under 4 million in the

1

first ten months of the campaign – and at home the economy was in a tailspin. The chasm between the governing and the governed was finally unbridgeable, whether it be between the tsar and the people or the generals and their inadequately armed conscripts. "The spirit of the army is such that news of a *coup d'état* would be welcomed with joy. A revolution is imminent, and we at the front feel it to be so" came the gloomy, and prescient, report from one general. The latent fear that overthrowing the tsar may bring more hardship than benefit was replaced with the feeling that things simply could not get any worse. The fact that the upper echelons of St Petersburg society still appeared to be having such a gay old time (the court jeweller, Carl Fabergé, boasted that he had never done such good business as in the winter of 1915-16) didn't help one bit.

Everything began relatively quietly, and with sufficient spontaneity to take the hard-core revolutionaries by surprise. On 23rd February 1917, public buildings were taken over, prisoners released, housewives came out onto the streets, and the police and soldiers mutinied. Those of the army who remained at their post refused to open fire on the demonstrators – indeed, such was the shortage of ammunition, they may have been unable to do so. After a three week standoff, Nicholas II announced his abdication in favour of his younger brother, the Grand-duke Michael. Clearly no fool, Michael refused to take the throne: so ended the Romanov dynasty, and for the first time since the Troubles, Russia was without a tsar. A Provisional Government was hastily lashed together, but it was essentially powerless, and ended up subordinate to the resurrected St Petersburg Soviet, now the Petrograd Soviet of Workers' and Soldiers' Deputies.

Lenin, who had fled Russia following the 1905 false start, returned to Petrograd (St Petersburg's de-Germanised wartime name) the following month, still unaware of the extent of the uprising. As his sealed train, organised by a German government keen to weaken Russia further, neared the Finland Station, the Bolshevik leader's main concern was whether he would still be able to get a taxi at that time of night. In the event, he was transported by armoured car away from the multitude

The First World War

The February Revolution

who had turned out to greet him to the Bolsheviks' headquarters, a palatial house belonging to one of Nicholas' former mistresses. The following morning he announced his April Theses, formulated during his journey back to Russia, and he was not messing about. Capitalism must be overthrown; the Provisional Government was to be wound up; the land and banks must be nationalised; no parliamentary republic could be countenanced; finally, the means of production and distribution must be taken forthwith into the hands of the Soviets, or Workers Councils.

The Soviet Union

The October
Revolution

Lenin was not to have it all his own way, however: Alexander Kerensky, the Minister of Justice in the Provisional Government, made a brief attempt to suppress the Bolsheviks, and to discredit them as agents of the Germans. Trotsky, just back from Siberian exile, was arrested again, Lenin fled back to Finland, and the revolution spluttered once more. It was, ironically, an attempt by the remaining loyalists in the Russian army to snuff out the revolution once and for all that set the final chain of events in motion. After a concerted propaganda campaign by the Bolsheviks, the counter-insurgency fizzled out before it reached the capital, and support swung back in favour of the new order.

Lenin knew the time had come: "History will not forgive us," he said, "if we do not seize power now." On 20th October the Petrograd Soviet took the decision to initiate an armed insurrection, with the date fixed for the night of the 6-7th November. Again, the uprising was at first quiet: people even continued to visit the opera and the ballet as around 25,000 troops occupied the railway stations, the State Bank, and the telephone exchange. Britain's Ambassador, strolling towards the Winter Palace on the afternoon of November 7th, remarked that "the aspect of the quay was almost normal, except for the groups of armed soldiers stationed near the bridges." The only real sounds of war came from the naval guns "bombarding" the Winter Palace, but even this posed no risk to passers-by: as with the shot from the cruiser Aurora that had signalled the insurgents to move the night before, the guns were using blanks.

The All-Russian Congress of Soviets convened to confirm a Bolshevik government, to be known as the Council of People's Commissars. Lenin read out two decrees from the Council: peace would be sought with Germany without delay, and all private property in Russia was henceforth nationalised. The second decree was in reality an acceptance of what had already happened: the rural population had been busily seizing land for months. The next stage of the revolution set the political tone in Russia for the next few decades: the will of the people was to be determined by the election of a Constitutional Assembly, for which all sides, Bolsheviks, Social Revolutionaries (now themselves divided into Left and Right) and Mensheviks, had vigorously campaigned. The November elections did not exactly go the way Lenin and his colleagues intended. On the basis of a 60% turnout, the Bolsheviks won less than a quarter of the vote, while the Social Revolutionaries found themselves in a commanding majority with over half the available seats. The Council of People's Commissars had no intention of ceding power to their more moderate comrades, and at its first session in January 1918 the Assembly was dispersed by Red Guards. A new dictatorship had replaced the old.

The Council of People's Commissars

Two months later, Lenin's decree on peace with Germany was formalised by the Treaty of Brest-Litovsk, with spectacular territorial losses for the new state. Russia lost one third of its population, a similar proportion of its agricultural land, over half of its industrial capacity and more than 80% of its coal mines. Cut off again from both the Black Sea and, apart from through Petrograd itself, the Baltic, Russia had ceded the territorial gains of nearly three centuries in a single document. Lenin's response to the many voices raised in outrage at this seeming capitulation was that Germany herself was already "pregnant with revolution", and that all notion of national territory would soon be irrelevant in the wake of a revolution which would ultimately make the whole world communist. In any case, although he said this less stridently, with no remaining capacity to fight, Russia had no choice but to accept crippling terms.

Russia's withdrawal from the war with Germany was equally unpopular with the remaining allies, for whom a further eight months of brutal fighting still lay ahead, now against a Kaiser who could throw all his forces west and south. Britain, France, Japan and the US decided to intervene in Russia in the hope of uniting the nationalist Whites into a force capable of defeating the Bolsheviks and rejoining the struggle against Germany. The fate of the deposed Tsar and his family, who could still act as a rallying point for the anti-revolutionary forces, was sealed. In the early hours of 17th July 1918, they were herded into the cellar of the house in Ekaterinburg where they were being held, and shot. Grand Duke Michael was executed the same year on the outskirts of Perm'. With the German surrender in November 1918, one reason for the interventionists' presence on Russian soil evaporated, but the threat of revolution spreading beyond Russia's borders remained. The Civil War that ensued technically lasted until 1923 when armed resistance in the Far East district of Ayano-Maysk was finally extinguished. By this point the foreign interventionists had long since pulled out, but the bitter conflict had already set the tone for relations between the Soviet state and its neighbours to east and west. Russian losses during the conflict were also monstrous: where the First World War had accounted for around 5 million lives, the Civil War's total exceeded that three times over.

Civil War

It is testament to the astonishing resilience of Russia (indeed, of Russians) that the country did not melt down altogether. To take just two examples from industry, steel production and manufactured goods stood respectively at five and thirteen per cent of their pre-war levels. In an attempt to revive the economy, Lenin was forced to compromise his principles and allow the return of a measure of capitalism to give output a shot in the arm. The New Economic Policy (NEP), justified by Lenin as "one step back, two steps forward" encouraged agricultural production by incentivising peasants to produce a surplus and allowing a degree of free trade in the countryside, although industry and manufacturing – the "commanding heights of the economy" – were kept within the control of the state. By 1928, both agricultural and industrial production had, miraculously, returned to their pre-war levels. The NEP signalled a fundamental change at the top of the Bolshevik power structure from the idealism to pragmatism, and parallel

NEP

with this went an inexorable shift in power from Lenin, the ideologue, to the former Commissar for Nationalities (his Georgian roots made him an ideal candidate for the post) and, from April 1922, General Secretary of the Communist Party Central Committee – Josef Stalin.

Lenin realised too late the amount of power that Stalin had gathered around himself during the early 1920s, and the testament he left after his death in 1924 proposing that the General Secretary be removed from office was ignored. Revolution had not, in the event, spread beyond Russia's borders, and Stalin now set the country on a radically different course, to create socialism in one country. What ensued was nothing less than a second revolution, a shock industrialisation that had not been seen since the time of Peter the Great. Power was again centralised in the hands of a single autocrat, now back in the Kremlin (Moscow had been re-established as the capital in early 1918), who would let nothing stand in his way. Stalin's preferred method of policy-enforcement was terror, and the excesses of his henchmen far eclipsed those of even Ivan the Terrible's *oprichniks*. The relative freedom of the NEP was over – every element of society was brutally yanked back under state control.

A more subtle, but no less powerful, motivator was the fear of external aggression and encirclement, part of Russia's cultural memory since the days of Genghis Khan, and industrial output was directly correlated to the capacity to fight. When Germany reneged on the 1939 Molotov-Ribbentrop non-aggression non-agression treaty and fell upon Russia in June 1941, this capacity would be put to its ultimate test. Anyone visiting Russia for the first time may be surprised to learn that the conflict of 1941-45 is usually referred to as the Great Patriotic War, rather than the Second World War – this is partially a result of Stalin's (very effective) policy of appealing to nationalist feeling to repel the invasion, but just as much because it was a very real fight for national survival. Nazi ideology ranked the Slavs alongside the Jews and the Gypsies as *untermenschen* – sub-human – and fit only for slavery or annihilation. Leningrad, as Petrograd had been named after the Bolshevik leader's death, endured a siege of 900 days, losing an average of one thousand citizens every twenty four hours; the

"Great Patriotic War"

1

lower-Volga industrial centre of Tsarytsin, renamed Stalingrad in 1925, witnessed the single bloodiest battle in human history, with the deaths of over 1.5 million people over an 18 month campaign. The most recent research puts total losses to the Soviet Union throughout the war at just over 23 million people – just over half were civilians. In other words, by the middle of 1945 the Soviet Union had lost just under 14% of its remaining population, and was faced with rebuilding itself once again.

The reconstruction plans following the war required, if anything, still more coercion of an exhausted people than did the industrialisation of the 1930s. The Soviet Union, hitherto seen by the West as a vital ally in defeating the Nazis, rapidly became the new enemy as the battle lines in Europe were re-drawn. Germany, indeed the entire continent, was sliced in half between the victorious powers, who now eye-balled each other from either side of the newly erected Iron Curtain. With the successful test of the Soviet Union's first atomic bomb in 1949, and its emergence as the world's second industrial power after the US just a year later, the Cold War – economic, technological, political, and ideological – had begun.

The Cold War begins

Stalin's death in 1953 did nothing to alleviate the Soviet Union's isolation, although it marked the end of the worst excesses which had characterised the preceding three decades. He was succeeded as First Secretary of the Communist Party by Nikita Khrushchev, a long-time ally and veteran of the Stalingrad campaign. Khrushchev denounced his predecessor in 1956, prompting a near-revolt by the more conservative elements of the Party, but he emerged victorious and in 1958 he also replaced Nikolai Bulganin as Premier of the Soviet Union, thereby uniting leadership of Party and State. Under Khrushchev's leadership, the Soviet Union continued its relentless march forward. Two important psychological victories were scored over the United States, with the launching of the first satellite, Sputnik I, in 1957, and Yuri Gagarin's first flight into space four years later. The two countries' rivalry was not just confined to space, however: in 1962 events nearly spilled over into nuclear war when the Soviet Union stationed missiles in Cuba, within striking distance of the American mainland, in retaliation for the stationing of US missiles in Turkey.

Internally, Soviet Russia under Khrushchev became a more peaceful place to live, although freedoms were still heavily circumscribed. In 1964, he was replaced while on holiday in Georgia by Leonid Brezhnev, a smooth, professional politician who it was felt would be a much safer pair of hands than the increasingly erratic Khrushchev. Brezhnev ushered in what became known as the *zastoy*, or stagnation, although we are speaking in relative terms here. Brezhnev's premiership was comparatively uneventful, but still included the Prague Spring in 1968, a narrowly-averted war with China in 1969-71, and the invasion of Afghanistan in 1979.

The Prague Spring

Economically speaking, though, the Soviet Union really was stagnating: the supreme effort of reconstruction in the post-war years had given way to a fundamentally unbalanced economy, with inefficient agriculture and heavy industry, unsustainable military spending and little or no capacity to meet the ever-growing needs of a modern consumer society. The centralist state left no room for the kind of small- and medium-scale economic activity that drove prosperity elsewhere, and the body politic was riddled by corruption at all levels. Yuri Andropov, the former head of the KGB who succeeded Brezhnev in 1983, attempted to press through measures to jump start the economy, but was in office for just 15 months, to be succeeded by the ailing Konstantin Chernenko, who was in power for an even shorter period before he too passed away in March 1985. Clearly, a younger man was needed at the helm if the Soviet Union were not to just meander on between increasingly frequent state funerals, and the baton passed from Chernenko to the relatively youthful Second Secretary of the Communist Party, Mikhail Gorbachev.

Mikhail Gorbachev

Having turned 54 just two weeks before his inauguration, Gorbachev was the first Soviet leader to be born after the Revolution. He embarked on a series of reforms aimed at reviving both the economy and the state. *Uskorenie* ("acceleration") soon gave way to the less readily-measurable *glasnost* (typically paraphrased as "openness", although it really embodies the idea of everyone having a voice) and *perestroika* ("restructuring"). Historians will argue for decades over how much this relaxation of the levers of power

Glasnost and Perestroika

contributed to the ultimate downfall of the Soviet Union in 1991. In the event, a combination of economic and political factors, not least a fall in global oil prices and consequent loss of foreign currency earnings, along with a relaxation of state control in other communist states and the reunification of Germany, undermined the Soviet Union piece by piece.

Whether the economic reforms enshrined in *perestroika* would have led to riches later will forever remain a matter for conjecture. As it was, the stripping away of the outer layers of the Soviet economy revealed a core more rotten than anyone, perhaps least of all Gorbachev, could have predicted. By the end of the 1980s, food rationing (yes, *food rationing*) had been brought in, gold reserves had been reduced by 90%, and the Soviet Union's external debt had grown from zero to US$120bn. Moreover, while the restructuring was having less success than intended, *glasnost'* was, if anything, turning out to be only too successful. The relaxation of Moscow's grip led many to find their voice, principally to advocate secession from the Union. The remaining hardliners in the Politburo staged an abortive *coup d'etat* on 19th August 1991, placing Gorbachev under house arrest, but history was not with them. After mass protests throughout the major cities, in which three people died, the ringleaders were arrested on 22nd and 23rd August. One of the conspirators, Minister of Internal Affairs Boris Pugo, shot his wife and then himself before he could stand trial.

The August Putsch

Gorbachev returned from house arrest to a very different Moscow. The speed of developments, after decades of "stagnation", was nothing short of breathtaking. In the early hours of 24th August , the statue of "Iron" Felix Dzerzhinsky, founder of the Cheka, forerunner to the KGB, was taken down from its plinth in front of the KGB headquarters, the Lyubyanka. The same day, Gorbachev resigned as General Secretary, while the President of the Russian Soviet Federative Socialist Republic, Boris Yeltsin, transferred the archives of the Communist Party to the Russian state archives. In a second decree, Yeltsin nationalised all Communist Party property on Russian territory. But perhaps the final hammer blow to the Soviet Union came not from Moscow at all, but from Kiev. Before the day was out, Ukraine's Supreme Soviet had passed an Act of Declaration of Independence, subject to a popular referendum. This was a world apart from the secessionist rhetoric of Lithuania or Azerbaijan – this was the country of birth of Khrushchev, Brezhnev, and any number of leading lights of the revolution, what's more Kiev was the original capital of the first Russian state. The other republics, emboldened, followed throughout the remaining months of 1991. On Christmas Day, Mikhail Gorbachev resigned as Soviet President, and the hammer and sickle flag was lowered atop the Kremlin to be replaced with the Russian tricolour. The Soviet Union had officially ceased to exist.

The Russian Federation

Russia's new president, Boris Yeltsin, inherited – yet again – a whole pile of economic trouble. A return to the command economy was no longer an option – the state was already too impoverished, and in any case, the people would not stand for it. Yeltsin opted for a different approach – the introduction of a free market. His 36-year-old deputy prime minister Yegor Gaidar called for "shock therapy", a broad-based relaxation of economic controls, monetary policy (including the exchange rate) and foreign trade, accompanied by the withdrawal of state expenditure on industry, construction and social welfare. The entire Russian economy, bereft of the rickety structure that had shored it up for decades, bombed. Your author, a student in Moscow at the time, can well remember the hyperinflation, flourishing black market, and any savings that hadn't been hurriedly converted into dollars at swingeing rates being wiped out overnight. Even in the capital, the economic powerhouse of a major industrial power, doctors and state officials were standing outside metro stations selling flowers and old collections of Pushkin to make ends meet.

Boris Yeltsin

The government quickly factionalised into those who believed that shock was the only therapy, and those who, in the words of vice president Alexander Rutskoy, saw the reforms as "economic genocide". The conflict came to a head in March 1993 with Yeltsin's announcement, in the face of increasing intransigence from his opponents, that he was adopting "special powers"

1

to continue the reforms. Within a week, the Congress of People's Deputies had voted to impeach him, but fell just short of the required majority. The battle continued to seethe throughout the summer until Yeltsin announced his intention to disband both the Congress and the Supreme Soviet and rule by decree. The Russian legislature, based in Moscow's White House, removed Yeltsin from power for breaching the Constitution, swore in Rutskoy as the new acting president, and locked the doors.

The 1992 Constitutional Crisis

Once again, the people came out onto the streets of Moscow, this time it was against the Russian president. The man who had famously climbed on top of a tank in 1991 to address the crowds now sent the army in to bombard his own parliament building, and blast his erstwhile allies out. Yeltsin survived the constitutional crisis, but his credibility was in tatters. In December of that year, elections were held for the newly-formed State Duma, with the Communist Party taking the single largest share of the vote.

Not everyone suffered poverty and deprivation in Russia during the 1990s, of course. Visitors to Russia today are generally struck by the amount of conspicuous wealth there, particularly in the larger cities. Yeltsin's era saw the rise of the oligarchs, a new class of hyper-rich whose wealth far outstripped that of their spiritual antecedents, the boyars. Broadly speaking, the oligarchs profited from two key policies: the voucher privatisation of state industries, and the "loans for shares" scheme.

The Rise of Oligarchy

The intention of privatisation in the early 1990s was to return state-owned industry to the people: Russian citizens were issued with vouchers with a nominal value of 10,000 roubles, redeemable against shares in state-owned companies. In the prevailing economic conditions, however, what people needed wasn't vouchers, it was cash. The result was predictable: those few who had ready money bought up vouchers at knockdown prices and rapidly accrued massive holdings in large companies. Oleg Deripaska, at the time of writing Russia's wealthiest man, with a personal fortune estimated at $28bn, began his rise dressed in a leather jacket, leaning against a beaten-up car outside the gates of an aluminium plant, buying shares off the workers as they went home for the evening. Within months he had sufficient equity in the company to become its Financial Director. Across many other sectors, particularly natural resources, power utilities and construction, it was the same story – fortunes were made almost literally overnight.

The lucky few who had benefited from the first wave of privatisation were well placed to make an even greater killing from the second wave, this time motivated as much by political as economic necessity. By the middle of the decade, it had become obvious that shock therapy was not working. Furthermore, opposition was mounting against further privatisation, which had clearly brought no financial benefit to the state. The solution offered by a syndicate of Russian financiers led by Vladimir Potanin, head of the investment group Interros, was as simple as it was well-timed. They would lend the Russian state US$2bn in return for managing the state's remaining share in a selection of leading companies, including behemoths like Norilsk Nickel, YUKOS and United Energy Systems. The stakes would be released at auction to the highest bidder, with the state retaining the right to pay off the debt up to 1st September 1996, at which point the shares could be sold on, with the new owners retaining 30 per cent of proceeds above the credit initially extended. Yeltsin, desperate for an injection of cash both to service state debt and to fund his forthcoming election campaign, issued a decree on 31st August 1995. Some of Russia's largest enterprises were "leased out" at knockdown prices to bidders who knew full well that the government would never be able to buy the shares back. Where the voucher-privatisations had made a few hundred people very rich indeed, loans for shares (a round dozen state enterprises were sold off in the end) made a handful of people wealthy beyond all dreams of avarice. With the support of the oligarchs, Yeltsin was duly elected for a second term in 1996, beating the Communist candidate Gennady Zyuganov by just over three per cent in the first round, and a more emphatic 13.5% in the second.

A couple of billion dollars, welcome though they undoubtedly were, did little to solve Russia's economic problems – worse was to come. Government debt continued to rise, and by May 1998 it had reached

Loans for Shares

US$140bn in foreign currency and just under half that figure in roubles. Revenues had declined to three billion dollars a month, while servicing this debt was costing a billion dollars every week. A shot of cash of the order provided by loans for shares was suddenly peanuts: Russia needed around $35bn to avoid total collapse, and no one was ready to stump up that kind of money. The oil giant Rosneft was offered in desperation for two billion dollars, but no one wanted it. Ten years later, in May 2008 Rosneft's market cap hit $129bn. Two things happened: on 14th August 1998, Yeltsin declared that there would be no devaluation of the rouble; three days later, a moratorium on payment of foreign debts was announced, and the rouble was devalued by half. With any remaining confidence from investors gone, the rouble sank below its devalued rate of 9.5 to the dollar, and kept on going. Any savings that people had managed to accrue in the past few years were wiped out again – a lucky few had managed to withdraw their cash from the bank, convert it to dollars and stuff it under the proverbial mattress. Those who had just converted their savings and left it in their accounts suddenly found that they could no longer get at them.

It had fallen to Sergei Kirienko, Russia's 35-year-old prime minister at the time, to announce that Russia was defaulting on its foreign debt. Less than a week later, he was gone, dismissed along with his government after just three months in office. The post of prime minister in Yeltsin's Russia had become a fairly short term one for many – only Viktor Chernomyrdin lasted longer than eight months throughout the entire period (he was at the helm for a very impressive five and a half years, from the end of 1992 until March 1998). So it was probably with no little trepidation that a relatively youthful former deputy mayor of St Petersburg and ex-head of the KGB, Vladimir Putin, accepted both the office of Premier and Yeltsin's blessing as Russia's future president just a year later. This latter was seen by many as the kiss of death, such was Yeltsin's unpopularity at this point. Nevertheless, on New Year's Eve 1999, with deep symbolism, Yeltsin announced that he was stepping down, and that henceforth Putin would be acting president until the elections in March the following year.

Putin did, of course, win the elections of 2000, even avoiding a second ballot by just under three per cent. He was faced with a Russia on its knees – you may want to check back through this chapter to see if you can find a Russian leader who actually did inherit a healthy economy. Russia's new president had studied law at university, but undoubtedly his schooling under the Soviet Union's remarkable education system, perhaps the greatest achievement of the Soviet period, had left him with a thorough grounding in history, and it is likely that he saw the parallels. Soviet schools also taught English literature, which may also have come to mind: "When sorrows come, they come not single spies, but in battalions," – the former KGB man would surely have appreciated Shakespeare's choice of metaphor. Putin's predecessors over the centuries had been confronted with the same problems, but generally not all at once. The governing structures were in disarray; the economy lay in ruins; the treasury was more or less empty; Russia's international standing was at rock bottom. Putin also had to contend with a powerful new class of independently minded industrial, financial and media barons who had grown very used to calling the shots, and his options for dealing with them were not the same as those available to Ivan the Terrible.

He could, however, make life very uncomfortable for anyone perceived as a threat, but first he had to arrange his own insurance. This he did on two fronts simultaneously: within the Kremlin, he promoted his old colleagues, whether from the security services or the St Petersburg government to positions of power. The KGB faction became known as the *siloviki*, a Russian word that doesn't easily translate into English. *Silovik* is a blanket term for anyone working in defence, security or law enforcement, "enforcer" is probably close, but the Russian word is less dramatic. In Putin's inner sanctum, though, the enforcers' job was clear: to take orders from their patron, and to ensure they were carried out without question. Alongside the strongmen, Putin needed effective administrators, and this is where the St Petersburg government came in – technocrats ruling alongside autocrats. The only potential problem with this approach was that it would bring with it an inevitable

The KGB

1

element of infighting as ideologically-opposed camps jockeyed for position and influence on policy. Time would show, however, that Putin, with experience of both worlds, also had a rare ability to walk between them.

Putin's second line of defence was, from the very beginning, his mass appeal. He knew that what the vast majority of the electorate wanted was not a leader they would necessarily like, but one they would respect, perhaps even slightly fear. Some of Putin's decisions may have made him less than popular with other world leaders, but his approval meetings at home are the stuff of dreams: returned to power in 2004 with 71% of the vote, in June 2007, less than a year before leaving office (when most US presidents would already be a lame duck), Putin's approval rating was a staggering 81%. He achieved this through pushing a number of the right buttons with the electorate, some of them more palatable to international observers than others. Among them were a strong, Russia-first stance on foreign policy, frequent appeal to Russian patriotic (sometimes nationalist) sentiment and regular televised carpetings of his own

Crises

ministers when they failed to deliver results. Standing above all this was a level of control over the media not seen since the days of Brezhnev.

It would be wrong to say that Putin's regime has entirely escaped without criticism. Among other crises, the loss of the Russian submarine fleet's flagship, the *Kursk*, in 2000, the *Nord-Ost* theatre attack in 2002, the banking "mini-crisis" and the Beslan school siege in 2004 all brought accusations of arrogance, incompetence, or both. Whatever happened, though, Putin ended up being seen as part of the solution, not the problem. Even in the wake of the monetarisation of state benefits in early 2005, which left millions of Russia's most vulnerable citizens materially worse off, and where thousands of pensioners came out on the streets with banners saying "Hitler deprived us of our youth, Putin of our old age", the hard kernel at the centre of government emerged largely unscathed. At no point during his entire term in office did Putin's approval rating dip below 65%.

As to the oligarch "problem", Vladimir Putin's talent for delivering punishment and patronage proved as successful with business figures as it did with his political cohorts. While some of the oligarchs from the 1990s continue to prosper, staunch in their support for the Kremlin, those few who have stepped out of line are now either in exile or, in the case of Mikhail Khodorkovsky, co-founder of YUKOS, once the jewel in the crown of the Russian oil and gas industry, in a Siberian prison. It is tempting perhaps to draw a comparison between the boyars and the *pomeshchiki*, but the Russia of the 21st century is a very different place from the Muscovy of the 16th.

The principal factor underpinning Putin's popularity, and the most important to readers of this book, is simple: for whatever reason (and there are too many to go into here), Putin delivered prosperity to Russia again. Later on we will look at Russia's key sectors in more detail, but for now we will limit ourselves to the headline figures. Economic growth has been, for so large a country in such deep trouble at the start of the third millennium, little short of miraculous, averaging 7% per annum without let-up. Clearly, spiralling oil prices have been of immense benefit to Russia as the world's second largest oil exporter (which also holds around 80% of the world's proven reserves of natural gas), but any temptation to start a fiscal spending spree has (so far) been resisted. Instead, Russia has used the opportunity to put its house in order, wiping out foreign debt, and accruing record currency reserves – by August 2008, Russia had nearly US$600bn in cash, more than any other country apart from Japan and China.

Prosperity

Between 2007 and 2008, Russia's net capital inflow doubled to around US$80bn. Russia's new president Dmitry Medvedev (one of the St Petersburg technocrats) became one of its first leaders in history to take the reins of a healthy economy. "In late 2008, as this guide went to press, Russia had to confront the uncomfortable reality that, for all the progress its economy had made since 2000, it was far from immune to the vagaries of the global market. At the beginning of 2008, the Russian Central Bank's over-riding concern was that the rouble's strength would hurt exports. At the end of November the bank's head, Sergei Ignatiev, announced that the country's reserves of cash has shrunk back to US$475bn – a 20% reduction in the space of three months –

Dmitry Medvedev

1

following the state bail-outs of several major companies and attempts to shore up the national currency.

The fall in global demand has led to oil prices plummeting from almost US$150 a barrel to around US$50, and falling prices of other commodities such as aluminium (down by nearly two-fifths on the year) and steel (down by nearly half since July 2008) will have a major impact on a country still over-reliant on mineral exports. Russia's economic growth prediction for 2008 has been pegged back from 7.3% to a still highly impressive 6.8%, but any remaining feeling that the country could remain aloof from the global crisis evaporated in the autumn, when trading on both Mocow's stock exchanges was suspended to prevent share values being wiped out entirely. The International Monetary Fund has already predicted that net capital inflow to the country for 2008 will be between US%15bn and zero. Russia is many things, but it is never boring.

This fairly superficial overview of the history of Russia should give you some sense of how it has become the country it is today. It may read a little like a roller-coaster ride, but if you plan to do business here, be in no doubt that you will have to hold on tight through both the ups and the downs. The one certainty is that the journey will be a memorable one. Any nation is best understood in the context of its own history, of course, and nowhere is this more true than in Russia. If, as I hope, you intend to experience this remarkable and fascinating country at first hand, the following chapters are there as your guide.

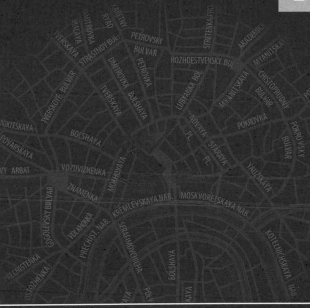

2

investigating the potential market

investigating the potential market

An outline of some of the myriad organisations which exist to assist the exporter, along with an assessment of their focus and likely relevance

Sources of information

You don't need me to tell you that thorough research is vital when entering any export market, and nowhere is this more true than in Russia. In the heady, chaotic days of the 1990s, fortunes were made by companies who were clever, lucky, or both. To take a fizzy example, the importers of the soft drink Irn-Bru were lucky, at least in their timing. Irn-Bru launched a major billboard advertising campaign in Moscow in late 1998, just before the government's default on foreign debt and subsequent economic crash. Suddenly, no one had the budget for large-scale advertising, nor was anyone prepared to take down the existing adverts. As a result, the Irn-Bru billboards continued to enjoy free exposure months after they were supposed to be replaced.

For every winner, though, there have been many losers, generally those who have either not done their homework in the first place, or haven't had the reserves of cash or determination to hang on during the tough times. Many investors in Russia tend to make at least one of the following three mistakes: firstly, they assume that they are pioneers, and that the market is just waiting for them to go in and conquer; secondly, they think that results will come quickly; thirdly, and probably worst of all, they think that Russia, as an emerging market, is therefore unsophisticated. Those cold war images of grim-faced workers trudging through urban snowscapes with battered shopping bags still persist in the eyes of some.

We should get this clear straight away: nothing could be further from the truth. The Russian market, and the consumer market in particular, is probably more sophisticated and savvy than most markets you will find in the west. Goods will not be bought simply because they come from overseas, nor will services be used just because they are provided by a western company: Russians have (and always have had) a keen eye for quality, but an even better one for anything that is substandard.

On the other hand, for those companies which deliver the goods there is every chance of success, given time. Russia is not a market that you can expect to dip in and

2

out of: if you decide to enter the territory, you should be doing so with a view to being there long-term. Otherwise, you are wasting your time, and you will spend a lot of money finding this out. To quote Lennart Dahlgren, former Country Manager of IKEA, still one of Russia's largest investors, "You have to have a belief in the future of this country. If you come here just because you see others coming here, I doubt you will be successful – you will be disappointed. You will have many more problems than you anticipated, and many discussions about leaving".

Even once you are established, you must keep in mind that, as in any young market, things can move fast: smart operators keep their ear to the ground at all times. Make sure you also build up a good network of contacts: sharing of information and news of developments will be very important as time goes on.

Fortunately for the business traveller, there is no lack of resources available which can help you find out what you need to know, and this section is intended as a guide to the main sources available.

Russian embassies and consulates

UK

Embassy of the Russian Federation in the United Kingdom
7 Kensington Palace Gardens
London W8 4QP
Tel: +44 (0)20 7229 6412
            +44 (0)20 7229 7281
            0845 868 11 99   *(from the UK)*
            +44 203 0511199   *(outside the UK)*
Fax: +44 (0)20 7727 8625
E-mail: office@rusemblon.org
Website: www.great-britain.mid.ru   *(Embassy)*
            www.rusemblon.org   *(Consular section)*

Consulate General of the Russian Federation in Edinburgh
58 Melville Street
Edinburgh EH3 7HL,
Tel: +44 (0)131 225 7098
Fax: +44 (0)131 225 9587
E-mail: visa@edconsul.co.uk

2

The Embassy website has a series of links to information for business people, accessible from the Country Profile button on the main page. It is a little heavy on the numbers, as is often the way with government information, and some of it is only in Russian and/or out of date. Depending on what you are looking for, you may at least find some useful statistics here.

Trade Delegation of the Russian Federation in the United Kingdom
32-33 Highgate West Hill
London N6 6NL
Tel: +44 (0)20 8340 1907
           +44 (0)20 8340 4491
           +44 (0)20 8340 3272
Fax: +44 (0)20 8348 0112
E-mail: info@rustradeuk.org
Website: www.rustradeuk.org

The Russian Trade Delegation essentially exists to represent the interests of Russian companies active in the UK. As a foreign company going the other way, you are not their target audience as such, but the Trade Delegation is staffed by helpful people who will at least give you advice. The delegation's website has information generally from the RF Ministry of Economic Development and Trade: Special Economic Zones, state-sponsored investment projects and the like. You will also find links to pages covering economic indicators and foreign investment statistics.

US

Embassy of the Russian Federation in the United States of America
2650 Wisconsin Avenue NW
Washington, DC 20007
Tel: +1 (202) 298 5700/01/04
Fax: +1 (202) 298 5735

Similar information here to Russia's London embassy, but with a useful links page to other trade promotion bodies (admittedly, some are more useful than others).

2

Trade Representation of the Russian Federation
2001 Connecticut Avenue NW
Washington, DC 20007
Tel: +1 (202) 232-5988
            +1 (202) 234-7170
            +1 (202) 232-0975
Fax: +1 (202) 232-2917
E-mail: rustrade@verizon.net

Canada

Embassy of the Russian Federation in Canada
285 Charlotte Street
Ottawa
Ontario K1N 8L5
Tel: +1 (613) 235 4341
Fax: +1 (613) 236 6342
E-mail: rusemb@rogers.com
Website: www.rusembcanada.mid.ru

Trade mission of the Russian Federation in Canada
95 Wurtemburg Street
Ottawa
Ontario K1N 8Z7
Tel: +1 (613) 789 1222
            +1 (613) 789 1066
Fax: +1 (613) 789 2951

Australia

Embassy of the Russian Federation in Australia
78 Canberra Avenue
Griffith ACT 2603
Tel: +61 (02) 6295 9033
Fax: +61 (02) 6295 1847
E-mail: rusembassy.australia@rambler.ru
Website: www.australia.mid.ru

The addresses of Russian embassies and trade delegations
in other countries are contained in Appendix 1.

Ministries and other government agencies

2

UK

UK Trade and Investment (UKTI), a division of BERR (the Department for Business, Enterprise and Regulatory Reform, formerly the DTI), is the UK government agency responsible for promoting export and encouraging inward investment. At the time of writing, Russia is one of the countries identified as a High Growth Market, and as such there are additional resources available to UK companies wanting to work there.

UKTI

On the Russia page of UKTI's website (www.uktradeinvest.gov.uk/ukti/russia), you will find a range of data, from general economic statistics to travel and health advice. There is also information on relevant events, conferences and exhibitions, whether they be in the UK or Russia. If you register on the site, you can also have access to a number of reports produced by the in-country sector specialists, and you can sest yourself up to receive alerts on forthcoming events and report updates. Currently there are a number of "priority" sectors, where UKTI has identified particular overlap for British companies in Russia, such as power and energy, sports and leisure infrastructure (no surprise, given that London will host the Olympic Games in 2012, and Sochi in Southern Russia will be the venue for the winter games in 2014), and financial services. Airports, construction and the creative industries are among other areas where specific opportunities have been identified. It is best to keep a weather eye on the website – as with any government agency, new policies and initiatives will come in from time to time, some of which may be particularly relevant to you or your company. Some of the key programmes available are described below.

UKTI runs a "Passport to Export" programme ("P2E"), intended to help first time exporters get the basics right. A series of trade guides is available to download, with the most recent Russia edition being from 2007 – a 2009 guide should be available by the time you are reading this. The trade guides have a little more information in them, and some useful contacts.

"Passport to Export"

2.

ITA

You can also use UKTI's website to locate and contact your nearest International Trade Adviser (ITA). An ITA I know described himself as being a little like a family doctor, and this is a pretty accurate comparison. Their role is to give you general advice and help guide you further through the range of resources and services available. Bear in mind that ITAs are not necessarily Russia specialists: UKTI used to operate on a system of country "desks", each staffed by a specialist team, with perhaps a secondee from industry as an Export Promoter, but this is no longer the case.

ITAs will also be able to put you in contact with the in-country trade teams, who work out of the British Embassy in Moscow, and the Consulates in St Petersburg and Ekaterinburg. There is also a representative covering Siberia and the Far East. The in-country teams (or "Posts" in UKTI parlance) can produce market research reports for you, containing information specific to your sector, and a series of contacts who will be of use – they will even be able to arrange meetings for you, although

OMIS

they cannot actually be present to facilitate discussions. The service is known as OMIS (the Overseas Market Introduction Service), and costs will vary depending on how much you want done – the most recent brochure quotes somewhere between £500 for a short report with a list of companies to contact to a few thousand pounds for something more in-depth. In any case, the service is subsidised, so will be significantly cheaper than going to a commercial market research company.

HGMP

UKTI has also recently introduced a High Growth Market Programme (HGMP), which currently covers 17 countries including Russia. The HGMP is targeted at mid-capacity UK companies, with annual turnover of £20-100m and/or between 250 and 1,000 employees, thereby plugging the gap between smaller companies who will be more interested in the services described above, and bigger companies who will be working on another level altogether.

TAP

Another programme which may be of interest is the Tradeshow Access Programme (TAP), through which UK companies can obtain financial assistance for exhibiting at a range of events in Russia. The programme is administered by a number of Approved Trade

2

Organisations (ATOs), so you need to apply to them in the first instance. A list of the TAP-supported events together with contact details for the relevant ATOs is available as an excel spreadsheet from the UKTI main website. For tradeshows not supported by the TAP, there is a parallel scheme called SOLO, with a maximum grant level of £1,000.

BusinessLink (www.businesslink.gov.uk) is a government-funded resource for UK companies, offering a range of information through various interactive sections of the website. Again, keep in mind that this is a non-specialist agency, so don't expect an Aladdin's cave of answers. If your enquiries get too specific, it tends to get a bit flustered and send you back to the UKTI site. You can, however, get in touch with your nearest Business Link and find out some general information on trade tariffs and the like.

UKTI HQ

UK Trade and Investment
Kingsgate House
66-74 Victoria Street
London SW1E 6SW
Tel: +44 (0)20 7215 8000
Website: www.uktradeinvest.gov.uk

Scotland, Wales and Northern Ireland have similar programmes available, some using the main UKTI services, with additional services available for local companies in some cases. You will find contact details for the agencies in Appendix 1.

Credit guarantees

The Export Credits Guarantee Department (ECGD) is the UK's official agency offering guarantees to companies competing for overseas orders and contracts. The ECGD's services are fairly specialised and complex, and will not be for everyone: a quick look at guarantees issued since 2000 for Russian contracts shows such beneficiaries as Airbus, Motorola and Thales plc, so draw your own conclusions. It is an arguable point that if the level of risk is sufficiently low that the ECGD will provide a guarantee, it may not be worth it for the exporter to pay the premium involved. You can ascertain

ECGD

2

whether the ECGD could be useful for you and your company by contacting the relevant business manager.

ECGD
PO Box 2200
2 Exchange Tower
Harbour Exchange Square
London E14 9GS
Tel: +44 (0)20 7512 7000
Fax: +44 (0)20 7512 7649
E-mail: help@ecgd.gsi.gov.uk
Website: www.ecgd.gov.uk

The European Union

The Enterprise and Industry Directorate General is part of the European Commission, and offers a range of support to European businesses focusing on, among other things, bringing improved access to finance for Small and Medium sized Enterprises (SMEs). The stated aim of the directorate is to improve the competitiveness of European companies both at home and internationally, and to encourage entrepreneurship, innovation and job-creation. Since 2003 the EU definition of an SME has been a company with fewer than 250 employees, and a turnover of less than €50m (balance sheet total less than €43m).

If your company falls into this category, you may be eligible for business support of some kind, but a lot of this will depend on your industry sector and prevailing policy at the directorate.

European Commission
Enterprise and Industry DG
Communication and Information Unit/R4
BREY 13/ 092
B - 1049 Brussels
Belgium
Tel: 0800 6789 10 11 (Europe Direct)
Website: http://ec.europa.eu/enterprise

EU funds are available to help with exporting to certain markets, but at the time of writing Russia is not one of them. UK companies are advised to make contact with the Commercial Section of the United Kingdom permanent representation in Brussels (UKRep), which exists to help companies understand and participate in the various programmes. The Commercial Section also provides notifications of forthcoming projects and invitations to tender, and offers a "Country Tracking" service on future opportunities in particular regions around the world.

Both the above services are considered part of the OMIS programme and are therefore chargeable. If EU project tenders are of interest to you or your company, you may want to register on TED (Tenders Electronic Daily), part of the European Commission Publications Office. Here you can receive for free regular updates of new opportunities – go to http://ted.europa.eu.

TED

You can also download from UKRep's website an annually updated directory of UK consultancy companies who have experience of working on the EU's external aid programme.

United Kingdom Permanent Representation to the European Union
10 Avenue d'Auderghem / Oudergemselaan
1040 Brussels
Belgium
Tel: +32 2 287 8211
Website: www.ukrep.be

US

US companies wanting assistance and advice on working in Russia should contact either the US State Department or the Department of Commerce. Both provide a wide range of market research information, from general exporters checklists, through detailed Country Commercial Guides to online seminars ("webinars", would you believe) and sector specific briefings. Your best starting point is the US government's export portal, www.export.gov, which brings together all the available resources into one place.

The Country Commercial Guides, while they are for obvious reasons mainly aimed at US companies, offer a great deal of general information applicable to all, and can be downloaded or ordered on cd-rom from the National Technical Information Service (www.ntis.gov). The down-

2

loaded version costs for US$25, the CD will set you back US$40. Better still, go to www.buyusa.gov/russia/en, where you can download the guide for free, as well as accessing a vast market research library of off the shelf publications and market reports, which you can search for by region, country, sector, date, or any combination thereof.

As with the UK, if you want to engage the services of US Commercial Service in-country teams, you can do so on a chargeable basis. Broadly equivalent to UKTI's OMIS programme, the Customised Market Analysis Program is a bespoke market research service providing exporters with information on marketing and selling their specific product, including price details of equivalent products, key competitors if any, existing promotion and distribution practices and possible business partners. Prices range from around US$500 to US$5,000+ depending on the amount of work involved.

CMAP

Additionally to CMAP, the US Commercial Service offers an impressively comprehensive series of other programmes which US companies would do well to look at. A full list is available at www.buyusa.gov/russia/en/products_services, below are a few examples:

The Gold Key Matching Service is broadly similar in intent to the CMAP, but includes a briefing and de-briefing from local staff as part of the trip. The charge at the time of writing for SMEs (fewer than 500 employees according to the US definition) is US$700, half that if you are using the service for the first time. International

IPS

Partner Search (IPS) provides details of potential partners, agents and distributors, and International Company Profile (ICP) is a more detailed due diligence on a particular company, including management details, financial condition, market coverage and credit-worthiness.

US Commercial Service
US Embassy Moscow
23/38 Bolshaya Molchanovka
Building 2
Moscow 121069
Tel: +7 495 737 5030

Fax: +7 495 737 5033
E-mail: moscow.office.box@mail.doc.gov
Website: www.buyusa.gov/russia/en

The US Commercial Service has branch offices in
St Petersburg, Vladivostok and Yekaterinburg.
Full contact details are in Appendix 1.

Canada

Russia is one of 13 priority export markets for Canada,
and bilateral trade between the two countries has
roughly quadrupled since 2002, reaching CAN$2.5bn
(approximately US$2.3bn) in 2007. Key opportunities
for Canadian companies have been identified in oil
and gas equipment and services, metals and mining,
agriculture, and construction. In 2007 Canada closed
its Consulate in St Petersburg, although it retains a
presence in Vladivostok and, of course, Moscow.

The range of services available to Canadian companies
is limited to market reports and sector profiles, all
downloadable from the Trade Commission's website,
in addition to which you will find a list of recommended
service providers, and travel reports similar to those
provided by other nations. There is also a link to an
export finance guide, which takes you through the
various financial issues of exporting, and points you
towards any resources that may be available for
particular sectors. There is not sufficient space to
go through all the variables here, if you think this
may be relevant to you, visit
www.edc.ca/english/exportfinanceguide/efg.htm.

Additionally, you can access a Virtual Trade
Commissioner by registering on the main website.
This is an interactive service designed to guide potential
exporters through the questions they need to ask
themselves, everything from export-readiness to
general information on import tariffs.

Virtual Trade Commissioner

Foreign Affairs and International Trade Canada
Embassy of Canada Moscow
23 Starokonyushenny Pereulok
Moscow 119002
Tel.:   +7 495 105 6000

2

Fax: +7 495 105 6004
E-mail: moscow@international.gc.ca
Website: www.russia.gc.ca

Australia

Australian companies have become increasingly active in Russia in recent years, and not only in the sectors that you would expect, such as metals and mining. Australia's relative geographical proximity to Russia's Far East has given it a particular advantage in working with companies far from Europe and Moscow. The agency supporting Australian exporters is Austrade, which in Russia is headquartered at the embassy in Moscow, with representatives also in St Petersburg and Vladivostok. Austrade's website has a decent amount of information on Russia, with special focus on a number of priority areas such as food and beverages.

EMDG

Austrade also administers the Export Market Development Grants (EMDG) scheme, which allows companies with an annual turnover of less than AUS$30m to claim back up to half of their export promotion expenses (up to a maximum value of AUS$15,000 at the time of writing), including costs incurred hiring marketing consultants and producing free samples.

Austrade also has offices in all the Australian states, as well as in many countries around the world. Some of the states also have their own separate trade promotion agencies, not all of which are based in-country. The Queensland government's Russia specialist, for example, is based in London as does a representative from the government of South Australia.

Austrade Russia/CIS
Australian Embassy
10A/2 Podkolokolny pereulok
Moscow 109028
Tel: +7 495 232 3257
Fax: +7 495 232 3298
Website: www.austrade.gov.au

Non-governmental organisations, Chambers of Commerce

2

Russo-British Chamber of Commerce (RBCC)

RBCC

Founded in 1916, with perhaps not the best sense of timing, the RBCC is an independent, bilateral membership organisation that seeks to develop business ties between Russia and the UK. With offices in London, Moscow and St Petersburg, the chamber is first and foremost a good network to access if you are working in Russia for the first time. The RBCC runs a series of events throughout the year, from simple evening networking receptions to high level business forums, and produces a monthly magazine for its members. Although it isn't a particularly big or powerful organisation, the chamber occupies an ideal position bang in the middle of Russian-British business, so becoming a member can be a handy way to get contacts where otherwise you might struggle. Russia is no different from a lot of other export markets in that good contacts are vital. The RBCC also provides chargeable consultancy services to its members, and can put together bespoke trade missions complete with market research, meeting facilitation and follow up.

The Chamber's London office is also staffed by a permanent representative of the Russian Chamber of Commerce network (RFCCI), generally an experienced Russian official from the Ministry of Trade. Russia, like many other countries, has an extensive network of Chambers of Commerce and Industry. I recommend that you always make a point of contacting your local CCI, especially if you are looking at investing outside of Moscow or St Petersburg – it is an excellent and underused resource. Some are more active than others, of course, but all should be able to provide you with useful contacts and information on local market conditions. Through the RFCCI website (www.tpprf.ru) you will be able to find contact details (and in most cases, individual websites) of the 175-odd chambers spread throughout the Russian Federation.
At least some will have information available in English.

RFCCI

2

Russo-British Chamber of Commerce
Willcox House
42 Southwark Street
London SE1 1UN
Tel: +44 (0)20 7403 1706
Fax: +44 (0)20 7403 1245
Website: www.rbcc.com

The American Chamber of Commerce in Russia (AmCham)

AmCham

AmCham, first established in 1991 as the American Business Club, is similar in concept to the RBCC, although it emphasises its role as a lobbying organisation, representing the interests of US companies working in Russia. Headquartered in Moscow, the chamber also has a "Chapter" (makes it sound like a biker gang, doesn't it?) in St Petersburg. Unlike the RBCC, which has an international membership base, AmCham's members are made up principally only of US and Russian companies. Again, it is a useful network to plug into. In common with other business associations, AmCham runs regular social events, so it is worth going along to a couple before you decide whether or not to join.

AmCham also produces a monthly members magazine, AmCham News, and a bi-monthly newsletter to which non-members can also subscribe. The chamber also runs a series of briefings, seminars, trade missions and regular sector-specific committees which offer a good way of keeping up-to-date with developments and making new contacts.

The American Chamber of Commerce in Russia
Dolgorukovskaya Ul. 7, 14th Floor
Moscow 127006
Tel: +7 (495) 961 2141
Fax: +7 (495) 961 2142
Website: www.amcham.ru

Below is a list of the other main international business support associations active in Russia. This is by no means an exhaustive listing, but covers the main organisations with which you may want to make contact.

2

The Association of European Business (AEB)

Krasnoproletarskaya ul. 16 bld 3
(4th floor)
Moscow 127473
Tel: +7 (495) 967 9765
Fax: +7 (495) 967 9779
Website: www.aebrus.ru

Similar to both AmCham and the RBCC, although the AEB only has a permanent presence in Moscow. The Association runs a series of briefings and networking "open" events, and also has a research department producing a series of sector and regional updates, along with an annual How to Invest in Russia guide.

The Canada Eurasia Russia Business Association (CERBA)

CERBA-Moscow
c/o Ronald A Chisholm Intl
Bolshoi Strochenovski, 15a
Moscow 113054
Tel: +7 (495) 937 4760
Fax: +7 (495) 937 4763
Website: www.cerbanet.org

As its name implies, CERBA does not only cover Russia, but also provides support to Canadian companies working with Ukraine and Kazakhstan. In addition to its Moscow office, CERBA has representation in Toronto, Calgary and Montreal.

The US-Russia Business Council

Ulitsa Bolshaya Nikitskaya 21/18
Building 1, Office 201
Moscow 125009
Tel: +7 (495) 291 2105
Fax: +7 (495) 291 2150
Website: www.usrbc.org

Headquartered in Washington, DC, the US-Russia Business Council is similar in appeal and approach to AmCham, concentrating principally on lobbying activities. The council website has some useful information on the Russian regions, special economic zones (see Chapter 5) and technoparks.

SPIBA

The St Petersburg International Business Association (SPIBA)
36 Shpalernaya ul.,
St Petersburg 191123
Tel.:   +7 (812) 325 9091
Fax: +7 (812) 279 9789
Website: www.spiba.ru

Specialising in St Petersburg and NW Russia, SPIBA runs regular committees on various sectors (HR, marketing and so on), and also acts as a conduit of information from both international and Russian companies active in the region to the St Petersburg city and Leningrad oblast authorities.

Industry-specific trade associations

There is a trade association for pretty much every conceivable business activity, and depending on the level of relevance to the specifics of the market, some of these will be actively promoting their members in Russia. A few of them will even have permanent representatives based in Russia, and many organise trade missions to particular regions of interest. Obviously, an association's level of activity in Russia will depend to a certain extent on the sector, and how much potential business there is in the market: organisations such as the Manufacturing Technologies Association, the Society of Petroleum Engineers, and British Expertise (which promotes UK professional services companies) are examples of bodies particularly active in Russia at the moment. The best advice is to contact your own industry association and see if they are working with Russia – if you see it as a target market, there is every chance that they will too.

Informal business networks

In addition to all the above, most of the major Russian cities, and particularly Moscow and St Petersburg, have thriving informal networks of foreign business people. Although Russia is hardly the Wild East that perhaps it once was, there remains an element of camaraderie in any expat community, and if you can make some good contacts among the more experienced operators, you will find this invaluable. Some of these networks have become organisations in their own right, such as the British, Jewish and Danish Business Clubs.

Online communities such as Expat.ru (Moscow-only), can provide useful information as well, and can help with everything from finding a private Russian teacher or a restaurant to converting clothing sizes. The site even has an online doctor and dentist for those late-night "what's that ringing sound in my ear?" moments.

The internet

Russia, and the Russians, have embraced the internet with open arms. The sociologist in me sometimes wonders how much of this is down to the fact that centuries of authoritarian rule have engendered a cultural predisposition to virtual networks. It is certainly the case that in Soviet times there was a kind of magical grapevine of information exchange, manifesting itself in everything from Muscovites almost instinctively knowing when a shipment of good quality shoes appeared in a department store, to the ready availability of officially banned Western music. Remember that one of the inventors of Google is Russian. Whatever the reason, there is an incredible amount of Russia-related information on the worldwide web. As always, though, much of it will be unchecked and may well be inaccurate, so tread carefully.

Exhibitions and conferences

In the 1990s, a number of business conference and exhibition organisers turned their attention to the emerging market economy of Russia, and a few more sprang up to specialise in events covering Russia and the countries of the former Soviet Union. Nearly two decades on, many of the latter have fallen by the way side, and now there remains a handful of organisers who have regular programmes of events and conferences either in Russia or elsewhere.

Business events

As regards cost of attendance, there are a very few events that are free to attend, but for the most part you will have to pay. It won't be cheap either – if you find an event where attendance is less than a thousand pounds, you are doing well (although you may want to ask yourself why it is such an apparent bargain). For your money you will get a two or three day event, generally with high-level industry speakers and ample opportunity for networking and contact building. In some cases an

2

exhibition will be attached to the conference, but there are also a range of events held at the major exhibition centres in Moscow, St Petersburg and the other major cities. Exhibitions are obviously much cheaper (or free) to attend, as they are principally financed by the exhibitors themselves, and they can be a very good way of gauging the market and seeing who the main players are. As described above, you may also be able to claim government support to meet some of your costs if you decide to exhibit.

It must be said that the days have long gone where people would flock to any event just because it involved Russia, and in recent years a few of the more general events have become shadows of their former selves. The smarter organisers have altered their approach to make their events more specific: you will generally find one that is relevant to your sector, unless you are into beekeeping or something like that.

Details of some of the major Russia-related events organisers can be found in Appendix 1.

Market Research

Economic and Country Guides

Once you have a handle on the general picture of doing business in Russia, you may want to obtain some more in-depth analysis and intelligence on your particular sector. This will obviously cost more, but it may well save you from possibly unpleasant (and definitely more expensive) surprises later on. Russia is a fast-moving place, so do not be over-reliant on information in annual market intelligence reports. They are excellent for background, but there is no replacement for keeping your ear to the ground.

There are, you will be unsurprised to know, a number of organisations producing regular detailed reports. Below is a listing of some of the main sources:

Dun & Bradstreet (D&B)

D&B

Long recognised as one of the industry-standard market research companies, and in existence since 1841, D&B produce a number of publications with economic and

2

risk analysis of Russia. The most comprehensive is the annually updated Country Report, which covers everything from general political risk to an assessment of the likelihood of your getting paid. More general information is available from the Export Guide, also produced annually, and you can additionally subscribe to a monthly (and slightly sketchy, in my view) Country RiskLine update. All are available as downloaded pdf files and in hard copy. For further information go to www.dnb.com.

The Economist Intelligence Unit (EIU)

Founded a year after the end of the Second World War, the EIU is part of the Economist Group, and provides a broadly similar range of reports to D&B. The EIU's flagship is the Country Report, updated monthly in the case of Russia, to which you can either subscribe for a full year, or purchase singly for slightly less than half the price of an annual subscription. Alongside the Country Report sit the Country Profile (an annual publication covering background information and historical context), a Country Risk Service providing ongoing assessment of credit risk with a rolling two-year forecast, and Country ViewsWire, a monthly analysis of the latest developments. With the exception of the online-only Country ViewsWire, all products are available either in electronic or hard copy format. The full range of EIU products can be seen at www.eiu.com.

EIU

In addition to the above companies, Business Monitor International produces a series of regional and industry reports, as well as a range of company directories and databases (which also include profiles on leading executives) in CD-Rom format. Datamonitor provides a number of overall sector reports which will include the Russian market, as well as a number of SWOT analysis reports on some of Russia's leading corporations. Snapdata, acquired in 2008 by Mintel, produces a series of Snapshots reports on some fairly precise sub-sectors – if you want an 11-page report on Russian home laundry appliances, or ice-cream, this is the place for you. Marchmont Capital Partners, a relatively recent arrival on the market from 2005, is essentially a corporate finance advisory firm which offers subscription-based access to its market and region reports, as well as a general Russia investment guide. Interfax Group was formed in the early 1990s as a Russian alternative to the established western information agencies, and produces a range of regular sector reports as well as a subscription news service in addition to its own online open-access newsfeeds. Some of Interfax's marketing is a little strange – I've never seen a line from a Tom Clancy novel used as a plug for an information agency before, certainly – but it is a viable option. Interfax also has a very comprehensive Russian company database, with over 4.5m legal entities listed.

There are a few information resellers out there, which can be a useful way to see what else is out there – www.mindbranch.com is a good example. Just make sure you get the report at the best price: generally it is best to order direct from the source.

Keeping up to date

Aside from the report-based sources, there are a handful of fairly sophisticated media-monitoring based business intelligence services available, such as Dow Jones Factiva, Lexis Nexis and Meltwater. All can be used to provide in-depth media information, both current and archived, to give you a better picture of the activities in sectors relevant to you.

There are also a number of companies providing their own content, including ISI Emerging Markets which, while not being focused solely on Russia, produces editorial content through its Intellinews service. The company additionally offers a number of media monitoring and research products. Slightly more specialized, Mergermarket is an independent M&A intelligence service using its own network of journalists to produce analysis of dealflows worldwide – particularly useful if you want to dig a little deeper behind the news from the standard news sources. bne (Business New Europe) is one of the very few independent specialist services which solely produces its own content, including analysis from a number of industry expert commentators, and offers a number of products for you to choose from depending how much information you need, and how frequently you need it.

For general online news in English, RIA Novosti, one of the major Russian news agencies, provides good coverage of both business and politics, as well as a number of subscription newswires. RIA Novosti also produces Russia Profile, an English-language magazine available both online and in print form, the latter being published 10 times per year. The Russian business daily Kommersant publishes an English version both in print and online, and you would also be well advised to check out the English-only Moscow Times and its sister publication in St. Petersburg.

All of the above (and more – there is no shortage) can be valuable for both background information and, perhaps more importantly, for keeping abreast of developments that may affect your business in Russia – competitor activity, legislative changes and the like. The best policy is to look at them all and decide which fits your business best.

My advice if you want to really keep up to speed on Russian developments is to look at an independent, specialist service – one that uses both Russian and international sources. With media coverage of Russia being what it is, you really need to see both sides of the story. To illustrate what I mean, when I was a student in Moscow in the early '90s, I knew of a correspondent working for a highly-respected international news organization who was filing a story on the almost complete lack of information on HIV/AIDS in Moscow. When a friend of mine asked the journalist whether he would mention in his piece the posters on every train carriage in the Moscow metro warning of the dangers of the disease, including a helpline number, his reply was along the lines of "Oh, you wouldn't catch me on the metro here."

From the other side, the media in Russia, while it enjoys marginally more freedom that it did a few years ago, is still a long way from being truly independent: there are powerful interests around which may influence coverage, just as in some cases there are in the west. The only way to be sure is to read as much information as you can, and draw your own conclusions.

2

More specialised information

You may find that, even armed with the information from the above sources, you still require more specific information on your industry, and particularly on prospective partners, which will not be available off-the-shelf. Again, there are a number of companies that can do this, although the cost of such information will obviously now be rising sharply. Make sure that, before you commission a report of this kind, you have already done fairly extensive research yourself. This will allow you to be very specific in terms of the information you request, thereby hopefully reducing your costs.

FCO

More importantly, if you are already *au fait* with the sector or company on which you have asked for additional checks, you will be in a better position to put this new information into context. You will also be able to demonstrate to the provider that you know what you are talking about, and this may well be reflected in the quality of the information you get.

A brief list of the main providers is below – most have offices in the US, the UK, Europe and Russia. Remember that if your company already retains the services of a law firm, you may want to approach them to perform a due diligence report for you, especially if they have a Russian office or partner.

Control Risks Group
Website: www.crg.com

Kroll
Website: www.kroll.com

Diligence LLC
Website: www.diligencellc.com

Drum Resources Ltd
Website: www.drumresources.com

Risk Advisory Group
Website: www.riskadvisory.net

GPW Ltd
Website: www.gpwltd.com

Travel advice

The UK's Foreign and Commonwealth Office and US State Department, along with the Ministries of Foreign Affairs of Canada and Australia, all provide travel advice through their websites. Some of this advice borders (excuse the pun) on the alarmist, but it is as well to know the risk of wherever you travel to in the world. The common theme running through travel advice from all countries is to avoid the Northern Caucasus – Chechnya, Ingushetia and Dagestan – and to exercise extreme caution in the surrounding areas.

Bear in mind that all advice from government sources may reflect at some level the prevailing political relations between that country and Russia. I would wholeheartedly agree that the Northern Caucasus is, and sadly looks set to remain for some time, pretty much a no-go area for foreigners (as it is for many Russians), but the accounts in some cases of gangs of marauding youths targeting hapless foreign businessmen in Russia's larger cities are fairly wide of the mark. Exercise the same caution and common sense that you normally would in a big city at home, and you should be fine.

Conclusion

Probably the final piece of advice I would give you is to be careful who you take advice from. Just because you are reading this text in a book with a cover and some pictures does not necessarily mean you should take it as fact. Russia continues to generate a lot of background noise, and to this day I am still regularly asked questions by people going there for the first time which suggest that their main knowledge of the place still comes from a John le Carré novel.

As with any export market (indeed, any foreign country), there is no substitute for running the soil through your fingers. All the above sources of information are useful, but only in the context of your own direct knowledge and experience of the country. Russia continues to confound first-time visitors – I have never taken a delegation to the country without them expressing surprise (usually pleasant surprise) at some unexpected detail or other. I have been travelling there for 20 years

2

now, and it continues to surprise me, as does the persistence of out-dated views among agencies which should really know better by now. Be especially careful of anyone who tries to convince you that you cannot hope to do business there without the contacts that they will be able to magically provide. In some cases they may be of real value, but until you go there yourself you will not be in any position to judge – the best thing is to get there yourself, and that is what we'll look at in the next chapter.

getting to Russia

getting to Russia

The various considerations
in arranging travel to Russia
from getting a visa to tips on
health and insurance

Visas

With very few exceptions, as a citizen of a foreign country you will need a visa to enter Russia. Do NOT fall into the trap of thinking you can just obtain a visa on entry, or that you can leave your application until the last minute. Most airports will not let you board a plane to Russia without a current visa, but if you do end up at a Russian point of entry without the necessary documents, you will not be allowed into the country, full stop. You will also have to pay for your return travel. Equally, while you can get certain types of visa turned around in a day, it will be an expensive business. People still make this mistake time and again when going to Russia for the first time – don't become one of them. Depending on your requirements, you may need well over a month to obtain your shiny new Russian visa.

Procedures vary slightly from country to country, but generally you will require at least the following documents:

*   A current international passport with validity of at least six months beyond the visa's expiration date and at least two adjacent and opposite blank pages
*   One recent passport-sized photo
*   A completed official visa application form (in the UK you will have to complete the form online and print yourself a copy, otherwise the form is downloadable from the website of your local Russian embassy or consulate – see contact details in Appendix 1)
*   Depending on the type of visa, a private or official invitation or tourist voucher

There are several types of visa available: a transit visa (which generally does not require an invitation or voucher) will enable you to travel through Russia to a third destination, provided that you have the correct documentation to complete your journey; a tourist visa, for general travel within Russia; a private/visitor visa, should you be seeing friends or family, and not staying at a hotel; a business visa, for work-related travel (this can be issued for single, dual or multiple entry); and finally a working visa or work permit should you be permanently based in Russia. This last document

Documents required

3

involves a whole series of other procedures, which we will deal with in more detail in Chapter 6.

Transit, tourist and private visas are issued for single entry and exit only, and you will have to specify the date of entry and return. Generally it is a good idea to make your visa valid for at least a week either side of your intended travel dates in case of delay – if you are still in Russia when your visa runs out, you may be stuck there for several weeks while a new one is issued. It generally takes around seven working days to process all these types of visa once you have submitted your passport, although you can get it done the same day for a surcharge.

If you are on your first recce trip to Russia, it is probably easiest just to book yourself a travel/accommodation package with a tourist visa included. Use a specialist travel agency, or at least one with experience of arranging bookings to Russia, as they will generally be familiar with the vagaries of visa processing locally and will make sure you get your documents on time. Start with the members of one or other of the business organisations mentioned in the last chapter, and you won't go far wrong.

A private visa is only really an option if you have a friend or contact in Russia who is prepared to officially invite you. They can generally only do this through an approved agency in Russia, and will have to send you the original invitation document, not a photocopy or fax copy. By the time you have reimbursed your contact for the courier charges and the agency fee, you might as well have just got your travel agent to arrange the visa in the first place. If you really don't want to stay in a hotel (and there are plenty of serviced apartments which you can stay in), just pay the extra to get your travel agent to issue the visitor visa with no hotel booking. If they really are a specialist they will be able to arrange the invitation.

More flexible (and more expensive) is a business visa, which can be issued on either a single or double entry basis, valid for one or three months, or as a multiple entry visa valid for one year. This last type is by far the most convenient, but it is not cheap – if you can get it for anything significantly below £500 or equivalent complete with all support documents, you are doing better than me.

3

For a business visa you will need, in addition to the main documents, a letter from your employer confirming the reason for your trip, and if necessary explaining why multiple entry is required. Once you have all this together, an invitation can be issued in three days for a single or double entry visa, while a multi-entry can take up to a month. The organisations that can issue invitations for business visas all have to be a registered representative of the Russian Foreign Office, so this really is something best left to the experts. Once you get established in Russia, your local Chamber of Commerce and Industry (not the foreign chambers like AmCham or RBCC) can issue an invitation for you. This will save a lot of money, not least because when the first year's invitation period runs out, they can generally just extend it for a reduced fee.

The application form itself is the same regardless of the type of visa involved, and you will need to provide basic personal details, information on any previous trips you have made to Russia, and a list of the cities you intend to visit.

Consular fees vary, and it is best to check on the website of the Russian embassy in your country. At the time of writing, the fees for business visas look like this:
You can go through the entire process on a shoestring if you really want to, and bypass the agencies, but ask yourself first if you really want to queue up outside the

Country – Type	6-10 working days	3-5 working days	Next working day	Same working day
UK – Single	£45.00 (7 days)	n/a	n/a	£95.00
UK – Double	£55.00 (7 days)	n/a	n/a	£105.00
UK – Multi	£110.00 (7 days)	n/a	n/a	£160.00
US – Single	$131.00	$150.00	$200.00	$300.00
US – Double	$131.00	$200.00	$250.00	$350.00
US – Multi	$131.00	$300.00	$350.00	$450.00
EU – All types*	€35.00	n/a	€70.00 (1-3 days)	n/a
Canada – Single	CAN$75.00 (15 days)	n/a	n/a	n/a
Canada – Double	CAN$100.00 (15 days)	n/a	n/a	n/a
Canada – Multi	CAN$200.00 (15 days)	n/a	n/a	n/a
Australia – Single	AUS$110.00	AUS$150.00	AUS$200.00	AUS$400.00
Australia – Double	AUS$170.00	AUS$200.00	AUS$285.00	AUS$485.00
Australia – Multi	AUS$370.00	AUS$400.00	AUS$460.00	AUS$600.00

*Pursuant to the EU-Russia visa agreement of June 2007.
Does not include citizens of UK, Ireland, Denmark and Iceland

3

Russian consulate at 6:30am behind a courier from the very agency you could have gone to. He or she will very likely have a pack of 20-30 applications, perhaps the last ones the processing department will take that day. I've done it, and I suggest that you do not. In some countries it is possible to make a postal application, but remember that if your application form has been wrongly filled in, or there is an error in your supporting documents, you will lose your fee. Better to save a lot more money once you get there by taking the train from the airport instead of a taxi (see "On arrival" below).

The visa system has long been a point of discussion among business travellers to Russia, not least because it has led to more than one high profile foreign businessman being effectively barred from working in the country. There are no signs at present that it will undergo any significant changes or streamlining in the near future, although there is a faint glimmer of hope on the horizon. When Ukraine won the Eurovision Song Contest in 2004, the authorities suspended the visa regime for EU citizens the following year, when it occurred to them that they wouldn't be able to cope with the extra volume of applications for people coming to Kiev. The move was so successful in terms of encouraging overseas visitors that Ukraine never reinstated the system. In 2008 Russia won Eurovision, so hope springs eternal.

Getting to Russia

Working on the assumption that you will be flying to Russia, if you are travelling to Moscow you will most likely arrive at either Sheremetyevo or Domodedovo airport, which lie 30km north west and 22km south east of the city respectively. In recent years Vnukovo airport, just under 30km south west of the centre, has started taking international flights – particularly some of the no-frills carriers like German Wings. Most of the major international carriers have daily direct flights to Moscow, and Russia's flagship carrier, Aeroflot, operates scheduled services to around 50 countries. St Petersburg's single international airport, Pulkovo, has daily flights to and from most of the European capitals, as well as Beijing. Flight times to Moscow are around 3½ hours from London, 9 hours from New York, and 2½ hours from Berlin. Further afield, airlines such as bmi, Austrian Air, Lufthansa and Air France operate less frequent services to major Russian cities like Yekaterinburg, Kazan', Rostov-on-Don, Nizhniy Novgorod, and Novosibirsk. If your destination is smaller still, the most flexible option is to fly to Moscow and catch a domestic flight from there. Russian internal flights are generally not the most luxurious – sometimes you half expect to glance around and see a guy at the back wearing a parachute and playing a harmonica – but the schedules are generally reliable, and the quality of pilot-training in Russia more than makes up for the low-tech hardware. The smoothest landing I ever experienced was in 1991 on a flight from Moscow to Tashkent in a venerable Tupolev. In any case, a lot of the Soviet-era fleet has now been replaced by Boeings and Airbuses, and a new Russian regional jet, the Sukhoi Superjet 100, will be entering service over the next few years.

As to cost, prices will obviously vary greatly depending on the airline and destination. With some of the larger carriers it is worth staying an extra night in Russia so that your trip includes an overnight stay on Saturday. If you do not, you can be charged the full "company is paying for the ticket" price, so it may be a better idea to save yourself (or your company) a few hundred pounds by having a day's sightseeing once the business part of your trip is over. The visa system means that Russia is not really a weekend or short-break destination, so there are not many budget carriers operating there yet.

Flight costs

You can get to Russia by rail if you wish, either from Finland into St Petersburg, or from central Europe into Moscow. There is a daily service from Cologne to Moscow, although as the journey takes thirty six hours it is really only an option for chronic aerophobics. The train goes through Germany, Poland and Belarus, and offers passengers a unique insight into 19th century European history as the carriages are taken one by one into a siding on the Poland-Belarus border to have their wheels changed. Russian gauge, around three inches wider than the rest of Europe, was allegedly adopted by Nicholas I in the 1850s to thwart a rail-borne invasion by hostile powers.

3

Passengers travelling from Finland to St Petersburg have to endure no such inconvenience, as the Finnish gauge is just 4mm broader than in Russia, a difference small enough to allow through-running. If you take the train to Moscow via Belarus, you will also need a transit visa for the latter, not to mention a head for heights as the carriages are all lifted two metres into the air to change the wheels with the passengers still on board.

On arrival

Within 72 hours of your arrival in Russia, regardless of the type of visa you have, you will have to register with the authorities. You will need an immigration card – a small A6 piece of paper which fits into your passport – which can be obtained either on the plane or in the confused-milling area in front of passport control at the airport. Fill in both sides – it is basically just personal and passport/visa details, purpose of visit (which should match the type of visa), and the address where you will be staying in Russia. The smiling border official will check the details, stamp the left-hand (entry) side of the form and keep it, handing the exit side back to you. They will also put a stamp in your passport either on your visa (if it is single entry) or on the page opposite. Keep the exit part of your immigration card, you will need this throughout your stay.

Registration

Registration itself is easy if you are staying at a hotel – when you check in, reception will take your passport from you ("augh, I've only been here an hour and my passport has already been confiscated!") and hand it back to you either later that day or the following morning with a registration stamp on the reverse side. Check this – it should be for the full period of your stay.

According to the Russian Federal Migration Service website, Host Parties (ie. whoever does the registration on your behalf) no longer have the right to take your passport from you, they may only take a copy, but most hotels still take your passport in the same way that they always did, so do not be unduly alarmed. Just don't forget to collect your passport when you are next passing reception. As a very charming and efficient hotel receptionist once said to my father when he was visiting

3

me in my student days, "Sorry, Mr. Gilbert, I know it doesn't make sense, but this is the Soviet Union, and if you didn't have a sense of humour, you shouldn't have come here."

If you are not staying in a hotel, you will need to register in some other way. Fortunately, there are a number of expat services companies who will do this for a fee – it can take a day or so, and generally they will just take a copy of your passport so you are not separated from it for too long. At the same time, get them to take a copy of your immigration card and give it back to you so that you have at least something to hand until you get the stamped one back. Legislation came in at the beginning of 2007 to streamline immigration rules, meaning that now only border officials can check your immigration documents, but this news has not yet filtered down to all levels of the police, who just might want to see your papers on the street, or in the metro. For this reason, make sure that you have your passport with you at all times when you are in Russia.

Before you can register, though, you have to get to your hotel. If you are staying in Moscow you may already have a car organised to collect you at the airport. If not, do yourself an enormous favour and take the train into the centre. Russia's capital has seen the number of cars on its roads rise astronomically since the fall of communism, and traffic jams are now legendary, especially on Leningradsky Prospect which you will have to take if you are coming from Sheremetyevo. A journey of a few kilometres can easily take three hours (I know of someone who took a full eight hours on this particular trip).

Much better to stride purposefully past the thronging taxi-drivers and touts and go to the express train terminal. From here you can take a modern train into the centre of town for a fraction of the cost, and more importantly, in a fraction of the time (from Domodedovo the journey time is around 45 minutes, from Sheremetyevo – 35 minutes). Both trains will take you to one of Moscow's main stations, where you can pick up a cab and sit in a traffic jam for a far shorter span of time. Taking the train will not only save you time

Getting from the Airport

3

when you arrive, it is also a good idea to get familiar with the service now, as it will be far more important to you when the time comes to go home and you have a plane to catch. In the unlikely event of your arriving at Vnukovo, you will be glad to know that a similar train service operates there.

If you are flying into St Petersburg, for now at least you are stuck with either a car from the airport, or if you are feeling more adventurous, a bus transfer to the nearest metro station. At least the traffic from Pulkovo airport isn't (yet) in the Moscow league, but still allow a good hour and a half at least for the 15km you will have to cover. You may be lucky and do it in twenty minutes, in which case you will wonder who this idiot is who told you to leave so much time – all I can say is that I lived there for a couple of years and the journey was never the same twice. An overland express rail link is currently being built which will go to the airport but mysteriously bypass the centre, but it will at least get you to a metro station. The link should be in service by 2011.

If you are flying into anywhere else in Russia, the best option is to arrange for a car to pick you up at the airport – the traffic won't be nearly so bad, and if you can book through your hotel or travel agent it will be one less thing to worry about.

Health and insurance

Travellers to Russia, even to the larger cities, should be immunized at least against tetanus-diphtheria, typhoid, and hepatitis A and B. Tuberculosis is becoming an increasing problem in Russia, and if you are travelling to outlying rural areas you should also think about getting jabs for Japanese and/or tick-borne encephalitis, a serious disease related to meningitis which leads to inflammation of the brain, and can kill you. Travel health advice can be sought either on the UK Foreign Office or US State Department websites (see previous chapter) or through a number of international travel-advice sites, like www.mdtravelhealth.com.

Opinions vary on whether you should drink the water in Russia – the FCO currently advises that you shouldn't, even in Moscow (whereas the US State Department says Moscow is OK), although I have done so for many years without any obvious ill-effects. As to the food, take the same precautions you would anywhere else, in other words, be sensible. Lukewarm meat pies bought at train stations are probably best avoided in Moscow just as they would be in London or New York, and the deeper you go into the countryside, the more cautious you should become, more than anything because you will be further from a chemist. One trick that will be familiar to veteran travellers is to have a generous-ish slug of vodka or similar before going to bed. No need to overdo it (of course) but the alcohol can neutralise any unfamiliar bacteria before they wreak havoc with your insides. You should always take out travel insurance wherever you go, and Russia is no exception. The level of cover is up to you, but it should at least include medical care, as private clinics are not cheap – Russia has an agreement with some western countries, including the UK, by which citizens of the latter can be treated for free in Russian hospitals, but the treatment will be limited. Insurance costs as a rule will be slightly higher than for Europe.

In the next chapter, assuming I haven't put you off, we will deal with the nitty-gritty of getting around Russia, both geographically and commercially, in a little more detail.

4

the ground rules

the ground rules

This section takes the reader by
the hand and talks through the
nitty-gritty of everyday life, from
how to get around to how much
to tip the bell-boy. Knowledge
of these essentials provides the
confidence to go out and do
business effectively.

4

Climate

Before we get on to more business-related matters, and at the risk of making you even more reluctant to go to Russia, it is worth spending a few moments to discuss the weather conditions you may encounter, and how to deal with them. Russia's continental climate means extremes of temperature, and even brief exposure to temperatures of -20°C is unpleasant, if not downright dangerous. Imagine the air being so cold that you cannot breathe too quickly for fear of scorching your lungs, and a spiky sensation developing in your nose as your nostril hairs start to ice up, and you will get the picture. Russians have a saying – "there is no such thing as bad weather, only bad clothing"*, and you will likely receive more or less constant upbraidings from your local colleagues and friends for not being sufficiently wrapped up against the elements. The reason is simple – cold of this nature can, and frequently does, kill people. To complicate matters further, buildings in Russia are generally kept heated at a much higher temperature than you may be used to, so you will be forever struggling in and out of clothing and heavy boots.

To deal with the cold effectively, you need to remember three things – layers, gaps and extremities. The more layers of clothing you have on, the more insulating air you will trap between the layers – air is a very poor conductor of heat, so each layer will be progressively warmer the closer you get to your skin. If you're going to be out for a while, wear long-johns or thermals under your trousers, and a cotton t-shirt under your shirt, and always make sure that the outer layer is thick and windproof. Secondly, gaps: even on a still day, cold will find its way through any chink in your thermal armour, and the difference between your body temperature and the air is such that you will lose massive amounts of heat at every weak or ill-defended point – you will find this out very quickly if you don't muffle up with a scarf.

Finally, and probably most important of all: the extremities. The most dangerous condition for anyone is

---

Footnote: Students of the Russian language may be interested to know that there is an alternative version to this phrase – "There is no such thing as bad weather, just not enough vodka."

4

when the body starts to lose its core temperature, but if your head, hands and feet are not protected against the cold, any efforts you make to keep the central portion of your body warm will be futile. The amount of heat you will lose through your skin will be generally proportional to the amount of surface area exposed, but if you run for a bus without wearing a hat, the increased blood-flow to your brain can mean you lose up to half your body-heat through your scalp. If your shoes are not warm enough, no amount of stamping will get the feeling back to your feet, and if you don't wear thick gloves, your fingers will be next to useless in a couple of minutes. Mittens are warmer than gloves due to their lower surface area, and fur-lined winter shoes make a big difference. For your head, wear at least a woollen ski-hat, and ideally a proper Russian fur hat (a *shapka*). Take the thickest winter overcoat you can find, preferably pure wool, and think about buying a fur-lined jacket (*dublyonka*) when you are there – you can get all the items mentioned above made with artificial fur.

This might seem silly, but remember where we came from as a species, and that we have had precious little time to evolve to deal with severe cold: your dog and your cat are both much better cold-warriors than either you or your thousand-generations-distant descendants will ever be. Winter conditions in much of Russia are such that your body is simply ill-equipped to replace lost heat if you do not take proper measures to protect yourself. The good news is that in the middle of a real cold snap you are unlikely to get ill, as most germs and viruses will be either dead or dormant under these conditions.

Currency

The Russian unit of currency is the Rouble, which is made up of 100 *kopeks*. During the Soviet era the rouble had various artificial exchange rates against world currencies, and was not traded internationally. With the collapse of the Soviet Union in 1991 and the subsequent emergence of a free market economy, the rouble could no longer be shored up, and it duly nose-dived as the Russian economy faltered, reaching its nadir in the thousand-fold devaluation of 1998 (see Chapter 1). Since then, prudent monetary policy has seen the rouble recover substantially, to the extent that in recent years the main concern became whether its growing strength will cause problems for Russian exporters. The recent global turmoil has reversed this trend. However, with Russia's Central Bank currently foced to prop up the Rouble, at the end of 2008, rates are approximately 41 to the British pound, 28 to the US dollar and 36 to the Euro.

4

Money

The rouble is Russia's only legal tender, and unlike in the 1990s when shops would happily accept "hard" currency, especially US dollars, you will now have to use roubles pretty much wherever you go. Coins are available in 1, 2, 5 and 10 rouble denominations, and banknotes come in denominations of 5, 10, 50, 100, 500, 1,000 and even 5,000. The two lowest paper-note denominations are currently being phased out in favour of the coin equivalent, although they remain legal tender for now.

You can obtain roubles before you arrive in Russia, but the rates will generally be fairly outrageous: take a little with you, at least enough for your train ticket from the airport, but it is generally best to take in the bulk of your cash in either dollars or euros, which are the most commonly-exchanged currencies in Russia and therefore have the lowest buy-sell spreads. Sterling is still ok ish, at least in the larger cities, but for other currencies it is generally better to buy dollars or euros before you go – even though you will be paying commission twice, you will still get a better deal in the long run.

Exchange points are plentiful throughout the cities, and as a rule it is better to change your money in the centre rather than the outskirts, as competition between the various dealers will be higher and the rates therefore fairer. For a good few years now you can of course also just use a cash machine, although remember that you will be hit for commission each time, and your bank will probably be using a less than favourable rate. Another option is to open a current account at Citibank – you can create an account which works in several different currencies at once, and if there is a Citibank ATM where you are (at the time of writing you will find them in 7 Russian cities, including Moscow and St Petersburg),

4

you can withdraw cash with no commission and generally at a decent rate. The only problem is that you are tied to Citibank cashpoints if you want to avoid commission, but there you go.

If you are a regular visitor to Russia you may want to think about opening a bank account locally – foreigners, even if they are non-residents, can open accounts in Russian banks, and there is a handful of international banks with extensive networks in Russia: the Austrian bank Raiffeisen (RZB) has been in Russia for many years now, and is by far the most established of the international groups. The French banking group Société Générale has been in Russia in its present form as BSGV (Banque Société Générale Vostok) since 1993, and the Italian group Unicredit is another example of a foreign bank with a branch network in Russia. Other major international players are somewhat belatedly coming to the market: one of the limiting factors, on the retail side at least, has been the fact that the Central Bank of Russia will only issue a retail banking licence to a Russian-registered bank, and even then it will take a long time. This means that the quickest way for an international bank wanting to get in on the act is either to buy out a Russian bank which already has a licence, as with Barclays's acquisition of Expobank in mid-2008, or to go through the lengthy process of applying for a licence for a Russian-registered subsidiary as in the case of HSBC Russia the previous year.

The Russian banking sector

Aside from the foreign banks, you can also look at a range of Russian institutions offering retail services – you will not be short of choice if you decide to open a local account. In fact, one of the major problems with the Russian banking sector as a whole is that there are simply too many banks, very few of which have until recently had sufficient capitalization to work efficiently. The Russian Central Bank's register of credit institutions for 2008 showed a total of 1,250 companies, and we can expect to see a great deal more consolidation of the sector in the coming years. Even some of Russia's largest banks listed below have had to receive State bail-outs in recent months to shore up their positions.

Sberbank Founded in 1842, with over 20,000 outlets throughout the country, Sberbank is majority owned by the Bank of Russia, with a further third of its shares belonging to institutional investors and 5% in private hands in the wake of a secondary listing on the Russian stock market in 2007. Once the sole provider of retail banking operations in Russia, increased competition in this sector has seen Sberbank's market share drop to around 50% in 2008. Sberbank remains by far Russia's largest bank, with a capitalisation not far off the rest of the top ten put together.

VTB Formerly Vneshtorgbank, or the Bank of Foreign Trade (*Bank Vneshnej Torgovli*). Established in its present form in 1990, during the Soviet period the forerunner to VTB handled all payments for goods imported to and exported from the USSR. VTB relocated its headquarters from Moscow to St Petersburg in 2005, and is expanding aggressively on the retail, consumer credit and mortgage markets through its subsidiary, VTB24. It acquired the London-registered Moscow Narodny Bank at the end of 2005, re-branding it VTB Europe Bank plc in October the following year. VTB is reported to be eyeing further acquisitions in Europe to extend its international footprint.

Gazprombank Established by Russia's state-owned natural resources giant Gazprom in 1990, Gazprombank's principal function is financing the operations of its founder and main shareholder. The bank has also expanded in both the retail and corporate sectors in recent years, and has offices in 51 regions across the Russian Federation. In 2008 Gazprom announced that it would be reducing its stake in the bank to 25%, either selling the remaining 17% to an institutional investor (or syndicate) or through a public offering.

Bank of Moscow Founded in 1994 by the Moscow city government, which remains the main, if not majority, shareholder. Third only to Sberbank and VTB24 in terms of retail deposits, Bank of Moscow's growing presence on the market meant that in 2008 it became a contributing bank to the MosPrimeRate, the key indicator on the interbank lending market for the Russian rouble.

Russia's Top Ten Banks

4

4

Alfa Bank Russia's largest private bank, founded in 1991 by Mikhail Fridman, one of the country's principal business figures. Fridman remains Chairman of the supervisory board of Alfa Group, of which the bank forms part. Alfa Bank's network includes subsidiaries in Ukraine, Kazakhstan and the Netherlands, and representative offices in the UK and the US.

Rosbank Now majority-owned by the French giant Société Générale, Rosbank was founded as "Nezavisimost'" ("Independence") in 1992, and acquired in the wake of the 1998 crash by another of Russia's business barons, Vladimir Potanin, who still retains a blocking share. Initially focused on corporate banking, Rosbank has extended its retail business in the last few years since its acquisition of the OVK group.

Uralsib Founded in 1993 by the government of the Republic of Bashkortostan in SE Russia, and initially called "Bashkreditbank", Uralsib was re-branded under its current name in 2002. The following year, the oil investment company NIKoil acquired just under three quarters of the bank's shares. Rumours circulated in early 2008 that Gazprombank was planning a buyout of Uralsib, but these were swiftly dispelled by both sides.

Promsvyazbank Joint-owned by brothers Alexey and Dmitry Ananyev, Promsvyazbank was originally founded in 1995 by a consortium led by the Moscow Telephone Exchange. Primarily a corporate bank, Promsvyazbank has in recent years increased its retail presence on the Russian market.

Ursa Bank Another fast-growing regional financial group, Ursa Bank was founded in Novosibirsk in 1990 as "Sibakadembank". In 2004 Sibakadembank entered a strategic alliance with Uralvneshtorgbank, and the two companies merged in 2006, rebranding under their current name in September the same year.

MDM Bank MDM, or "Moskovsky Delovoy Mir" (Moscow Business World) Bank, was founded in 1993, and for the first five years of its existence was in the top five Russian banks for currency operations, before investing in the wake of the 1998 crisis in some of

Russia's larger industrial groups. Today more than three quarters of the bank's shares belong to Russian businessman Sergey Popov, co-founder of TMK and Eurochem, two of the bank's major investments.

In late 2008 as this guide was going to press, the URSA bank and MDM bank announced their merger, which will create a private bank holding smaller only than Sherbank and VTB. It is likely that mergers and aquisitions in the sector will only increase as banks seek to protect themselves from the global downturn.

Russia is nearing the end of marathon negotiations regarding accession to the World Trade Organisation, of which more below. It is probable that when Russia eventually enters the WTO, there will be an element of liberalisation of the banking sector, and in particular a relaxation of the limits currently imposed on the activities of foreign banks in the country.

Transport
Around Russia

The Russian Federation occupies such a vast territory that generally the only way to get from one city to another is by air. Fortunately for the business traveller, the regional air service in Russia is extensive – you can fly to over 75 regional cities from Moscow, around 50 from St Petersburg. As stated in the previous chapter, don't expect too much luxury, and you won't be disappointed – it will still be generally a better experience than a lot of the no-frills airlines operating in the west, and the services are very efficient. You should be able to order tickets from your hotel, if you are staying in one, alternatively there are plenty of ticket desks in the big cities. Sorry to state the obvious, but remember that in some cases you will be travelling long haul – Moscow to Khabarovsk, for example, is around eight hours. Remember also to leave plenty of time if you are going by road to the airport either in Moscow or St Petersburg. Russia's national carrier Aeroflot splintered into a number of regional carriers in the early 1990s, but still serves most of the major cities, the others being covered by regional carriers (more often than not, using Aeroflot's old planes). Flights to all destinations from the

By Air

4

big cities will generally be at least once-daily (between Moscow and St Petersburg there are flights every hour), but you should generally try not to leave booking to the last minute. Fares are reasonable, even to far-flung destinations.

The alternative to air-travel between cities, if you are not travelling too far, is the train. Even here, with the exception of the odd express service, you will generally be travelling for at least eight hours, and most likely it will be an overnight train. Rail travel in Russia is a little like stepping back in time, and if you do not experience a slight thrill at the sight of a 15-carriage train stretching along the platform into the night, with a crisply-uniformed guard standing to attention at the entrance to each carriage, then you've got something missing. There are three main types of carriage: the cheapest is *platzkarte*, an open-plan carriage with benches which double as bunks; next up is a *kupe*, a corridor sleeper-car with four-berth compartments, and finally *SV* (*spal'ny vagon = sleeper car*), also made up of compartments, but with only two people sharing. You are most likely to travel in a *kupe*.

Depending on your destination, and indeed, your luck, your initial warm feeling at the return of romance to long-distance travel may be replaced by creeping horror that you are about to spend a whole night in a small, locked compartment with three total strangers who probably all know each other. If you don't speak any Russian, the fact that you cannot understand what they are saying may only deepen this feeling. Don't worry – overnight train travel is common practice in Russia, and the carriages quickly turn into a series of temporary living-rooms as passengers don their slippers (you may want to get yourself a pair of these, they make the whole experience a lot more comfortable) and the guard walks up and down the corridor handing out towels and offering tea. You are much more likely to be travelling with a middle-aged piano teacher en route to see her sister in Nizhnevartovsk, or a businessman catching the red-eye to an urgent meeting, than to open the compartment door to a gaggle of noisy youth halfway through their third bottle of vodka.

Be smiley and friendly with the guard – generally they are female, of a certain age, and rule their carriages with a maternally iron hand. A few hundred roubles may well ???? you into a compartment of your own if you are feeling either nervous or unsociable. A few security tips to the wise: if possible, when you book your ticket, get a lower bunk. When you get into your compartment, lift your bunk and place any easily portable valuables (like a laptop) in the large box underneath. If you get a top bunk, put said laptop in the space above the door, with something heavy like a suitcase in front. Secondly – keep your passport on you, and when you go to sleep, put it under your pillow. Just don't forget it in the morning. Finally, there is a flip-up catch set into the door which locks the compartment from the inside. If your travelling companions haven't already done so, flip this up once everyone has turned in for the night.

4

Security Advice

Most likely you will have a great time – Russians are incredibly friendly and convivial travelling companions, and you will find that any language barrier is quickly overcome. Your key advantage lies in the fact that you are foreign: your native compartment-mates will be simultaneously impressed by your pluck in taking the train in the first place, and interested to know about where you're from, and what you think of their country. Congratulations, you have just become exotic, so enjoy it – you will like as not meet as strangers and part as friends. Even if you don't end up chatting the night away, it is the done thing to give a cheery *do svidanya* as you leave the compartment in the morning. In mixed-sex compartments, the men will retreat politely into the corridor around 11.30pm to allow the women to get changed and get into bed – leave around fifteen minutes and remember to knock lightly on the door before you go back in. Men generally get changed either in the bathroom, or in the compartment itself with the light out when the womenfolk are safely tucked up and averting their eyes. If you want to have a wash and brush-up in the morning, set your alarm for around an hour before arrival so you can get into one of the bathrooms at either end of the carriage without too much queuing. One other thing, if you smoke: the smoking compartment is at the other end of the carriage from where the guard sits – don't make the mistake of lighting up at the wrong

Train Etiquette

end, or you will understand the true meaning of the
expression "if looks could kill", and all your smiles
will count for nought.

Around town
Moscow

Unless you are keeping to the very centre, Moscow is
not a walking city. A few years ago some colleagues and
I decided that it would be jolly pleasant to walk back to
our centrally-located hotel after we had had some dinner
near Red Square. Setting off briskly, we finally reached
our destination around three hours later – and that was
without getting lost. Getting around by car can also be
problematic: the boom in car use since the 1990s has far
outstripped the best efforts of the city authorities to build
more capacity. There are getting on for 3.5m cars in
Moscow today, with the number growing by at least
150,000 per year. Even with three ring-roads at various
distances from the centre, gridlock is a more or less
constant threat – nor is Moscow the sort of city where
a clever driver can dodge the jams.

Driving

If you want to go round Moscow by car, it is generally
a good idea to hire one with a driver – there are plenty
of agencies that do this. There is also any number of taxi
firms, one of which even uses London black-cabs. If
you're feeling confident, and you have a little Russian,
you can just flag down a private car. It tends to come as
a surprise to first time visitors to Russia (and much of the
former Soviet Union) that you can do this at all, let alone
that it is so commonplace and easy. On a busy stretch of
road you will generally be waiting for no more than a
minute: tell the driver where you need to go (ideally have
the address written down in Russian), and agree a price
before you get in. Haggle – halve whatever sum they
come up with first. Your accent and generally lost
demeanour means that you will be paying more than
a local, but it'll still be cheaper than a taxi. As I say,
thumbing down a car is very common, it's not like in
Europe where you would doubt the motives of any driver
willing to let a total stranger into their car – generally it
will be someone either on their way home or on some
other errand who will be glad to take you a few miles
for a small consideration, provided it is not too far out

4

4

of their way. I wouldn't recommend you to do it if you are on your own until you have been there for a while, though, and if you have any doubts about the safety of either the car or the driver, just wave them on. You may be lucky and get an off-duty embassy driver (this does happen), in which case you will arrive at your destination in some style.

Aside from private cars, Moscow has a thriving community of *marschrutki,* or licensed private minibuses which follow most of the bus routes. These buses are generally 12- or 14-seaters, and can stop anywhere to pick up or drop off. The fare is fixed, generally between 14 and 20 roubles, and you pay the driver as you sit down. If you don't have the right change, don't worry, *marschrutka* drivers have an uncanny ability to drive, smoke and calculate change all at the same time. Remember that you can ask the driver to stop wherever you want, but give him a bit of advance warning, and be specific – most of the minibuses have a notice inside saying "This bus does NOT stop 'somewhere around here'."

Marschrutki

Should you be tempted to drive in Moscow yourself, and I don't recommend it, get an international driving permit – this is a universally recognised document which you can pick up at the post office or through your local automobile association/club for around five pounds or equivalent, provided you have a driving licence. Car hire is not well-established in Moscow at all, there are very few people who want to drive a car there if they don't have to, and the number of accidents on Moscow's roads is such that insurance is prohibitive. Driving in Moscow really is not for the novice, nor is it for the faint-hearted: traffic rules are loosely observed, and Russian traffic police are still notoriously corrupt, especially when it comes to foreigners. Add to this the fact that the roads are shared between slow-moving Ladas and wealthy young things red-lining their Lamborghinis along the main boulevards, and you can quickly see why someone is killed on Russia's roads every fifteen minutes.

International Driving Permit

Happily, Moscow is also served by one of the most comprehensive metro systems on the planet. A masterpiece of totalitarian engineering, with some stations that will truly take your breath away, the

4

The Metro

Moscow metro carried over 2.5 billion passengers in 2007, more than double the numbers of London and second only to Tokyo. Indeed, if you ever find yourself changing lines at Kievskaya station during rush-hour, you may be forgiven for thinking that they are all using it on the same day. A lot of people blanche at the very idea of using the Moscow metro, and it can be a little fraught at busy periods, but it remains the quickest way of getting from A to B in the city, without exception. There is a bewildering choice of tickets available, generally the most convenient one is a single card which entitles you to a maximum number of journeys – you pay a single fare for each journey, irrespective of whether you are hopping one stop or travelling from one end of the city to another. The trains themselves are fast, capacious and frequent – on some stations in rush-hour they will be more frequent than once a minute. The rolling stock is none too modern, although on some lines new trains are slowly being brought into service. It can be crowded, and people will bump into you – not out of malice, mind, Muscovites just have a less keen sense of personal space than a lot of other people, probably as a result of daily use of one of the world's busiest transport systems. Don't get offended, just bump them back.

St Petersburg

The centre of St Petersburg is a much easier place to get around on foot. Bisected by the main thoroughfare of Nevsky Prospekt, and criss-crossed by a series of canals, you will find the city to be a far more pedestrian-friendly place. Russia's second city also has a metro system, although it isn't nearly so extensive as in Moscow, with only four lines against Moscow's twelve, and around a third of the number of stations. Having said that, it still carried more passengers in 2007 than the Shanghai metro. St Petersburg's location on marshland also means that the metro system is one of the deepest in the world, especially those stations which are near the river. Sometimes you can spend longer on the escalators than you do on the trains. Taxis, *marschrutki* and private cars are all as readily available as they are in Moscow, and traffic jams, while still severe at certain times of day, are still not at the chronic level of the capital. The airport road is pretty bad (see previous chapter), as are the embankments of the canals, but considering it is Europe's third most populous city after Moscow and London, St Petersburg is really not too bad, no matter what the locals may tell you.

Expect the situation to improve in the next few years as some major infrastructure projects, including the long-overdue completion of the ring-road and a tunnel under the river, come on stream. This second project will call an end to one of the peculiarities of St Petersburg: during the months that the river Neva is ice-free, all the bridges are raised at night to allow shipping to pass. If you are on the wrong side of the river when this happens, you can be well and truly stuck, as by the time the bridges go up the metro will also be closed. There is a suspension bridge at the eastern end of the city, but it is a long round-trip, so be warned. Aside from that, driving in St Petersburg is far less fraught than in the capital, although in my experience finding somewhere to make a left turn can take up the best part of an afternoon.

The City of Open Bridges

Other cities

Elsewhere in Russia, you should be spared the traffic chaos that haunts the capital, and many of the larger cities have rapid-transit underground systems (Novosibirsk, Kazan' and Samara are examples). All will have good transport infrastructure, although a lack of investment since the fall of the Soviet Union means that the road surfaces will generally leave a great deal to be desired, as will the condition of the buses. There is no doubt though that as Russia is becoming more prosperous, this situation is improving, but give it time.

Communications

Postal service

The Russian postal service (Pochta Rossii) is extensive, but slow, especially when it comes to international mail. Delivery time within cities is generally around three days for first class items, and between three and five days between regions, which is not bad when you come to consider the distances involved. Postal rates are also reasonably inexpensive, and it is a good way to send non-urgent correspondence. The service has a fairly comprehensive and unexpectedly user-friendly website – www.russianpost.ru/portal/en/home. If you don't speak any Russian, though, it is a good idea to take a translator with you when you actually go up to the counter.

Courier services

Russia is well served by most of the major courier companies, including DHL, FedEx and UPS, in addition to which you will find a wide range of independent courier companies in the big cities which are a useful way of getting urgent documents around. There is also a handful of companies who can take secure items into Russia for you. In a later chapter we will talk about the specifics of the Russian customs system, and you will be well-advised to use a specialist service for important documents and packages, as the tracking services of some of the bigger companies still sit slightly uncomfortably alongside the realities of customs clearance in Russia.

The internet

As stated in Chapter 2, the internet is massively popular in Russia, and although the penetration of the services in 2007 stood at just over 20%, around 30m people, the country remains the fastest growing internet market in Europe, growing by just under a quarter in 2007. No slowdown in this growth is expected until 2010, and a project is currently ongoing to have internet access available in every settlement throughout the Russian Federation with a population of over 500 people – something to bear in mind should you find yourself in some remote enclave and you need to check your emails. Any hotel worthy of the name will have internet access, as will many restaurants and cafes – in many places Wi-Fi access will be free. Broadband is still limited in the main to the bigger cities, and even in Moscow it hovers around 20% for corporate users, and a lowly 3% for domestic. However, expect these figures to change quickly – billions of dollars are being invested in the ICT sector as a whole, with an increasing proportion coming from Russian companies. Market penetration is matched, if not outstripped, by a concomitant increase in the amount of information on the Russian web: in 2007 the number of .ru domains crossed the million barrier, at the end of a year which saw the total number of registered domains more than double.

Fixed line telephony

Russia's copper network is struggling to recover from many years of under-investment, and has failed to keep up with the country's shifting settlement patterns. Direct fixed lines are currently available to just over a quarter of the population – less than 40m people. By the end of the first decade of the 21st century, the plan is to have the network fully digitised with a new 10-digit standard for fixed-line numbers, and major investments are now being made to reduce the number of people still waiting for fixed-line access.

Mobile communications

In direct contrast to the fixed-line story, and partially as a result of the lack of capacity in the static network, mobile communications continue to boom in Russia. At the end of 2007 there were 30m more SIM cards than the total population of the country, although territorial penetration is still less than half. Russia has also benefited from the fact that it came to the mobile table relatively late in the development of the technology, meaning that it could use state of the art equipment straight away. This is in contrast to countries like the UK which invested heavily in early technologies only to see the equipment become obsolete after a few years. When you use your mobile in Russia, you should notice the difference in quality straight away. If you are a Londoner, you will also be pleasantly surprised to know that you can use your mobile on the underground as well. The market is dominated by three operators, MTS, Beeline/Vimpelcom and MegaFon – you would do well to consider getting a local pay-as-you-go SIM card to control costs.

3G is still in its early stages in Russia, a pilot rollout is currently in place in St Petersburg offering 3.6Mb/sec – again, the market moves very fast so expect the network to be much more extensive by the time this guide is published. Mobile email through Blackberry-style devices was initially delayed by Russian anti-terrorism legislation, which requires that unhindered access to all communication media be available to the security services, something that the strong encryption used by the handsets did not allow. At the end of November 2007 an agreement was reached between the authorities

4

3G

4

and the operators, and the sector is now growing at breakneck speed, particularly in Moscow.

Dialling codes

The international dialling code for Russia (and, interestingly enough, Kazakhstan) is +7. City codes are generally 3- or 4-digit numbers, followed by a 7- or 6-digit individual number respectively. As stated above, a new standard is being brought in for terrestrial numbers post-digitisation. Most cities have just one code, although Moscow already has 495 (previously 095) and 501. Depending on where you are dialling from in Russia, you may have to dial 8 and wait for a different dialling tone before making a national call. If you are calling abroad, you need to dial 10 for the international exchange. Mobile number codes are all three-digit, begin with 9, and will depend on the mobile service provider, and you can also get a "city" code for your mobile phone when you open a contract – the monthly line rental and connection charge tend to be slightly higher for these numbers and they are still considered something of a status symbol.

Television and radio

There are no major English-language radio stations in Russia, although the satellite/cable station Russia Today is available in most countries and broadcasts primarily news and current affairs. Founded by RIA Novosti, one of Russia's main news agencies, it can be a useful way of picking up local news, and particularly the Russian media-line on events, which does not always coincide with that in the West.

Public holidays and working hours

Conventional office hours are as elsewhere in Europe, ie. an eight-hour period sometime between 8:30a.m. and 6:30p.m. In the cities most shops are open until 8 in the evening or even later, although they will not necessarily be open at 9 on the dot. Russia is not short of public holidays, having inherited a number from the Soviet period which have since been augmented by a few Russia-only holidays.

The main dates are listed below:

1-5 January	–	New Year
7 January	–	Orthodox Christmas
23 February	–	Defender of the Fatherland Day
8 March	–	International Women's Day
1 May	–	Labour Day / First Day of Spring
9 May	–	Victory Day
12 June	–	Russia Day
4 November	–	National Unity Day
12 December	–	Russian Constitution Day

In addition to the above, there is the ever-moving Orthodox Easter (generally around two weeks later than the Catholic/Protestant festival), and a dizzying number of other specific holidays – Transport Police Day on 18 February, and Baltic Fleet day exactly three months later are just two among dozens. As in other countries, if the holiday happens to fall on a weekend, the nearest Monday is also taken off. The situation becomes slightly more complicated if it falls on a Tuesday or a Thursday, in which case it may happen that either a Saturday or a Sunday becomes a working day in order to preserve a 3-day break. You will also find that the proximity of 1 May and Victory Day, both very important dates in Russia, means that a lot of people tend to take time off to coincide with both these dates. Don't plan any business trips in the first week and a half of May if you intend to have a lot of meetings, and get used to the fact that your Russian counterparts will start to talk about things happening either before or after "the May holidays" as early as the first half of April.

Similarly, at the very end of the year the close juxtaposition of December 25th, New Year, Orthodox Christmas and even "Old New Year" (January 13th is January 1st by the Julian Calendar, used in Russia until the adoption of the Gregorian standard in 1918) produces a hiatus of activity of up to three weeks.

4

4

Business etiquette, do's and don'ts

Conventions of doing business in Russia differ little from elsewhere in the world: your established instincts will serve you well here. However, there are a few common mistakes made by people new to the country which are worth considering and, ideally, avoiding in order to make your experience of working in Russia as smooth as possible. If you are travelling to Russia regularly and reporting back to colleagues who haven't had the benefit of reading this book, it is also in your interests to make them aware of the information below, all in the name of international understanding.

Business Meetings

First of all, do not expect your first trip to Russia, even to Moscow, to be crowned with a triumphant briefcase full of firm orders or representation agreements. Your initial meetings will all be very much information-exchange sessions, and if you try to pressure your Russian counterpart into making any kind of commitment too early, you might as well not bother. They will want to know that you are serious about working with them, and will expect you to be direct, but not pushy. You will also generally be under examination from the beginning – your meeting may at first seem off-hand, but this is in most cases a default-setting, let it wash over you and walk out smiling and confident. Do not be surprised, either, if your enthusiastic punctuality is rewarded with a twenty minute wait in reception.

Follow-up

Always follow up your first meeting with an email or preferably a phone-call thanking your contact for their time, and say that you will be visiting again soon and that you look forward to meeting with them again. They will generally agree to another meeting, and you will almost certainly find a much warmer reception at the second instance – if not, they are either just impolite, or genuinely not interested. If the signs are good, then it is from here that you will generally be able to get down to business – I say generally, you may need to do a little more dancing and juggling first. If you can, try and elicit some information about hobbies, interests, family etc. and arrive at your second meeting with a modest gift that shows you have put some thought into them as a person. You may well find that by the time of the third meeting they have done the same.

Here we touch on a wider aspect of the Russian character which you will not necessarily be expecting if your instincts are more European or Anglo-Saxon, and it is something to bear in mind throughout your time in Russia. Russians are generally very reserved, suspicious even, where strangers are concerned, even if they are fellow-Russians (in fact, especially if they are fellow-Russians). However, once you break through that initial barrier, you will find them much more friendly than your countrymen back home. The same principle applies to officialdom – whereas going through Heathrow immigration you are generally treated with polite disdain from start to finish, at Sheremetyevo you will likely be met with a scowl and seen off with a grin as you try out your heavily-accented Russian for the first time. It doesn't always work like this, mind, and don't expect a friendly bear-hug from a traffic cop if you run up and playfully knock their hat off, but the principle remains.

Back to business: having established that you shouldn't expect concrete results from your first meeting, do not fall into the trap either of thinking that you are even necessarily talking to the right person. This is a phenomenon by no means limited to Russia, of course, but be aware that your first meeting may well be with someone who is in no position of authority to decide whether the company will work with you or not. This is a familiar game, and if you want to get anywhere, you have to play it: whatever you do, do not make it apparent that you have rumbled them and that you are therefore no longer interested in the meeting. Carry on (apparently) regardless: your new aim is to get the person sitting opposite in the best position to convey positive signals to the decision-maker who lurks behind the scenes – in other words, make them your ambassador. Then you start again, from the paragraph before last.

Thirdly – and this is slightly contradictory, I know – at the same time as being prepared for the long haul in Russia, be equally ready to react if things happen quickly. I once brokered a meeting with a mid- to high-level buyer at a major Russian company only to have the president walk in halfway through to see what's what. You may find that your potential customer likes the cut of your jib and places a big order on the spot. If you're

The Gatekeeper

4

not ready for it, you and your company will lose credibility, so if it is relevant to you, make sure you read the next chapter on import documentation and the like before you go in and start selling.

Other than that, the rules of doing business and making the correct impression on your potential clients and partners apply in Russia as they do everywhere else. As Russia becomes more familiar with working with international companies any gaps of perception are, if anything, narrowing. For example, not so long ago it wasn't always a good idea to shake hands with a woman, as this was seen as not entirely appropriate – this may still be so with women over a certain age, but the younger generation will expect you to shake their hand.

One final practical point: we started this chapter with advice on how to deal with the severe frosts that a Russian winter can deal out. When in gets warmer in the spring, you will have a second enemy. Slush. In a city, months of exhaust fumes, road salt and urban grime that have been absorbed by the snow since November make their way to the surface and onto the shoes and trouser-legs of the unwary as the melt begins. The Russians nickname it "porridge", and with good reason. Even if you are being dropped by your driver opposite the entrance of every building where you have a meeting, keep a rag handy to give your shoes a last wipe before you go. If you're in a business centre or a hotel, you may well find a shoe-cleaning machine in reception.

Language

As an English-speaker, you are in the privileged position that most of the people you deal with speak your language already, especially if they are professionals under forty years of age. However, it remains the case that many people in more senior positions (including the above-mentioned decision-makers) may not be so comfortable in your language, and certainly not when it comes to commercial negotiations. When your company is more established in Russia you may well have a local agent or representative who will do the negotiating on your behalf, but until then, take an interpreter with you: apart from anything else, it shows you're serious. In fact, even if you are a Russian-speaker, and a good one at that, it is still advisable to have someone with a native command of the language with you, as they will be able to pick up asides or nuances that you may miss. There is no shortage of agencies with freelance interpreters on their books – as with the travel agents, and any other service company, it is a good idea to approach in the first instance those companies who are members of one of the business support organisations or chambers of commerce.

4

Socialising

Assuming you are getting on well and forging ever-closer links with your Russian partners, sooner or later you will likely be invited to lunch or, more likely, dinner. The West is slowly losing this tradition, more's the pity, but in Russia the idea of entertaining clients at a restaurant is still very much alive. If you are invited to a meal, go unless you have a very compelling reason why you physically cannot be there. It is a very important stage in cementing a professional relationship, and while a refusal will be taken graciously, it will also be considered impolite.

An important element of the meal will be toast-giving, but don't let this fill you with dread if you are not a particularly confident public speaker, it is not a formal requirement to stand up and relate a witty fable. Russians are aware that toasting is one of their traditions and they will not be expecting you to compete. You should at least propose a toast at some point during the meal to thank your host and to say that you look forward to a long and fruitful business relationship together – anything more will be regarded as a bonus, and if you can work up a couple of Russian words to throw in, it will be warmly appreciated. There is much written about the traditional order of toasts, but don't let this worry you unduly: the Russians don't. The only one that is observed almost universally is that the third toast is generally in honour of the fairer sex – if you are a woman, have an answering toast ready and you can go fourth. If you are a man, also have something prepared and try and get your toast in here, and suspend any worries you may have that complimenting women on

Toast-giving

their looks (in a general sense) may be construed as sexist – it's an easy toast, and a good way to earn approbation and brownie-points.

Assuming that all the above has gone well, and that you are edging towards the reality of doing your first piece of business, the next chapter will take you through the more technical aspects of working in Russia.

5

getting down to business

getting down
to business

A general guide to Russia's business
climate, covering the legal framework
for investors, import tariffs and
customs regulations.

The Russian economy today

Even the most cursory glance at Russia's recent main
economic indicators will tell you that the country has
performed a remarkable *volte-face* since the economic
meltdown of 1998. Real GDP growth has averaged
6.5% since 2000, average incomes have almost doubled
in 10 years, and in 2007 the country ran a very healthy
budget surplus of 5.5% of GDP. While it is undeniable
that the recent high oil and gas prices have helped this
growth no end, the share of key sectors in Russia's
overall GDP have remained more or less constant
throughout. According to the World Bank, an
increasing proportion of Russia's strong growth
stems from domestic consumer demand borne along
by the increased liquidity brought by the country's
position as a major oil and gas exporter.

Russia has also done much to put itself in a good
position to capitalise on the bounty of high oil prices
since 2003. The first decade of the millennium has seen
significantly more political stability in the country, and
various reforms to taxation and budgetary institutions,
as well as (some) progress in removing administrative
barriers to business, have had a beneficial effect on
prosperity. Corporate Russia has also performed well;
between 2000 and 2006, the capitalisation of Russian
public companies went from 15% of GDP to over
107%. The largest of Russia's corporations, Gazprom,
reported revenues in 2007 of US$98.6bn, slightly lower
than the GDP of Kuwait. Russia has had an investment
grade rating from all three major agencies since the
beginning of 2005, and its overall performance in
terms of investor confidence continues to be strong.

Overall, the IMF placed Russia as the world's 11th
largest economy by nominal GDP in 2007, 7th if
adjusted for purchasing power parity. By 2050, it has
been estimated that the country will overtake the UK,
Canada, Spain, Germany, Italy and France to claim
6th place on nominal GDP. A lot can happen in four
decades, of course, and these predictions are based on
a number of assumptions, but we should be aware that
Russia is today a serious global player, and we can be
fairly certain that its importance will only grow as we
move through the century.

5

5

That is not to say that the country does not face significant challenges ahead, though: Russia is a big ship, and will take a long time to turn round. On the macroeconomic level, strong growth brings with it the risk of inflation, which in Russia hit 11.9% (CPI) at the end of 2007. This is in spite of efforts to contain money supply through the creation of the Reserve Fund (originally known as the Stabilisation Fund), capped at 10% of GDP, and the more recent National Welfare Fund, which was set up to absorb the "overspill" from its elder sibling. As mentioned earlier, Russia's tricky task now is to control the strength of the rouble while simultaneously keeping inflation within acceptable limits. The global downturn and subsequent fall in the prices of jey commodities has hit the Russian economy hard – as the wider economic crisis shakes out over the next few years, the country will have to tread very carefully to protect the gains made in the early years of the 21st century.

At the same time, major investment is still needed in the country's physical infrastructure to make conditions favourable for sustained growth, and to address the imbalance in prosperity between Moscow and the regions. To take just one indicator, the retail trade turnover of the Russian capital still exceeds that of the next ten largest cities, including St Petersburg, combined. Investment as a proportion of GDP, although increasing, still hovers around 20%, or half that of China. Growth in small and medium sized companies remains low, and other limiting factors on growth include enduring administrative and bureaucratic barriers, inadequate protection of property rights, and an overall shortfall in training and education. The situation was summed up neatly by President Medvedev in early 2008 when he identified the four 'i's which were key to Russia's future prosperity – Investment, Infrastructure, Innovation and Institutes.

More of a threat to Russia's continued economic growth than any of the above, though, is the simple fact that the country's population is slowly shrinking. A combination of low birth rate, poor life expectancy (according to 2006 World Health Organisation figures, 60 years and 73 years for men and women respectively), and emigration has reduced Russia's population by nearly 5m people

since the turn of the millennium. More alarming still
are the demographics hidden within these bare figures:
because most émigrés are those of working age, it has
been estimated that if current trends continue, Russia's
working population could be reduced by almost a fifth
before the third decade of this century is out.

Stock and currency exchanges

Since the mid-1990s two exchanges, the Moscow
Interbank Currency Exchange (MICEX) and the
Russian Trading System (RTS), have dominated the
nascent Russian capital markets sector. The former is
currently the largest exchange in Russia, the CIS and
central/eastern Europe, with total trading volumes of
over US$4 trillion in 2007. More recently, in 2008 a
commodities exchange was established in St Petersburg,
initially to deal only in petroleum products, with
construction materials, grain and mineral fertilizers
to follow at a later date.

The performance of Russia's capital and equity markets
has mirrored the country's steady economic growth,
although market indices have obviously been more
sensitive to transitory shocks, such as the banking
mini-crisis in 2004 and the conflict with Georgia in
August 2008. The latter led to a sharp fall as investors
pulled tens of billions of dollars out of the system in
response to a perceived heightened political risk, a
problem exacerbated by the global market crashes of
the following months. Both exchanges suspended trading
on several occasions to prevent runs on key stocks.

The climate for foreign investors

Being told that Russia's major corporations are
prospering is all very well, but it is a little like being
told that it is ok to swim in potentially shark-infested
waters because the whales don't seem all that bothered.
There have been several high profile cases over the past
few years of disputes involving foreign companies such
as the Bank of New York Mellon, Shell, TNK-BP,
PricewaterhouseCoopers and others which have
undoubtedly rattled those considering establishing
a presence on the Russian market.

5

In 2008, the Foreign Investment Advisory Council (FIAC), a body set up jointly in the mid-1990s by the Russian government and a number of foreign investors, conducted a survey of foreign CEOs, some already present in the market, some still considering entry. Asked whether they were optimistic or not about the future of Russia as an investment destination, most respondents were bullish, although concerns remain, particularly over the lack of qualified local personnel, and remaining administrative barriers. On this latter point, if you tell the average Russian businessman that in the UK it is possible to create a limited company in a couple of days, they will most likely not believe you – in Russia the average time to open a company has only recently dipped below a full month. Most of those questioned, however, felt that the overall investment climate had improved over the past few years, and perhaps more importantly, the consensus on whether it would continue to improve over the next decade was still more positive.

The Strategic Sectors Law

A theme which regularly emerges from this and other investor surveys is that companies working in certain sectors, particularly natural resources, tend to have a more ambivalent attitude to working in Russia. One of the issues particularly exercising the minds of foreign investors in some of these key sectors has been the snappily-titled Federal Law "On the Order [=Procedure] of Foreign Investment in Companies of Strategic Significance to National Security and Defence", better known as the Strategic Sectors Law, which came into force in May 2008. This particular piece of legislation identifies 42 sectors, including geological study in subsoil areas of "federal significance", nuclear facilities, fixed-line telephony and large-scale media, where foreign companies require special approval before they can invest.

It should be made clear that the law does not prohibit foreign investment in these sectors, although it does limit the share of ownership dependent on the sector and the nature of the investor. What must also be borne in mind is that Russia is more open to investment by foreign companies in strategic sectors than many other oil-rich countries, particularly in the Middle East. The reason for this is simple: Russia's immense mineral wealth is generally in hard-to-get-at areas, and it needs foreign expertise to develop these resources. At the same time, the Russian government, understandably, does not want to sell out cheaply to international conglomerates. A more robust position has been adopted with foreign companies in recent years, which has knocked investor confidence, but at least with the enactment of the 2008 law the ground rules are clearer. The key priority for the future will be to ensure that the law is clearly and consistently applied.

5

One of the recurring themes of the FIAC survey is the wide variance in the opinion of the respondents, from which the researchers could only take a median reading. Remember in Chapter 1 where I said that the one generalisation you could make about Russia was that it is impossible to generalise? As stated elsewhere in this guide, Russia rewards persistence and the long, wide and deep view. Also vital is preparation (Chapter 2) and careful choice of business partner (Chapter 6). To end on a positive note, the consensus of respondents from the FIAC survey was also that they found the investment climate in Russia to be much better than they had been expecting.

Legislative framework
Summary

Foreign investment in Russia is regulated by the 1999 Federal Law "On Foreign Investments in the Russian Federation". While this law does not cover investments into Russian banks, credit organizations, insurance companies and non commercial organisations, in the vast majority of cases this is the piece of legislation that will pertain to you. The objective of the law is to attract foreign investment by providing a stable framework for companies, guaranteeing their rights to invest, to receive revenues and to repatriate profits made. The law also sets out to bring Russia into line with international standards on the rights of foreign investors.

One of the key features of Russian legislation on foreign investment is that it emphasises both the federal and regional element, and indeed it is one of the peculiarities of investing in Russia that there is such a level of competition between the regions for attracting overseas companies. The Samara, Nizhny Novgorod, Sverdlovsk, and Leningrad regions (*oblasts*), as well the city of St Petersburg and the wider territories of Krasnodar Krai and Khabarovsk Krai have all been particularly proactive in creating favourable legislative conditions for investors.

5

Special Economic Zones

A recent development which combines federal and regional elements is the emergence of Special Economic Zones (SEZs), pursuant to the 2005 Federal Law "On Special Economic Zones in the Russian Federation". Six locations were selected in late 2005 to accommodate two types of zone: High Technology Incubation Zones (TIZs) will be located in the Moscow region (at Zelenograd and Dubna), St Petersburg and Tomsk in Siberia, and Industrial Production Zones will be created in the Lipetsk region in central Russia and in Yelabuga in Tatarstan. Since then, two more types of zones have been identified, focused on tourism and ports. The programme will take some time to implement, but the principal advantages to investors are a reduction in profits tax from 24% to 20%, exemption from Corporate Property Tax, Transport Tax and, where applicable, Land Tax for the first five years, as well as a favourable customs regime, including the ability to import goods and equipment without paying duty or VAT. Investors should also be able to expect improved infrastructure, physical and otherwise, in these regenerated areas.

Intellectual Property Rights

One of the remaining areas of concern for investors generally is Intellectual Property Rights (IPR) protection. As is often the case in Russia, the problem lies not in any lack of legislation, which is fairly comprehensive, but in the application and enforcement of existing laws. As with all things in today in Russia, this issue has to be taken in context: a couple of decades ago all property, whether intellectual or otherwise, belonged to the State, so the notion of its protection was not even relevant. The situation with IPR protection is undoubtedly improving, with extra impetus behind it coming from Russia's desire to enter the World Trade Organisation, but as you walk down St Petersburg's main street, Nevsky Prospekt and pass by the strangely familiar green and white sign of the Republic of Coffee, you will see that there is still some way to go. If you are an investor with a product vulnerable to IPR or copyright violation, be sure to avail yourself of all possible advice before you launch. Some money spent on legal advice early on could save you a great deal more in the long run.

Trade summary

On the experience of much of the last century, you may think that Russia's borders have been traditionally closed to the movement of both people and goods. Think again. Remember that the foundations of the state of Rus' were laid on commerce and the movement of goods, and throughout its subsequent history much of Russia's fortune, literally and figuratively, has been intimately intertwined with its access, or lack thereof, to international markets. Even during the chaotic months following the 1917 revolution, Russia remained a global trading presence, and throughout the Soviet period import and export remained active, even as the supra-national economy remained centrally planned. Post-1991, Russia's emergence as a free market economy has seen activity increase exponentially. According to official figures, in US dollar terms both exports and imports increased by around 400% between 1995 and 2007, with the former always comfortably in the van.

As you would expect, the bulk of Russia's exports are in the natural resources sector, with physical imports consisting mainly of manufactured goods and machinery. There's an old Russian joke about a delegation of Japanese businessmen being shown around the country in Soviet times who, when asked at the end of the trip what they thought the Soviet Union's finest achievement was, replied, "Definitely your children. They are the most wonderful children we have ever seen: intelligent, polite, hardworking, you should be proud of them. But the things you make with your *hands*…" This is something of an outdated joke, but it remains the case that Russia's consumer manufacturing sector, whether the product be cars or clothing, seriously lags behind that of other countries to the west and east.

Russia is, however, keen to avoid the dreaded "Dutch disease", i.e. over-reliance on natural resources to drive

5

5

the economy, and has taken advantage of the recent high commodity prices to invest heavily in the manufacturing, technology and service sectors. In addition, rising labour costs in western Europe and elsewhere, together with a burgeoning local consumer base, have led a number of manufacturers to open plants in Russia, particularly in the automotive sector: Ford, Volkswagen, Toyota and Nissan are all there in force. Recent progress has been significant, although the Russian economy still has some way to go to recover from the ravages of the last century or so.

Russia and the World Trade Organisation

Russia's path to accession to the WTO has been a long and arduous one, and a detailed account of the negotiations conducted since the country made its formal application to join GATT in 1993 would fill many books. At the time of writing, Russia looks set to beat China's record of just under fifteen and a half years from application to accession, a record that has stood since 2001. For a country to enter the WTO, it has to sign bilateral accords with all other member states who stipulate this requirement. Since the signing of a bilateral accord with Saudi Arabia in June 2007, the only two remaining countries with whom Russia has yet to reach a final agreement are Georgia and the US. The former has withdrawn its signature to a previous agreement over a range of territorial and trade disputes, and currently obstacles with the US persist in the areas of intellectual property rights, international access to Russia's finance and insurance sector, and issues over the import of US meat products.

I have lost count of how many times in the last few years announcements have been made that a US-Russia deal was close, and there is no guarantee that other problems won't surface before a final agreement is reached. Many senior figures have made themselves hostages to fortune by declaring that the end is in sight. Another complication surfaced in May 2008 with the accession of Ukraine, with whom Russia will also now have to negotiate a bilateral accord. It has to be said that Russia's negotiations with other WTO members have not been devoid of a geopolitical dimension on either side. Russia is keen to protect certain economic sectors, particularly finance and manufacturing, from sudden exposure to international competition, and it is perhaps no surprise that some WTO member states are being very cautious about admitting so large an economy with such vast natural resources into the club.

Importing into Russia

5

The current Russian Federation Customs Code was passed in April 2003 and came into force at the start of the following year. It was brought in to align customs legislation and procedures with both the new constitution of the Russian Federation, and with international standards and practices in anticipation of Russia's eventual accession to the WTO, of which more below. Although the previous code never presented insurmountable obstacles to importing goods, it nevertheless remained a cumbersome instrument which ran the risk of causing problems for Russia as the level of international trade increased.

The new code has streamlined procedures for appealing (through the courts) against the actions (or inaction) of the customs authorities, along with setting a time limit of three days during which a shipment has to be inspected before it must be released. The code also allows for the temporary import of fixed production assets, for which the importer will have to pay 3% of the duty payable per month for a period of 34 months, at which point the goods in question are automatically released for domestic use if they are still in the country.

Perhaps the key element of the new code, however, is that minor errors made in the customs declaration will not lead to a refusal to release the goods, provided that said error or omission has no effect on the actual duty payment made. To illustrate the importance of this provision, under the old code a company I once worked for had a valuable shipment of perishable goods impounded for six weeks because it had ended up in the wrong warehouse at Novosibirsk, even though the importing agent was ready (and increasingly desperate) to pay the duty.

5

It remains the case, however, that shipments can be stopped as a result of an apparently trivial error, and even under the new, more importer-friendly code, problems still happen. If the officials dig their heels in, the best option may be to ship the goods back to where they came from and start all over again. As an exporter to Russia, you will make your life much easier by going to a specialist freight forwarder, who will have spent years building relationships with the customs authorities and will have a much better chance of getting the goods cleared. In my experience at least, some of the larger shippers are fine until something goes wrong.

Import duties

Even under the 2003 code, the complex system of import tariffs which exists under Russian law can be at first bewildering to a potential exporter. There are around 11,000 individual tariff lines covering every conceivable variation of goods imported – 34 for cotton alone, depending on the form in which it is imported. To make matters still more complicated, approximately 1,700 of these use the so-called "combined rate" tariff system, in that the goods in these categories attract both a specific rate and an *ad valorem* rate, the latter being applicable only to the monetary value of the goods, and not any

Tariff Codes

other measure such as weight or volume. In such cases, the customs officials will apply whichever rate is higher. The full list of tariff codes, including those with combined rates, is available, in Russian, from www.tamognia.ru/laws/law_1538.html – make sure you have at least 1,100 sheets of paper handy before you hit "print".

Mercifully, the tariff rates themselves are fairly consistently applied – all dairy products, for instance, attract 15% duty with the exception of baby-milk, which has a 5% duty so long as the fat content is below 10% and it is imported in packaging of less than 500g nett (tariff code 0402 29 110 0). Certain tariff codes include a fixed minimum amount per unit weight, while others have separate tariffs based on value: if you are a cheese producer, you will be importing your shipment of Tilsiter at a slightly different rate depending on whether you are selling it at above or below €1.65 per kilogram.

Amendments have also been brought in over the past decade and a half for specific reasons. In 2002, in an attempt to stem the tide of second-hand cars being privately imported in the 1990s, Russia brought in a punitive tariff on foreign cars over 7 years old. If you were to try to import a petrol-engined car over this age with a cylinder capacity of over 3 litres, you would be relieved of €3.20 per cubic centimetre at the border, unless you are a diplomat, in which case what on earth are you doing driving around in an old car?

Requirements for the consignee

In order to receive goods, the consignee has to be registered with the customs authorities at the point of entry – if you are airfreighting into Sheremetyevo, for instance, you need to be registered there. To do this you need to present a range of documents, including the state registration certificate for your company, the company statutes, and passport details of the company directors along with a sample of the company stamp. Stamps are generally very important in Russia – if you are thinking of establishing a permanent presence there, you will find that you won't get very far without one – more details in Chapter 7. The consignee generally has to be a Russian legal entity: as a representative or branch office of a foreign company you can import goods for office use, but not for re-sale.

Any original documents submitted for registration must either be in Russian, or accompanied by a notarised translation. If the originals are in Russian, they will still need to be accompanied by a notarised copy.

Documentation needed

You will need at least the following documents to import your goods into Russia:

- Sales contract
- Commercial invoice
- Packing list
- "Passport of the deal" (*passport sdelki* – from the bank)
- Certificate of Conformity (CoC) – Gosstandart if required (see below)

- Export Customs Declaration issued in the country of origin (fax/photocopy)
- Insurance policy (fax/photocopy)
- Price list of the producer/shipper

All documents have to be in Russian, most are pretty standard fare for exporters, although we will deal more closely with CoCs later on. The last three items are to confirm the dutiable value of the shipment – they MUST coincide with each other, as well as with the commercial invoice and any prices set out in the sales contract.

Certificate of Origin

In addition to the above mandatory documents, you may also need a Certificate of Origin for the goods, but generally only in those cases where certain countries have preferential duty rates (RF Customs Code 2003, Chapter 6, Art.37.1). For certain classes of goods you may also need an import licence, particularly on excisable goods such as alcohol and tobacco. You may also need a certificate from the relevant Russian ministry for some products – the Ministry of Telecommunications if you are importing telephones, the Ministry of Health if you are importing medical equipment etc.

If you are importing samples by air, a simplified procedure is available provided the value of the goods is less than US$100 – bear in mind that this will only apply when the samples genuinely look like they are less than US$100 in value. Any attempts to under-declare value will put you in all sorts of trouble.

It is beyond the scope of this guide to cover every eventuality – it is best to contact a specialist shipper who will be able to advise you exactly what you need.

Labelling, standards, testing and certification

Whatever you are importing, the descriptive labelling of the goods should be in Russian, either on its own or together with another language. Where relevant, any instructions for use either on the packaging or included with the items must also be in Russian. For consumer goods, whether they be food or non-food, Russian

language information either on or in the box must
include the following information:

- Product name
- Country of origin
- Name and address of manufacturer or any other
  relevant contact information
- How and where the product is to be used
- The main characteristics and description of
  the product
- Safety requirements (if applicable)
- Conformity certification and licensing
- Expiration date (if applicable)

5

The Russian government does not at present recognise
international standards such as the ISO-9000 system.
How WTO accession may affect this remains to be seen,
but for now around three fifths of goods sold in Russia,
whether they be locally produced or imported, have to
have a Certificate of Conformity of one kind or other.

GOST R Certificates

The most common type of certificate, covering
everything from oil and gas equipment to perfume
and cosmetics, is the **GOST R** certificate. These can
be obtained either for a single consignment or for serial
production and import, depending on whether you are
sending goods to Russia sporadically or exporting on
a constant basis.

The procedures involved in obtaining a GOST R
certificate vary depending on the product, but
can include analysis and evaluation of technical
documentation, product sampling, surveillance visits,
factory audits and even in some cases certification of a
product's quality management system. There is a very
limited number of organisations with the necessary
accreditation to issue GOST R certificates, perhaps the
best established is SGS, which has over 1,000 offices
around the world. You can find your nearest office by
visiting www.sgs.com.

Certification is neither straightforward nor cheap,
even for a single consignment, but the system is so
much part of Russian commercial life that importers
can exercise the option to voluntarily certify products
which do not require it, as a marketing tool if nothing

5

else. As stated above, for some classes of goods not covered by the GOST R certificate you may require separate certification from other government agencies, some examples are below:

- Sanitary-Epidemiological Conclusion Certificate (formerly known as a Hygienic Certificate) for products that come in contact with the human body;
- GOST R Ex-Proof Certificate for explosion-proof equipment and materials;
- Fire Safety Certificate for flammable or fire extinguishing products;
- Rosstroy Certificate for building materials;
- Telecom Type Approval Certificate for telecommunications equipment.

Pursuant to Federal Law 184 *On Technical Regulation*, which came into force in July 2003, by 2011 the existing 500,000 (that's right, half a million) state standards will be replaced by a distinctly more manageable 1,000 statutory regulations. This harmonisation with international practices is a requirement for Russia's WTO accession, and again, legislative reform will be just a single element of the process – implementation of the new standards and regulations can be expected to take some time to bed in.

Most likely your initial business in Russia will be conducted through a representative or agent, or you may be selling direct to the customer with regular trips to maintain the account. As time goes on, though, the prospect of opening a permanent representation on Russian territory may become increasingly attractive. The next chapter takes you through the steps needed to establish a presence in Russia, and includes some general information on the experience of running a Russian office.

6

setting up
a permanent
operation

setting up a permanent operation

For those looking to establish a long-term pressence in Russia. This chapter covers some of the main market entry strategies, types of legal entity and the fundamentals of Russian employment law.

In approaching a market of Russia's size and complexity, you will hopefully have a long-term business strategy in mind, and at some stage the question of establishing a permanent presence for your company will inevitably surface. Most companies working in export markets will go through a series of stages as their business develops, with initial work handled by a sales operative making regular trips to win new accounts and build order volumes. All being well, the time comes when there is sufficient business to justify appointing a local sales agent to represent the company on a rolling contract basis. In some cases, the appointment of an agent will be the first stage in the plan.

6

As the business becomes more established, it may make better economic sense to set up a permanent operation in the country as a bridgehead for further expansion. Under Russian law there are a number of ways to do this, and this chapter, while not intended as an exhaustive account of the ins and outs of each type of legal entity you can create in Russia, provides a general overview of the options available, as well as giving some information and advice on how to make your Russian operation successful.

Agents and distributors

The main advantage of working through an agent or distributor, and the reason why so many companies are happy to pay them commission, is that it is a quick way of plugging into an existing sales network. An established agent will already have a good idea of whether your goods will sell well alongside their existing portfolio, and will be vital in helping you formulate your sales strategy. Of course, you will need to choose very carefully when appointing someone to represent your company to a new market, and it is a good idea to make use of the services available either from the export trade team of your relevant country or from a company specialising in due diligence work.

I know of many companies who have handicapped their Russian business by appointing an agent in a hurry, and an equal number who have regretted rushing to put together a cooperation agreement. If you have already made several trips to Russia banging on doors in an attempt to sell your products, there is a strong temptation to be overly receptive to the idea that someone local will be able to instantly solve your problems and make the business take off. This is not going to be the case with everyone, and the last thing you want is to be lumbered with an agent who either has a bad reputation in the market, or will not be motivated to promote your company. The least you should do is to speak to other companies represented by the same distributor before committing. If the agent concerned is reluctant to put you in touch with their other clients, ask yourself why.

On the subject of the agreement itself, the general norm is to have a legal contract produced in English and Russian setting out the responsibilities of either side. This may sound like stating the obvious, but make sure you know that the Russian and English text both say the same thing. In the case of disputes further down the line, you may want to think about specifying the jurisdiction under which any conflicts will be resolved. For a court to settle a dispute in your favour is one thing, getting it enforced may be quite another, and will be subject to whether there is a reciprocal agreement between Russia and your home country. For this reason you may want to consider specifying international arbitration in any agreements. My intention is not, of course, to put you off, and the more time you spend making sure that you have found the right partner, the less likely such an eventuality becomes. Nonetheless it is worth taking the time early on (and getting legal advice, even if it is expensive) to ensure that your business in Russia goes as smoothly as possible from the off. If this is starting to sound like a mantra that you have read a dozen times in this guide already, good.

Foreign Legal Entities

The most basic form of legal entity under Russian law is the **Representative Office** (= *Predstavitel'stvo*), which a foreign company can establish to perform general support, marketing and ancillary functions on behalf of the parent. As originally envisaged under the legislation, a Representative Office is not permitted to involve itself directly in commercial activity, and is therefore not subject to profits tax. In reality it has become accepted practice that such an entity can sell goods and services,

Representative Office

issue invoices etc. so long as it registers itself with the tax authorities and submits accounts (...and pays tax!).

A **Branch Office** (= *Filial*) is slightly more involved in terms of registration requirements, but is permitted to fulfil any or all of the functions of the parent company, including sales, repatriation of foreign currency earnings, contracting with Russian entities and appointing a sales force. To all intents and purposes, in the eyes of Russian law a Branch Office is a fully-fledged subdivision of the foreign company.

6

Registration

Either of the above must, of course, be registered with the Russian authorities: there are a number of official bodies which can issue approval and accreditation for Foreign Legal Entities, the two most common being the State Registration Chamber of the Ministry of Justice (SRC) and the Chamber of Commerce and Industry of the Russian Federation (CCI). Two things to note: firstly, the CCI can ONLY issue accreditation for a Representative Office, not a Branch. Secondly, if you are planning to open either type outside Moscow or St Petersburg, you will also need preliminary approval from the local authorities before you submit documents for accreditation.

Branch office

You will remember from earlier in the guide that the average time to set up a company in Russia has only recently dipped below a full calendar month. The list of documents below, which are the minimum requirement to receive accreditation of your representative office, will probably go some way towards explaining why this is so. All documents in the list below must be legalised/apostilled in their country of origin and accompanied by a notarised Russian translation:

Documents for Registration

> • A written application for the establishment of the representative office, signed by an authorised representative, indicating the following:
> - company name
> - date of incorporation
> - registered address
> - nature of business

6

- purpose of establishment of the representative office
- details of business cooperation with Russian partners
- prospects for development;
- Extract from the Trade Register of the parent company's country of origin or other document confirming registration;
- Articles of Association (Memorandum of Association) of the parent company;
- Resolution of the parent company to establish a representative office in the Russian Federation;
- Original and a certified copy of the regulations of the representative office
- Certificate of creditworthiness from a foreign bank servicing the parent company in its home country, issued within the last 6 months;
- Two or more reference letters from Russian business partners, submitted on company letterhead, signed by the authorized person and including the company stamp;
- General Power of Attorney for the Director/Head of the representative office
- Power of Attorney issued to the person authorized to represent the interests of the representative office at the Federal State Institution, State Registration Chamber with the Ministry of Justice of Russia (this is required only if the authorized person is not the head of the representative office – in some cases this may be the accountant or book-keeper)
- A document certifying the address of the representative, i.e. a letter of guarantee or lease/tenancy agreement together with a certified ownership certificate from the landlord. If you are sub-letting, you will have to additionally produce a sublease agreement
- If the office is located outside Moscow or St Petersburg, an original document of consent from the local authorities
- Two copies of the application form/data sheet of a representative office of the foreign legal entity, signed by the legal representative of the foreign company

To register a Branch Office you will need a similar collection of documents, and depending on the nature of your business, you may also need to produce "expert opinions", either as originals or certified copies, from bodies such as the Russian Ministry of Fuel and Energy or the State Ecology Committee. Accreditation is issued for a limited period of time, after which you will have to apply for an extension. Accreditations for Representative Offices are issued for periods of 1, 2 or 3 years (this is specified on the application), a Branch Office accreditation can be issued for up to 5 years. According to the SRC itself, accreditation is normally issued within 21 working days of receipt of the application, but can be expedited to 7 working days in exceptional cases.

Registering employees

Foreign employees of either a Branch or Representative office must also receive accreditation before they can begin work, while Russian employees require accreditation only if they are head of the office. Approvals are issued by the same bodies as for office accreditations, and require a written application from the employer, a copy of the office accreditation certificate, a Curriculum Vitae of the person to be accredited, passport copy and relevant powers of attorney, along with either two or three passport sized photos, depending who you believe. The employee accreditation will last only as long as the office accreditation, and will have to be renewed in the same way. Note that this foreign employee accreditation is NOT the same as a work permit, which we will deal with later in the chapter.

As a rule, a Foreign Legal Entity can employ no more than five foreign nationals, unless it can justify to the accreditation body that the functions to be carried out cannot be performed by a Russian employee.

Russian Legal Entities

Russian law permits foreign companies to establish a local business entity, which can be either entirely owned by the parent company, or co-owned with a Russian partner or partners. There are a number of different

Registering Foreign Employees

6

options available should you wish to set up a Russian company, including general and limited partnerships, but the most commonly encountered types of Russian company are the Limited Liability Company (LLC) and the Joint Stock Company (JSC). The essential difference between the two is that the former does not issue shares in the form of securities, instead its start-up capital stems from "contributions" made by the founding parties. An LLC is therefore more straightforward to set up, and is often the weapon of choice for creating a wholly foreign-owned subsidiary. The JSC justifies the additional complexity of formation in providing a more stable trading environment in several key areas. In particular, under JSC law it is not permitted for one participant to leave the company and withdraw their shares without the consent of the other participants, nor do all strategic decisions require the unanimous approval of all participants to be adopted. Thirdly, participants in an LLC with a share of over 10% in the company can apply to a court to seek the expulsion of another participant, provided that they have grounds that the participant substantively hindered the company's activities and/or were in material breach of their obligations.

When you come to deal with Russian companies, you will probably notice a range of initials prefixing their names – these initials describe the type of company, as set out in the table below:

Russian Abbreviation	Type of Company	Full description in Russian	English Abbreviation
OOO	Limited Liability Company	Obshchestvo s Ogranichennoy Otvetstvennost'yu	LLC
ZAO	Closed Joint Stock Company	Zakrytoe Aktsionernoe Obshchestvo	CJSC
OAO	Open Joint Stock Company	Otkrytoe Aktsionernoe Obshchestvo	OJSC

Limited Liability Companies (LLC)

An LLC is formed by up to 50 participants (a participant may be either a person or a legal entity) who all make contributions to the company's Charter Capital. The minimum charter capital is presently set at 100 times the statutory minimum monthly wage (100 roubles), so according to current exchange rates you need to raise just over £200. Should the number of participants exceed 50 as the business expands, the LLC is required by Russian law to re-register as an Open Joint Stock Company within one year.

All participants have the legal right to participate in the management of the LLC and to receive a share of its profits, to sell all or part of their interest in the company to other participants, and to withdraw from the LLC without the consent of their fellow participants. They also have the right to receive a proportion of the assets of the LLC upon liquidation, once the creditors have been paid. Additional obligations can be placed upon the participants only by unanimous consent, except in the case where the additional obligations are placed upon only one participant who has agreed to these obligations. In this specific instance only a two-thirds majority is required.

Joint Stock Companies (JSC)

As explained above, the key difference between an LLC and a JSC is that the shares in the latter are deemed securities, and therefore have to be registered with the Federal Service for the Financial Markets of the Russian Federation (the FSFM). The number of shareholders in a closed JSC may not exceed 50, while an open JSC may have an unlimited number of shareholders. Minimum charter capital for a closed JSC is the same as for a LLC, for an open JSC it is ten times that, or 1,000 times the statutory minimum wage. Securities in the JSC can be issued in the form of shares (ordinary or preferred), bonds and issuer's options.

Existing shareholders in a JSC have a pre-emptive right to acquire newly issued securities in the company, whether the securities be privately or publicly placed, and are required to include their interest in the shareholders' register maintained by the JSC. A

Limited Liability
Companies

6

Joint Stock
Companies

shareholder in a closed JSC may sell their shares to a third party only after they have notified the other shareholders, who have in turn elected not to buy them up. Finally, open JSCs must appoint a licensed registrar to maintain the shareholders' register.

Registering a Russian Legal Entity

With the exception of registering securities with the FSFM, the procedure for registering a JSC or LLC is broadly the same, and is done through the local tax office. The documentation required is essentially what you would expect, there is little point in listing it here as you will no doubt be working with a lawyer if you are this far down the line with your Russian business.

6

Book-keepers

A general point which covers all the above before we go on: if you establish a company in Russia, in whatever form, one of the most important employees you will ever have will be your accountant. By this I do not mean the gentleman with the nice car who you have to take to lunch twice a year, but the in-house book-keeper who is pretty much a *sine qua non* for any Russian office. When I first came to work in Russia, I was surprised that my office of only six people had a full-time book-keeper, as I thought that simple things like invoicing and credit control could surely be left to the office manager. I was still more surprised to find that another office in the company had TWO book-keepers. Surely this was excessive? Boy, was I ever wrong. The amount of paperwork generated in the average Russian office on any given day can be nothing short of staggering: refer back to Chapter 1 and the section on the Tatar-Mongol Yoke and you will see where it all comes from. Legislative efforts are being made to reduce the administrative burden on companies working in Russia to bring it into line with international standards, but for now, at least, your book keeper will be vital to the smooth running of your office. These are highly trained specialists, who will be a far more valuable guide through the maze of Russian commercial and employment legislation than the expensive international firm your company works with everywhere else in the world. If you find a good one, hang on to them whatever you do, and don't forget to buy them flowers on their birthday.

Taxation in Russia
Corporate Tax

First, the good news. The rate of Profits Tax in Russia is 24%, making it significantly lower than both the US and many European countries. This rate is made up of a 7.5% rate payable to the federal budget, and 17.5% which goes to the regional coffers. The local authorities have a discretionary right to reduce this second portion to 13.5%, giving an overall rate of 20%. Profits Tax is payable on all sales and non-sales income generated by a Permanent Entity (PE), whether that entity be foreign or Russian.

In addition to Profits Tax, other withholding taxes may be levied on profits from share dividends, royalties and interest among other things. The amount you pay will depend on the presence or otherwise of a double taxation treaty between Russia and your home country. If you are a US company, for instance, you will not pay withholding tax on income from interest or royalties, but you will pay 10% on income from dividends on shares held in a Russian company, unless your company owns 10% or more of the share capital or voting power in that company, in which case the rate will come down to 5%.

Profits Tax

As an employer, your company will also have to pay a Unified Social Tax on the salary of all employees, whether they are Russian or foreign (prior to 2003, this tax was only levied on the salaries of Russian employees). This tax is calculated on a sliding scale from 26% to 2%, with the highest percentage applicable to the lowest portion of the salary, and the 2% rate being applied to earnings in excess of 600,000 roubles per month.

Unified Social Tax

Personal Tax

Again, we'll start with the good news: income tax in Russia is levied at a flat rate of just 13%. This rate will apply to all your Russian employees, and to any foreign employees who qualify as residents. As a foreigner, you are deemed a resident if you spend 183 days or more on Russian territory in the course of the year – you do this by sending your local tax office photocopies of each page of your passport, showing border entry and exit stamps.

Income Tax

6

Should you not qualify for resident status, the rate rises to 30%, again irrespective of how much (or little) you earn.

A curious result of this is that, as a foreign citizen, you cannot actually pay your income tax until such time as you can prove your resident status, i.e. at the end of your first year working in Russia. Your employer can either withhold the relevant portion of your salary, or pay you your full pre-tax entitlement on the understanding that you will be responsible for declaring your earnings and submitting your own tax return. Either way, you end up paying all your income tax for a year's earnings in one go. This can be quite a harrowing experience if, as I once did, you elect to pay your income tax at your local branch of Sberbank in cash. Again, just to reiterate, your full time book-keeper is the one to go to for advice on all these things.

Investing in property as a foreigner

As a foreigner you are permitted to buy, own and sell property in Russia, and generally you have the same rights as a Russian citizen, although there are restrictions on foreign ownership in border areas and of agricultural land, the latter of which may only be leased by a foreign entity for a maximum of 49 years. The Russian Strategic Sectors law (see previous chapter) can be seen as a result of the Kremlin's increasing scrutiny on foreign investors in the country as a whole, and if you are considering a major investment in Russia you should be prepared to spend a lot of time establishing how far your rights extend, and whether any forthcoming legislation may affect them.

Before you invest at all, even if you are just buying a flat near the office, it is important that you have established resident status, or you will end up paying substantial tax on both the purchase and sale of any property. Similarly, if you invest in a property and sell it on in less than three years, anti-speculation law means that you will be hit for 30% of the total sale price, not merely the portion that is profit.

Work permits for foreigners in Russia

All non-Russian citizens are required to obtain a permit to work in the Russian Federation. The work permit is sometimes also known as a working visa, but it should not be confused with a business visa as described in Chapter 3. The latter is issued only as a document to allow entry and exit to and from the Russia, it does not allow you to be employed there. This used to be a slightly grey area, as it was technically possible to be employed as a "consultant" for your company, work on a permanent basis in Russia and get around the work permit legislation. So long as the employee in question was receiving their salary overseas, and was not signing documents on behalf of the company that would require a Power of Attorney, they could perform all other necessary functions, qualifying for residency status merely by dint of the length of time spent in Russia (see **Personal Tax** above). As of 2008, however, the legislation was changed so that an annual multi-entry business visa would only allow you to spend a maximum of 90 days in Russia during each 180 day period.

Regardless of whether it is a Russian or Foreign Legal Entity, any company operating in Russia must also obtain a permit for employing foreign nationals before any individual work permits for employees of that company can be issued. If you intend to work in Russia for your company, or to employ foreign nationals, it is vital that you start the process of obtaining a permit as quickly as possible, as it can take a long time, in some cases up to six months from initial application to the issuance of an actual work permit. To obtain the company permit in the first instance, the following documents have to be submitted to your local branch of the Russian Federal Migration Service (FMS):

Company Permit

*   Permit application form;
*   Documentation to confirm preliminary agreement with the employee(s) to be hired, including details of salary, social and employment security;
*   Proof of payment of federal tax to employ foreign nationals – at the time of writing, this is 3,000 roubles per employee;

6

- Copy of Federal Tax Service registration (where relevant)
- For a Foreign Legal Entity, copy of accreditation certificate
- For a Russian Legal Entity, copy of company's entry in to the Unified State Register

Any copies submitted must be notarised. Once you are over the initial surprise at how many book-keepers there are in Russia, your second shock may come when you notice how many notaries there are, and how busy they all seem to be. Now you know why.

To obtain the employee work permit itself, the following documents are required, in addition to the application form and the company permit – again, any copies must be notarised and, where necessary, accompanied by a notarised translation into Russian:

- Passport photograph
- Proof of any professional qualifications, or document confirming level of qualification by Russian educational standards
- Proof of ID, valid at least 6 months from the date of application
- Guarantee letter from prospective employer confirming that the employee will leave the Russian Federation if required to do so by the FMS

As I write this, the fee to obtain a work permit is 1,000 roubles per employee. The permit should be processed by the FMS in 30 working days. When you go to collect your work permit, you must also have a medical certificate (which can only be issued by a limited number of hospitals and clinics) confirming freedom of infection from a range of diseases, including HIV, syphilis, tuberculosis and leprosy. The FMS will be able to give you a list of the approved establishments which will be able to issue this certificate. The only instance where this certificate will not be required is for employees who will be in Russia for less than 90 days.

Quotas for employing foreign nationals in Russia

At the end of 2006 the Russian government introduced a quota system for the employment of foreign nationals, specifying the number of people who would be issued work permits based on their skills and the sectors in which they would be working. If you're interested, the total number of foreign nationals requiring visas who would be issued with work permits in 2008 was 672,304. Just under double this number are available for foreign nationals not needing visas (citizens of Ukraine, Kazakhstan etc). Quota systems have a habit of ringing alarm bells, but as far as I know there has not yet been a case where the demand for work permits has exceeded the number available. The quotas are reassessed on an annual basis, and there is provision for increasing quotas during the year should employers be able to cogently demonstrate a business need. In other words, as a potential employer it is something you should be aware of, but not in a panic about.

Employment Quotas

6

Employing Russian nationals

If your intention is to staff your office solely with expats, you do not need to read this section, but from experience I can tell you that you are making a mistake. Nothing wrong with expats, you understand, some of my best friends are expats, but if you are working in Russia, you will definitely find that having a "home team" on your side will be a distinct benefit. Additionally, you will find that the Russian education system, particularly the universities and institutes, has done you proud as an employer – these are seriously well-trained people, and you will find that any commercial naivety which may in some cases have dogged their early post-graduation years will be long gone by the time they are in their mid-twenties. Still more importantly, your Russian employees are your guides in knowing how to do business successfully on a personal level. In other words, they are a vital resource, so use them. Best of all, it doesn't take months to get them on the books, although getting them off the books again can be another matter entirely – see below.

Russian employment law

Employment law in Russia is generally straightforward, although there are elements which might seem unusual if you are used to US or European practice. As an employer, the thing you have to keep in mind is that the system of rights for employer and employed is weighted overall in favour of the latter. All employees, whether Russian or not, must have a detailed contract setting out their rights and obligations, and any additions to the latter must be agreed in writing by both parties. The 2002 Labour Code of the Russian Federation (amended 2007) sets out a range of mandatory minimum guarantees which cannot be superseded or circumscribed by the employment contract. It is important that the employment contract sets out expressly the duties and obligations of the employee, as the latter will be fully within their rights to refuse any task that is not written down in black and white. As is so often the case in Russia, the reality tends to be more flexible than the letter of the law, but it is in your interests as an employer to make sure you are covered before you end up with a marketing assistant who refuses to use the telephone.

All your Russian employees will have a Labour Book, a little (generally red) ledger in which is contained their entire employment history. This you have to sign when they begin work, and on the day they leave. You are also required by law to pay your employees at least twice a month – the norm is to pay a fixed amount in the middle of each calendar month, with the balance payable on the last day. Another thing to bear in mind is that if you are used to thinking of salaries in gross terms, e.g. "I earn £40,000 a year", in Russia salaries tend to be quoted nett, monthly. So, if you include a salary of 1,000 euros in a job advert, your successful applicant will be expecting that amount to be transferred to their bank account each month. Income tax, Unified Social Tax, and a number of other little charges on top are considered the responsibility of the employer.

If it turns out that you have chosen a wrong 'un, be aware that it is VERY difficult to terminate employment in Russia. Put all thoughts of sweeping in to the office one morning shouting "you're FIRED!" out of your head right now, or you will find yourself at an employment

Employee's Rights

Terminating Employment

tribunal in very short order. If you do want to dismiss someone, you have to follow a set procedure of one verbal warning followed by two written warnings, and these warnings have to be for specific misdemeanours. Only once this process has been completed can you give someone their cards. That is not to say that no one ever gets fired in Russia, but very often employers prefer to go down the route of making an offer that can't be refused, generally a couple of months' salary. If your employee has a child under the age of three, their rights become even more sacrosanct, and you will only be able to fire them on the grounds of gross misconduct.

6

As an employer, you have the right to set a three month probation period on new hirings (six months for senior executive level positions), during which either party may terminate the employment in writing by giving three days' notice, without financial penalty. In these situations the employee may resign without giving a reason, but the employer must state the specific reason why the new person did not pass the probation. My record for a new hiring in Russia was one day! Employees are also entitled to 28 calendar days' paid holiday per year, which they can use in full after six months' employment. Holiday pay is calculated as an average of the previous three months' income before the start of the holiday, including any commission, so don't be surprised if your sales people take off for the beach soon after they land a big contract.

Probation Periods

Maternity leave is also generous, and progressive, in Russia: paid leave for the new mum begins not less than 70 days before the baby is due, and not less than 70 days after the birth. Maternity pay is funded from Unified Social Tax contributions, and is based on the employee's full basic salary up to a statutory maximum of 23,400 roubles per month (as at 1st January 2008). The child's care-giver, be they the mother, father or other relative, may also claim partially paid childcare leave until the child is three years old. During this time, they have the pre-emptive right to return to full-time work on the same terms as before, so you have to keep this in mind when hiring anyone to cover them during this period.

Maternity Leave

6

In conclusion

I am acutely aware, as a generally honest person, that I began this chapter with a breezy-sounding "this section is not intended as an exhaustive account" before proceeding to bludgeon you as my reader with seemingly interminable details on everything from the maximum number of shareholders in a CJSC (50, remember?) to the hassle you have to go through if you want to fire your office manager. Again, it is not my intention to put you off working in Russia, quite the opposite, but the more you know before you arrive, the better. In many ways Russia is no more bureaucratic than the UK or the US – some things are a great deal easier, as you will find if you ever compare notes on obtaining visas with a Russian national who has visited Britain. The key thing is to be aware of the system, and NEVER try to cut corners – that way madness lies.

A few observations in parting on office culture, particularly if you are the head of office. It is generally held that any "softness" on the part of the boss is seen as weakness, and while I do not hold with this entirely, it is something you need to bear in mind if your management style is very inclusive and democratic. You may have to shorten the leash, depending on the dynamic of your particular workplace. Birthdays and some national holidays are observed enthusiastically, particularly International Women's Day on March 8th, when all male directors will be expected to bring flowers, chocolates etc. for their female colleagues. Regular staff meetings are also more important in Russia than elsewhere, and the post-Soviet phenomenon of reluctance to show initiative persists yet, although things are much better than they used to be in this regard. The more a Russian office is aware of the parameters within which it operates, the happier it will be, and this will be reflected in productivity – any perceived slippage in standards, whether it be punctuality, the length of lunch-breaks or rambling personal phone-calls, will be difficult to reign in once it starts, so make sure that you get this right from the very start. If you want your colleagues to socialise with each other, you will also have to actively encourage this – it is a good idea to arrange the odd office lunch. Russian employees also like to have the opportunity to improve themselves through professional training courses, so have this in mind or they will start to feel neglected. Finally, bear in mind that inflation still runs in double digits in Russia, so you will be faced with frequent, and in fairness, understandable, calls/hints/demands for pay rises.

6

7

industry overviews

7

industry overviews

The aim of this section is to provide a general overview of some of the key sectors of the Russian economy which are of most interest to foreign investors.

Russia has been a free market economy for less than two decades. For the first half of the 20th century, the country's economic activity was geared largely towards fighting a series of debilitating wars and attempting to re-build shattered infrastructure during brief periods of peace. Post-1945, Russia's reconstruction and continued industrialisation took place against the background of an unprecedented build-up of the military-industrial complex in competition with the western powers. State investment was thus predominantly focused on large-scale industry and military technology, with the result that by the 1980s the Soviet Union could boast some of the world's most advanced combat aircraft and several miracles of construction and engineering, while at the same time lagging behind other countries in areas like agriculture, residential housing, light industry and consumer goods.

As stated elsewhere in this guide, Russia has made immense strides in a relatively short period of time to address some of the structural issues in its economy, and the general consensus of opinion is that the country is going in the right direction. In this chapter you will find brief overviews of some of the sectors in the Russian economy which are of key interest to foreign investors.

Agriculture

Around 10% of Russia's land mass is suitable for agriculture – in other words, Russia's total cultivable land area is roughly three times the size of France. You will remember from Chapter 1 that the question of land reform has dogged Russia throughout its history, and recent experience has been no different. Attempts at restructuring under both Gorbachev in the 1980s and Yeltsin in the 1990s brought little benefit, indeed 1995 saw Russia's worst grain harvest since 1963, with a total yield of 63.4m tons. The area of cultivated land in Russia also decreased by 30% during the 1990s to around 70m hectares, although more recent figures point to a degree of recovery here – at the time of writing estimates pointed to a 2008 grain harvest of 95m tons, 15% up on 2007, with a predicted 60% increase in grain exports.

7

The Russian government is aware of the need to boost production still further, particularly in view of rising global food prices, and has selected the sector as a priority for investment. The principal debate surrounds to what extent this should be achieved by more intensive farming techniques, and to what extent by simply increasing the amount of land made available for agriculture. The scope for improvement in both areas is vast: while around 7% of the world's arable land is owned either by the Russian state or by collective farms, around one sixth of this area, over five times the total cultivable land of the United Kingdom, lies fallow. Meanwhile, the average grain yield of those areas which are under the plough is less than a third of that achieved in the US and western Europe at 1.85 tons per hectare, although in places it does rival western averages.

Black earth

European Russia's most productive agricultural areas are in the Central and Volga economic regions – the land of *chernozem*, or black earth – where nearly two thirds of available land is devoted to agriculture. Beyond the Urals, it is mainly the more temperate southernmost areas of Siberia and the Far East which are turned over to cultivation. Obstacles to development in the sector include lingering uncertainty over land rights and the mass flight to urban areas during the 1990s, although agriculture still employs over 10% of the working population. Concerns have also surfaced among private investors that agriculture's status as a national investment priority may yet lead to heightened state involvement, or interference, depending on your point of view.

Land prices

The recent sharp rises in global food prices, together with the scope for expansion in the Russian agricultural sector, have not been lost on investors – you could say that black earth is the new black. Arable land prices almost doubled between 2006 and 2008, and have now comfortably passed US$1,000 per hectare. It is also worth remembering that Russia was once the world's largest exporter of grain. From the point of view of the foreign investor, the agricultural sector does not fall within the remit of the Strategic Sectors Law mentioned in the preceding chapter, although the dominant private agricultural companies, such as Razgulyai, Black Earth, and the London-listed Cherkizovo, are Russian-owned.

Particular opportunities for foreign companies lie in the sphere of agricultural equipment, where companies such as John Deere and Caterpillar have done brisk trade supplying modern, efficient tractors to farms keen to increase yields.

Table 7.1   Russian agricultural production 1992-2007 (figures in millions of tonnes unless otherwise stated)

	1992	1995	2000	2001	2002	2003	2004	2005	2006	2007
Grains (weight after processing)										
	106.9	63.4	65.5	85.2	86.6	67.2	78.1	78.2	78.6	81.8
Sugar beet (factory)										
	25.5	19.1	14.1	14.6	15.7	19.4	21.8	21.4	30.9	29
Potatoes										
	38.3	39.9	34	35	32.9	36.7	35.9	37.3	38.6	36.8
Vegetables										
	10	11.3	12.5	13.3	13	14.8	14.6	15.2	15.6	15.5
Cattle & poultry (slaughter weight)										
	8.3	5.8	4.4	4.5	4.7	4.9	5	4.9	5.2	5.6
Milk										
	47.2	39.2	32.3	32.9	33.5	33.4	32.2	31.2	31.4	32.2
Eggs, bln. pieces										
	42.9	33.8	34.1	35.2	36.3	36.5	35.8	36.9	37.9	37.8
Wool (physical weight), **thou. tons**										
	179	93	40	40	43	45	47	48	49	...

Source: Rosstat Russian Federal State Statistics Service

Metals and mining

Russia produces one fifth of the world's nickel, uranium and cobalt, and between 5% and 7% of its coal and iron ore. Following the privatisations of the 1990s and a number of mergers and acquisitions over the past decade, the sector is dominated by a small number of major enterprises, some of which are truly global players. Norilsk Nickel, founded in 1989 to agglomerate several of the Soviet Union's non-ferrous mining companies, has aggressively expanded over the past few years, and now

Russia's major
metals producers

has interests in Africa, Australia, Finland, Canada and the US, in addition to its core business in Siberia. It is said locally that when God was distributing riches around the world, his hands froze when he got to Norilsk and he dropped everything he had left. There is a 50% chance that the palladium in your car's catalytic convertor originally came from here. RusAl (Russian Aluminium), whose main shareholder is Oleg Deripaska, currently Russia's wealthiest man, accounts for over 12% of global aluminium output, producing among other things almost 200 tonnes of aluminium foil every single day. There was talk in 2008 that the two giants were discussing a merger, which would create a US$100bn behemoth to challenge the supremacy of BHP Billiton, although at the time of writing these talks have been put on hold. Steel production in Russia is dominated by a handful of companies: Evraz Group, Severstal, Novolipetsk Steel, Mechel and Metalloinvest, and in 2007 the country was ranked fourth in the world in overall production, behind China, Japan and the US.

Financial woes

Regardless of their considerable might, companies in the sector remain at the mercy of commodity prices, and the falls of the second half of 2008 hit the Russian concerns as much as anyone else. Norilsk even went as far as buying back its own shares at a 25% premium in an attempt to reinvigorate its stock, the value of which fell by a third between May and August 2008. The sector as a whole, however, remains robust, and the companies to emerge from the corporate battleground of the 1990s are generally sound and financially efficient – a world apart from their creaking state-owned forebears although some including Evraz, Severstal and Mechel received state bonus towards the end of 2008 to pay off foreign debts.

In the 1990s Russia's coalmining giants were, if anything, in an even worse state than their metallurgical counterparts, and so they were not privatised with quite the unseemly haste seen in other sectors. Propped up by massive state subsidies, the industry nonetheless shed more than half its workforce between 1991 and 2001. Russia's coal-bearing regions are spread throughout the country, from the Donestk Basin (Donbass) in the south west (shared with Ukraine) to the Lena Basin in eastern Siberia, which is considered to be the largest single coal

7

deposit on the planet. Russia lies second in proven coal reserves behind the US, with deposits of just over 157bn tonnes, but such a vast country could contain a great deal more – I have seen one report estimating a total of six trillion tonnes. In terms of output, Russia ranks fifth, with 314.2m tonnes extracted in 2007. At the shiny end of the carbon equation, Alrosa accounts for around 20-25% of global rough diamond production, with the vast majority of its mines located in Yakutia in north east Siberia. Exploration is also underway in the Urals and near Arkhangelsk in north west Russia.

Oil and gas

While the metals and mining sector is heavily dominated by Russian corporations, oil and gas has seen a much more significant level of activity from international companies. The sector has seen more than its fair share of controversy in recent years, with a number of foreign investors complaining of the level of state control/interference. Russia is nevertheless one of only a handful of major hydrocarbon producers to allow any degree of production sharing with international companies.

Russia is the world's second largest oil producing nation after Saudi Arabia, with up to 14% of proven global reserves, and as the home of over one third of the world's natural gas, it has no rival in this sector. The state-owned giant Gazprom accounts for 20% of total global production of natural gas, and controls all Russia's gas exports as well as the country's entire delivery pipeline infrastructure. Around 43% of the oil and gas consumed in Europe comes from Russia, something that gives the region's political leaders a severe case of the jitters on a regular basis.

Gazprom

Up to 90% of Russia's oil production is accounted for by just 10 companies, led by Rosneft, also state-owned. Major international investors in the country include Shell, with its multi-billion dollar stake in Russia's first offshore oil and gas project, Sakhalin-2 (a stake which was diluted by 50% in April 2007 with the entry of Gazprom to the project), and ExxonMobil, which has a 30% share in Sakhalin-1, a smaller project located off the island's north east coast. More recently, in separate

Foreign investors

7

deals made in 2007, the French and Norwegian giants Total and StatoilHydro acquired a combined 49% share in the development of the vast Shtokman gas field beneath the Barents Sea, which is estimated to hold over half as much natural gas as the entire Caspian.

TNK BP

All of the above are minority investments, but there is to date just one example of a 50:50 joint venture between Russian and foreign partners, that of TNK-BP, a company formed in 2003 by the Alfa, Access/Renova Group and BP to develop assets in Western Siberia. The middle of 2008 saw a storm of controversy as the two sets of shareholders aired their differences over the future strategic development of the company, a dispute which culminated in the departure of its CEO, Robert Dudley. The conflict did very little for investor confidence in Russia, where the perception remains that international companies do not enjoy a level playing field alongside their domestic counterparts, whether they be partners or rivals.

Nonetheless, the oil and gas sector remains an area of intense investor activity, and as stated elsewhere in this guide, Russia is keen to encourage foreign involvement in developing resources which are for the most part very hard to access. In engineering terms, both the Sakhalin projects go beyond what was thought possible in offshore development not so long ago, and Shtokman will be no less challenging. From the other side, naturally the oil and gas majors cannot resist the lure of such wealth sitting in the ground (or beneath the waves and shifting ice-sheets), even if they don't always get things their own way. The raw figures are fairly compelling: the market for field services and construction engineering alone was put at US$33bn in 2007, with expected growth of between 10% and 15% year on year. In a report commissioned by UK Trade and Investment in 2007, total investment required for full development of Russia's onshore oil and gas industry alone was put at around US$1 trillion.

Power

Increased energy consumption is an inevitable consequence of economic growth, and domestic energy demand in Russia increased by almost 40% between

1998 and 2007. The Russian power sector has gone through significant changes since the decision of the Russian government in mid-2006 to liberalise the sector. Central to these changes has been the break up of the RAO UES (Unified Energy Systems) monopoly on generation and supply, although the state retains control of the transmission and distribution network through the Federal Grid Company, in which it holds a 75% share. The Russian government's stated aim is that the entire sector will be liberalised by 2011, with the exception of a handful of elements in which the state will retain a majority shareholding. Among these is the Sochi Electricity Generating Station, which is considered a strategic asset.

The de-monopolisation of RAO UES

Elsewhere on the generation side, the state monolith has been divided into six Wholesale Generating Companies (WGC – Russian ОГК) and fourteen Territorial Generating Companies (TGC / ТГК). The international energy giants have, as you can imagine, been very keen to share in the bounty of Russia's newly deregulated sector, and investors so far include RWE and E.ON (Germany), Enel (Italy) and France's EDF. In 2007, the TGCs brought in US$24bn in private investment, and not just from abroad: Russian investors include Gazprom, Mechel, Norilsk and the Siberian coal producer SUEK. As elsewhere in the Russian economy, the promise of future income goes hand-in-hand with the immediate requirement for major investment in modern plant and equipment, with a figure of just under 1.5 trillion roubles cited in RAO UES's own investment programme for 2006-10. Long term, the plan is to double Russia's electricity output to 2 trillion kWh by 2025.

Foreign investors in the power sector

Alongside its coal-, oil- and gas-fired stations, Russia is planning a major expansion in its nuclear generating capacity in order to free up more of its mineral wealth for export. Of Russia's 31 nuclear power plants, just under half are nearing the end of their working life, and all are located in the European part of the country. On the other side of the Urals, with all those rivers, it is not surprising that Russia's renewable energy sector is dominated by hydroelectric power, with Hydro-OGK, the world's second largest hydroelectric firm, producing

nuclear and hydro-electric power

7

around 20% of Russia's total output from around 50 stations. Of the ten largest hydroelectric dams in the world today, four are in Siberia, although when China's Three Gorges Dam on the Yangtze becomes fully operational in 2012, it will put an end to Russia's supremacy, producing more power than all four combined. Hydro-OGK plans to double its generating capacity by 2020, with the bulk of the extra gigawattage coming from the Caucasus, Siberia and the Russian Far East.

In addition to feeding domestic demand, Russia is a major exporter of electricity, both to CIS countries and other neighbours including China, Poland, Turkey and Finland. Plans are also in place to supply Iran, Afghanistan and Pakistan from two new hydroelectric plants in Tajikistan.

Infrastructure, construction and real estate

Once again, this sector in Russia is characterised by an impressive surge in activity resulting from a combination of generally strong growth and the legacy of under-investment in the 1990s. A visitor to any of Russia's major cities today could easily be forgiven for thinking they have just wandered onto an enormous building site. The construction industry is one of Russia's largest employers, with a workforce of just under 5m people, or more than 7% of the total workforce.

Residential construction

The headlong migration to the cities since the fall of the Soviet Union triggered a massive boom in residential construction, with high rise blocks springing up on the perimeters of Russia's cities "like mushrooms after the rain", to borrow the local expression. To take just one official statistic, between 2000 and 2007 just under four million new flats were built throughout Russia, a total of slightly more than three hundred square kilometres of living space – around the size of Kansas City. Much of the newly built housing is replacing the low-quality apartment blocks built in Russia during the 1960s and 1970s, and certainly some of the larger cities have a brighter and more modern aspect today than they did even a few years ago. Demand still far outstrips supply, however, and this, combined with rising incomes and, crucially, the increased availability of mortgage credit, has seen prices rise exponentially. According to one estimate, residential prices in Moscow leapt 90% between mid-2006 and mid-2007. The scale of the task of housing Russia's increasingly affluent population is considerable: just to reach the European average of living space per capita, the country will have to increase its total housing stock by a third – or over three times more than what has been built so far.

Commercial
real estate

Russia's economic renaissance has also led to a vast expansion in commercial real estate, although for now the sector is also characterised across the board by lack of supply, vanishingly low vacancy rates and commensurately high prices – good news for investors, landlords and developers, less so for tenants. When you come to book a hotel in Moscow, or rent an office, you will see what I mean. A 2008 survey of prime office rental rates put the Russian capital second behind London's West End at over £1,000 per square metre per year, almost double New York prices. Moscow is famously expensive, so this may come as no shock to many readers – more surprising perhaps is that St Petersburg lies 11th on the same list, just ahead of Singapore. Both cities have numerous construction projects underway, notably the spectacularly ambitious Moscow International Business Centre, better known by its original name, Moscow-City. First conceived in 1992 by the Moscow city government (which will eventually make its home there) the Moscow IBC is due for completion in 2020, and among its skyscrapers it will boast the world's second tallest building, the 2,000 ft Russia Tower. The tower itself, designed by UK architect Norman Foster, is just one of many examples of international activity in the Russian construction industry.

Moscow City

Foreign money is, for now, flooding in alongside expertise: in 2006 over half of the investment in the entire sector came from overseas. Nowhere is this more obvious than in the hotel sector, another area of chronic undersupply – Moscow has only around 10% of hotel rooms per head of population compared with London

Hotels

or Paris, and Russia's other cities are even more sparse. Various surveys have estimated that both Moscow and St Petersburg will have to double their supply of hotel rooms by 2010 to catch up with demand. Many of the major international chains are already in Russia in force, as a glance at the following chapters will show, but there is plenty more to come: Hilton, International Hotels Group (IHG), Marriott, Accor and Park Inn are just a few of the companies with major regional expansion plans. One of the main things you will see over the next few years in Russia is a gradual replacement of the old Soviet-era hotels with modern buildings – the development of the sector as a whole is perhaps best encapsulated by the hotel that stands in the very centre of Moscow, on the corner of Tverskaya and Mokhovaya, looking onto the Kremlin and Red Square. Built as the Intourist in 1970, and known for years by Muscovites as the "Rotten Tooth", in 2002 it was torn down and replaced by the 5-star Ritz-Carlton Moscow. For the future, it is the regions, in particular the mid-priced sector, which will show the strongest growth, and the return on investment is predicted to be excellent. According to one expert opinion an operator can spend no more than US$100,000 per room to have the best hotel in town.

Construction in Russia is not confined solely to the cities, but continues apace between the major population centres. Towards the end of 2007 the Russian government announced a programme to invest US$1 trillion in infrastructure projects over the next decade.

Transport infrastructure

The rail network, which will forever remain a key infrastructure component in Russia's vast hinterland, will receive 11 trillion roubles of investment, just under US$440bn, by 2030. The pace of road-building will (it is hoped) reach 4,000km per annum by 2010, including a number of high-speed toll roads. Key projects include a 650km motorway between Moscow and St Petersburg, a spur road from the centre of Moscow to Domodedovo airport, and a 200km stretch of the Don highway which will link the capital to the Black Sea port of Novorossiisk via Rostov-on-Don.

A myriad of urban infrastructure schemes are also

7

either in the planning stages or already underway: St Petersburg alone has over US$10bn of projects on its books, including a tunnel beneath the River Neva, a sea passenger terminal on the Gulf of Finland, a 50km stretch of its ring-road and an elevated express railway. Another major sub-sector of construction in Russian cities is urban regeneration, as the country seeks to revive derelict areas and improve the public realm. In Moscow, the Soviet-era Hotel Rossiya, once the largest hotel in the world, is making way for a major mixed-use urban development covering almost 40 hectares, while the New Holland project in central St Petersburg will transform an artificial island originally completed in 1721, and since used variously as a prison, a naval arsenal and a submarine testing pool, into a culture and leisure complex housing a 2,000 seat concert hall.

Urban regeneration

Large-scale infrastructure projects, whether municipal or federal, require enormous amounts of initial capital investment, and in spite of the recent petrodollar bonanza the Russian government has already made clear its desire to attract private investment to help fund some of the larger development schemes. In recent years the concept of Public Private Partnership (PPP) has gained ground to the extent that almost no major project will be devoid of this element. Russia's Federal Law No 115-FZ, adopted in July 2005, sets out the country's stance on concession agreements with private investors, and is based on the UK PPP model.

Public Private finance

Yet another key area of undersupply is warehousing, and here the disparity between Moscow/St Petersburg and the regions is, if anything, even more stark than it is the hotel sector. Of Russia's entire stock of international standard warehousing, 75% is split between the two main cities. Volgograd, one of southern Russia's major industrial centres, has just 10m^2 per head of population, around 1% of that available in Budapest, for example. Current estimates are that the warehouse space will more than double by 2010, although this, as always, will still be insufficient to keep up with the demand generated principally by Russia's burgeoning retail sector, of which more below.

Warehousing and logistics

7

Consumer retail

Russia has one of the world's fastest growing consumer retail markets, driven by an increase in disposable income of 11% per annum since 2003. More important still than cash has been confidence: a pervading feeling among consumers that Russia's increasing prosperity is more than just a blip saw overall retail sales increase over the same period by just under 29% year on year, with a total turnover in 2007 of US$424bn. On arriving in Russia you will notice straight away the rapid proliferation of out-of-town hypermarkets and retail parks, and should you become a regular visitor it will seem to you that there are more with each trip – between 2006 and 2008 the amount of retail space in Russia almost trebled. As always, however, this expansion must be understood in context – Russia still has around a third of the retail shopping centre space per capita compared with the European average. Again, Moscow and St Petersburg have seen the bulk of the early development, followed by a progressive roll-out to the regional centres, and it is now the smaller cities which are seeing the fastest growth.

The consumer retail sector as a whole, whether food or non-food, is home to several major Russian and international companies, although it would be wrong to say that these companies are dominant. In 2006, the top four retailers in Russia could claim around 5% of market share, compared with around 85% in the UK, and it is predicted that there will be a fair degree of consolidation over the coming years. Key international players include Metro (Germany), Auchan (France) and IKEA (Sweden), while key absentees include, for the moment at least, the American giant Wal-Mart, which has been linked with a move into Russia for some time now. In August 2008 the Russian newspaper Vedomosti announced that Wal-Mart was on a shortlist to buy the Lenta chain of hypermarkets, and by the time this guide has been published the deal may well have gone through.

Lenta is just one of several major Russian retail chains, and in 2009 plans to have around 50 stores across the country (although none will be in Moscow). Of the other major companies in the sector, the largest in sales terms is the LSE-listed, Dutch-incorporated X5 Retail Group, which in 2007 turned over US$5.32bn through its various brands. The table below has some detail on some of the companies you will likely encounter on your travels in Russia. It is intended more as a representative cross-section than a comprehensive listing.

Table 7.2 Companies active in Russian consumer retail sector

| | | | STORES (at end 2008) | | |
| | | T/o 2007 | | | |
	Country	(US$mn)	Moscow	St Petersburg	Regions
Hypermarkets/Supermarkets					
Auchan	France	3,085	10	2	7
Dixy	Russia	1,431	139	121	165
Karusel	Russia†	831	4	16	6
Lenta	Russia	1,559	0	14	17
Magnit	Russia	3,677	599	104	1,697
Metro	Germany	3,571	10	3	35
O'Key	Russia	1,114	0	13	7
Perekrestok	Russia†	1,945	106	18	66
Pyaterochka	Russia†	2,946	277	251	151
Ramstore	Turkey	590*	28	5	17
DIY/Home improvement					
Castorama	France/UK	225 (est.)	1	2	4
IKEA	Sweden	1,000 (est.)	3	2	5
Santa Haus	Russia	35	3	6	8
Consumer Electrical					
Eldorado	Russia	6,000	42	28	862
M. Video	Russia	2,033	34	15	85
Tekhnosila	Russia	1,400	26	6	106

* figures for 2006
† incorporated in Holland

Information and communication technology

We touched on the subject of the internet and mobile telephony briefly in Chapter 4, but it is worth taking a

7

The internet

moment to examine the sector in a little more detail, not least because there are indicators of exceptional growth wherever you look. To take a few headline figures: against the background of overall GDP growth of 7.8% in 2007, sales of mobile handsets increased by 16%, the number of personal computers in the country increased by 35% to around 31m devices, and internet access increased by half, with actual internet traffic volume doubling. According to the Russian Ministry of Communications, the sector as a whole in 2007 was worth just over US$60bn, up from around US$38bn the previous year. Expansion in the sector for now shows no sign of abating, and is expected to continue at a rate of around 19%, outstripping all the other BRIC countries.

Mobile phones

Russia instantly embraced the mobile phone as a must-have accessory, and as a westerner, you will almost certainly notice that everyone else seems to have a much flashier model than yours. In fact, 40% of mobile sales in 2007 were "premium" handsets, with the more basic models accounting for only around 8% of turnover. All the main manufacturers are well represented, and the sector as a whole is ruled by three operators: MTS, Vimpelcom and MegaFon, which in 2007 divided the market up between themselves at 33.2%, 29.9% and 20.4% respectively. The mobile retail sector is burgeoning on the back of all this growth, the largest outlet being Euroset, which posted revenues of US$5.61bn in 2007 through its network of over 5,100 branches throughout Russia and the wider CIS.

Nanotechnology

Away from the consumer sector, the Russian government has identified nanotechnology as a key growth area for the future. In 2007 the non-profit Russian Nanotechnology Corporation (Rosnanotekh) was formed, and the state has pledged to invest US$8bn from the federal budget into the nascent industry by 2015, of which 75% has already been provided. Such vast amounts of investment in what is for now a fairly esoteric branch of science have raised eyebrows around the world, not least in the wake of comments by Vladimir Putin that nanotechnology would "lay the groundwork for new weapons systems". Research and development in Russia is by no means limited to molecular manufacturing, in fact there are two million Russians currently working in R&D, more than in any other European country. Many international tech companies have Russian centres, including Sun Microsystems, Boeing, Microsoft, IMB, Motorola and Intel. Russia's long-term investment in military technology has clearly stood it in good stead, as has the level of training in this field – the head of the last example's Russian operation summed it up in 2005 when he said, "We at Intel have a saying: give the urgent projects to the Americans, the big projects to the Indians, and the impossible ones to the Russians. The Russians can do anything." With this in mind, the country has set itself the goal of being one of the top three IT-services outsourcing destinations by 2010.

7

Automotive

If you skipped the section in Chapter 3 about taking the train from the airport, you will have plenty of time early on in your first trip to Moscow to reflect on the growth in the automotive sector in Russia. In fact, as you gaze at the thousands of cars thronging the Leningradsky Prospekt, you will feel more like you are part of a mass migration than a traffic queue.

The Russian auto-boom of the last few years has been fuelled by a heady mixture of economic growth, rising income, easier availability of credit and a general sense among consumers that a nice set of wheels is one of the joys of modern life. Remember the remarkable statistic about retail demand increasing by 29% year on year since 2003? For the car market, it is 38% and rising – in 2007 the market grew in value by more than half, to around US$53.5bn. In Europe, currently only the Germans buy more cars than the Russians, and in 2009 even they will be left behind – at least, they will according to Martin Winterkorn, CEO of Volkswagen. Winterkorn certainly hopes to be proved right, as he made the prediction at the end of 2007 at the official opening ceremony of his company's new production plant in Kaluga, 160km south west of Moscow.

Automative boom

Volkswagen is just one of many carmakers attracted to Russia by both the ready market and the lure of lower wage expectations for skilled labour: Ford, Toyota, Nissan, Suzuki, Hyundai and General Motors are all

7

either making cars or building plants in St Petersburg, and at the end of 2007 both PSA (Peugeot-Citroen) and Mitsubishi signed agreements to join VW in Kaluga by 2010. In Kaliningrad, Russia's tiny enclave on the shores of the Baltic, the Avtotor assembly plant has been turning out everything from lunking great Hummers to svelte BMW 5-series for many years now. A third advantage of Russia-based production or assembly is, of course, that it provides a way around import tariffs, and the Russian government has sought to further encourage foreign manufacturers with a range of regulatory measures, including Resolution 166, adopted in 2005, which allowed a specified quantity of components to be imported at favourable tariff-rates. More recently, the range of components eligible for import at reduced tariff was more than doubled in an extension to the resolution. One of the country's recently established Special Economic Zones (SEZ) in Elabuga, Tatarstan, will include facilities for auto component manufacture.

The influx of foreign carmakers in Russia has had a deleterious effect on the domestic industry, which has seen production decline since its peak of almost 1.1m units in 2001 to just over 800,000 in 2007. This is especially alarming against the background of such a high-growth sector, and when you come to consider that on average foreign brands are at least three times more expensive than the Russian product. AvtoVaz, the maker of Lada cars, still accounted for around a quarter of new car sales in Russia in 2007, followed at some distance by GAZ (maker of the Volga sedan and the Gazelle marschrutka, among others) with a market share of just 3%. GAZ, based in Nizhniy Novgorod, is currently part of the Basic Element investment group owned by Oleg Deripaska, who acquired the UK-based LDV light commercial manufacturer in 2006, and was reported to be considering a bid on Jaguar Land Rover a year later. Deripaska is not accustomed to working with unsuccessful companies, so it is reasonable to expect a degree of development from GAZ in the coming years. Both AvtoVaz and GAZ have created joint ventures with foreign manufacturers, the fruits of which have included the Chevrolet Niva light 4x4 and the GAZ Siber saloon, based on the Chrysler Sebring.

If you think the traffic jams in Moscow are bad now, the situation is unlikely to improve any time soon. Even with the rapid expansion of the past few years, Russia still has around only a third of the cars per head of population when compared to western countries.

The above sector summaries are not intended as an exhaustive analysis of the Russian economy today, but more to give the reader at least a general idea of where the country finds itself at the moment. If you need further information on any of the sectors in particular, or if your area of business has not been covered, then I strongly urge you to turn to Chapter 2 and examine the various sources of information available to you. The Russian economy continues to develop rapidly, and the importance of remaining up to date cannot be overstated. It is a complex place to do business, no doubt – in fact I heard someone say recently that he had been working in Russia for 20 years and felt that he understood it less now than when he started. At least by reading this chapter you will hopefully have a good understanding of some of the key sectors of the modern Russian economy, and a ready answer for anyone still under the impression that there is nothing out there but snow and oil.

7

Moscow

8

Moscow

Moscow

A brief history of Russia's
capital, with an overview of the
city today and a walk along the
city's oldest street.

Information on hotels and places
to eat

History

"Moscow," in the words of the guitar-poet Bulat Okudzhava, "is like a duchess who answers the front door in her dressing gown." This may have been true a few years ago, but a visitor to Russia's capital today may beg to differ on the choice of attire. Moscow is bright, brash, noisy (sometimes noisome) and never dull, and as it is likely to be your first destination in Russia, it is worth taking a little time to understand the present-day city in the context of its unique past.

The city shares with many of Europe's other great metropolises (London, Berlin, Paris, Prague) the distinction that no one can be entirely sure where the name came from. Unlike the above examples, Moscow is at least named after the river that runs through it, the *Moskva*, but this doesn't help us very much. One of the most popular theories is that the name is a compound of the Mari words (the Maris were a Finnic people, their descendents now live in Tatarstan and Bashkortostan) *maska* and *ava*, meaning "bear" and "mother" respectively. Nice though it would be to imagine Moscow as the mother of all bears, unfortunately the word *maska* did not pop up in the Mari language until the 14th century at the earliest, around 200 years after the city's name first appeared in the written record – and in any case, it is a borrowing from Russian. Other theories abound, variously translating *Moskva* as "dark water" or even, and this will appeal to English readers, as "ox-ford", but the most likely explanations are more prosaic. One uses the Old Russian root *mosk*- meaning "glutinous" or "swampy", which you can well understand if you ever visit the river's headwaters near Mozhaisk, while another hypothesis takes as the root of the name the Baltic words *mazg* ("knot/hub") and *vandou* ("water"), alluding to the geographical importance of the river, in linking the much more extensive Oka and Volga river systems and, consequently, the Dnieper and the Don.

Whether or not this last theory is the correct one, it is true that Moscow's convenient location within striking distance of so many trade arteries played a major part in its subsequent development. The first written reference to Moscow dates to 1147, with an invitation from the

8

Prince of Suzdal, Yuri Dolgoruky, to Prince Svyatoslav Ol'govich of Novgorod to "come, join me Brother, in Moscow". While there is abundant archaeological evidence of a settlement on the site of the centre of Moscow dating back to the third millennium BC, this historic meeting of the two princes is generally accepted as the moment the city was born. Although the meeting itself took place in April, Moscow today celebrates its birthday on the first weekend of September. It was another nine years before Dolgoruky ordered a small fortification to be built in the middle of the settlement, as just one link in a defensive chain across the south-western frontier of his relatively modest domains. A hundred paces would have taken you from one side of it to the other, but this unprepossessing wooden structure was the original antecedent of Moscow's Kremlin. Dolgoruky himself was an intriguing character – the name means "Long-Armed", but this had nothing to do with any physical attributes, rather his constant coveting of the throne of Kiev, whence he and his brothers had been scattered as rulers across Rus' by their father, Vladimir Monomakh.

Yuri Dolgoruky

8

A few historians have put forward the theory that Dolgoruky was the grandson of the Anglo-Saxon King Harold, and Vladimir Monomakh did indeed take Harold's daughter, Gytha of Wessex, as his wife after she fled England following the Battle of Hastings. Gytha was, however, merely the first of Vladimir's three wives, and in all probability died before Yuri was born. Vladimir's second wife, the more likely mother of the future founder of Moscow, is mentioned in the Primary Chronicle only as an unnamed Byzantine noblewoman. Whatever his genealogy, Dolgoruky was a prominent figure in the running internecine conflict between the various Grand Princes of Kievan Rus' in the 12th century which led to its ultimate fragmentation. According to one Russian commentator, if he really was half-English, this would at least explain some of the more hooliganistic aspects of his character. Yuri died in Kiev in 1157, most likely at the hands of the local nobility, and just a year after the building of Moscow's first Kremlin. His remains are still interred near the Kiev Pechersk Lavra (Monastery), where he is to this day an enduring source of controversy as Russian and Ukrainian politicians argue over his return.

A monument to Dolgoruky was erected in 1954 just off Tverskaya Street, directly opposite the Moscow mayoralty. Following a decision by the latter in 2005, passers-by are treated every December and January to the spectacle of the founder of Europe's largest and most populous city, in full armour and mounted on a charger, dressed up as Father Christmas.

It was to be some time before a settlement of any size or influence took shape around Dolgoruky's modest fort, indeed the territory of the Moscow Kremlin was extended only at the end of the 1330s by Ivan I, better known as Ivan Kalita ("Moneybags") for the acquisitive streak which he shared with his 12th century predecessor. Even so, Kalita's domains covered only around 1,500 square kilometres, and his authority of course remained secondary to that of the tartars. In 1367 Ivan's grandson, Dmitry Donskoy, completed the rebuilding of the Kremlin as a stone fortress, extending it almost to its present-day dimensions. Dmitry was also the first of Muscovy's rulers to successfully challenge the Tatar-Mongol hegemony, inflicting a major, albeit temporary, defeat on the Khan's forces at the Battle of Kulikovo on the banks of the River Don in 1380. Throughout the ensuing centuries, the Kremlin has gone through successive periods of construction and re-fortification, and today's structure, over two kilometres in circumference and with walls in places almost twenty metres high, owes its magnificence to both Russian and foreign (principally Italian) architects.

There is insufficient space here to describe all the treasures of this remarkable citadel, but a tour of the Kremlin should be a compulsory part of your off-duty itinerary in Moscow. Set aside several hours, although this will still be nowhere near enough to do justice to the cathedrals, palaces and museums ranged before you. The Kremlin is also home to the largest cannon never to have fired, and the largest bell never to have chimed. The Tsar Cannon, commissioned during the brief reign of Ivan the Terrible's son Fyodor and cast in 1586, weighs just under 40 tonnes and would probably have exploded had anyone been so foolhardy as to try and use it to propel any single projectile that would have fitted its 35-inch bore. Most likely it was built either as an ornate

8

Dmitry Donskoy

The Kremlin

showpiece or to fire grapeshot. The Tsar Bell, nearby the cannon, dates from the 1730s and was intended to hang in the Ivan the Great Bell Tower which overlooks it. However, during the Great Fire of 1737 the bell was still lying in its casting pit when attempts to extinguish the conflagration led to the bronze cooling too quickly, and a fragment broke off from its skirt. The damaged bell remained in its pit for another hundred years before finally being placed in its current position, along with the fragment which broke off. "Fragment" is probably the wrong word, as it weighs 11 tonnes, more than half the weight of the largest tuned bell in existence, which hangs in the Riverside Church in New York.

Fire has been a regular feature of Moscow's history, not surprising in view of the fact that it was only after the final city-wide holocaust in 1812 that widespread use of stone was made beyond the Kremlin walls. Apart from 1737 and 1812, major fires were recorded in 1365, 1443, 1547 and 1571, prompting the Russian saying "Moscow would burn down from a penny candle". By the 17th century, residents had grown so accustomed to seeing their homes reduced to piles of ash that a flourishing market sprang up on the eastern side of the city, where you could buy a prefabricated house, wooden of course, and have it delivered and built anywhere in central Moscow within three days.

The fires of Moscow did not arrest the city's slow but inexorable advance from its vanishingly humble beginnings to become the centre of one of the largest empires in human history. Nor, for that matter, did anything else. Between 1654 and 1656, half the city's population was borne away by the plague, and just a few decades later it lost its capital status to St Petersburg, but neither of these events presented more than a temporary setback. After Napoleon's departure in 1812, the cost to rebuild Moscow was estimated at 270 million roubles, more than the Imperial government's entire annual income at the time. But rebuild itself it did, principally from private funds, to become what was widely considered to be one of the world's most beautiful cities. In 1918, after a two-hundred year break, Moscow was again the capital of Russia (and the Soviet Union) and carried on as before. One of the things that strikes

8

The fires of Moscow

a visitor today is Moscow's all-pervading sense of resilience. With the fall of Constantinople in 1453, Moscow had inherited the mantle of the Third Rome (Byzantium had been the second), and the city is still imbued with a sense of its own destiny as a centre of history and civilisation. There is an old Russian proverb that says, "There is nothing above Moscow except the Kremlin, and there is nothing above the Kremlin except Heaven". Alongside this sits a healthy sense of perspective, even self-deprecation – what other city would plan to build the world's second highest building in its centre, and retain a vast medieval fortress as its seat of government, yet still quite happily adorn the statue of its founder with a red and white fancy dress costume each year?

Moscow today

if you look at Moscow on a series of historical maps, your immediate impression is of a place which has expanded organically through regular attempts to impose some sense of order onto its chaotic street plan within, and to fortify its increasing wealth against attack from without. North-east of the Kremlin, the outline of the residential and commercial quarter of Kitai-Gorod, whose walls were built in 1530s on the orders of Ivan the Terrible's mother, can still be made out, indeed fragments of the wall still remain near the Hotel Metropol and in the Zaryadye district by the river itself. Just fifty years after the completion of the Kitai-Gorod wall, it became apparent that the city needed more extensive fortifications, and in the late 16th century a new wall was commissioned, ten kilometres in length and built of white stone, surrounded at a distance by the *Zemlyanoy* Val ("Earthen Rampart"). Gradually Moscow grew beyond these fortifications too, and both were levelled in the early 19th century as part of the post-1812 reconstruction, with the inner stone wall replaced by a ring of boulevards known, predictably enough, as the Boulevard Ring. The earth fortification is now traced by the Sadovoye Kol'tso, or Garden Ring, an urban motorway 18 lanes wide in places, which retains the name Zemlyanoy Val on its southeastern section.

8

In the 20th century, Stalin's plan was to broaden the Ring still further, and to punctuate it with even more of the neo-gothic *vysotka* buildings which today characterise the Moscow skyline. Seven of these buildings were constructed in the end: the Ministries of Foreign Affairs and Communications, Moscow State University, the Hotels Ukraine and Leningrad (the latter is now part of the Hilton Group), and two apartment buildings.

Moscow's
"Seven Sisters"

In a sequence of events typical of Moscow's historical development, in 1937 construction began on a still more ambitious skyscraper, the Palace of the Soviets, a 415 metre urban centrepiece which was to be crowned with a 6,000 tonne, 100 metre high statue of Lenin. To make way for the palace, the Cathedral of Christ the Saviour, built to commemorate the victory over Napoleon and completed only seventy years previously, had been dynamited in 1931, with a full year needed to remove the rubble. After a series of attempts to lay the foundations, it became clear that the ground could not support such a building, and the project was eventually scrapped in favour of a giant open-air swimming pool, which remained operational all year round. It was said that the waters of the pool were sacred, and that therefore no one ever drowned there (a remarkable feat in itself, considering that the only way to access the main pool was through water-filled tunnels with heavy rubber curtains at either end). In 1995 the swimming pool was closed and an exact replica of the Cathedral was built on the site.

To capture the contrasts which characterise Moscow so well, I recommend you take a walk along one of its oldest streets, the Arbat. Begin at Smolenskaya Square, with the afore-mentioned Ministry of Foreign Affairs towering at your back, and the western section of the Garden Ring stretching out in front of you, most probably groaning with traffic. When you turn right into the street itself, you will move instantly from the roar and thunder of a 21st century metropolis to a narrow, pedestrian side-street lined with cafes, antique shops and market-stalls selling everything from nesting Russian dolls to KGB branded zippo-lighters. A couple of hundred metres down on the right, on the corner with Plotnikov Pereulok, you will pass a life-size bronze statue of Bulat Okudzhava, he of the dressing-gown quotation that began this chapter, and

A walk through
Moscow's history

whose most famous song is dedicated to the street.
Nearby is a monument to Pushkin and his wife, Natalia
Goncharova, who lodged in one of the Arbat's many
mansions in the early 19th century. On either side,
smaller and quieter side-streets radiate out, leading to
still more peaceful corners of old Moscow. The name
Arbat is first mentioned at the end of the 15th century,
and was once applied not just to the street, but to the
entire area. As with the city itself, there is no single
uncontested theory behind the term: the general
consensus appears to be that it comes from the Arabic
word for suburb, a root which it shares with Rabat, the
capital of Morocco.

Making your way along the Arbat, you may soon find
yourself lulled into an easy reverie, which will last just
until you are thrust out at the far end onto Arbat Square
and the modern city returns. To your left you will see the
Novy ("New") Arbat, formerly Kalinin Prospekt, a six-
lane highway lined with grey skyscrapers which was
literally cut through the northern Arbat district in the
1960s, while on your right Vozdvizhenka Street leads
down to the Alexandrovsky Garden and the Kremlin's
western wall. Dropping down towards the Kremlin, you
will come to the junction with Mokhovaya Street, and
turning left takes you towards Manezh Square, site of a
spectacular multi-story underground shopping centre
built in the 1990s. From here, you climb back to the
right into Red Square, and as you emerge onto the open
expanse, directly ahead you will see the Cathedral of St
Basil the Blessed, better known as St Basil's, and for
many people the most instantly-recognisable building
in the city. Completed in 1561, and commissioned by
Ivan the Terrible to commemorate his victory over the
Khanate of Kazan', St Basil's is in fact nine churches
in one, each dedicated to a saint on whose feast day
the Russian army saw victory. On your left is the State
Department Store GUM, completed at the end of the
19th century and now housing a 200-strong collection
of designer boutiques and fashion outlets. Directly
opposite GUM is the Lenin Mausoleum, a stark granite
and marble tomb built against the dying wishes of its
occupant in 1930, and the setting for countless politburo
group photos at military parades throughout the Soviet
period. In around half an hour, you will have gone from

8

15th century Moscow to 1960s modernism, forward again to the '90s consumer society and then back to the time of the dynasty of Ryurik, encapsulated by a structure flanked by two buildings which themselves symbolise the final days of Imperial Russia and the height of Soviet power. All stand in the shadow of the construction which, in one form or other, predates them all, and which gives the distinct impression that it will still be there long after they are gone.

The wilfully haphazard way in which Moscow has developed over the centuries means that there is no single area in the city which could be called a business district. Once it could be said that the Garden Ring circumscribed the commercial and administrative part of the city, but the Moscow International Business Centre mentioned in the preceding chapter will be located well outside this division, as will the majority of the city's other major construction projects. A third ring road has already been built in Moscow, and the city's circumference is marked by the MKAD, the Moscow Circular Automobile Road. Both hover on the edge of gridlock as Moscow's still-burgeoning population of motorists vie for space. It seems likely that Russia's capital will extend its horizons still further as time goes on.

Hotels and restaurants

Over the past few years Moscow has seen its hotel capacity expand considerably, although demand for international standard accommodation in the city has grown at an even faster rate. The business traveller today can choose from a wide range of hotels in all categories, from boutique private hotels in the centre to major chains on the outskirts of the city. In almost all cases, the prices will be high irrespective of the time of year, although by going to a specialist travel agent you may be able to strike a good compromise between price, location and comfort. Moscow is also well stocked with restaurants serving almost any type of food in any price range, from small intimate cafes to opulent pre-revolutionary nostalgia-houses and western fast-food chains. A comprehensive listing of Moscow's restaurants would, of course, fill a telephone directory and be out of date within a year, so I have included at the end a brief listing of some of the better known (and more permanent) places which you may want to check out.

Bear in mind that hotel rates will vary greatly, the numbers below are approximate figures based on a range of sources.

Luxury hotels
Ararat Park Hyatt *****
Luxurious hotel located in the very centre of Moscow, next door to the Bolshoi Theatre and a short walk from the Kremlin and Red Square. The hotel's neo-classical façade gives way to a modern glass and metal interior. Opened in 2001, the Ararat Park Hyatt is considered one of Moscow's most opulent, and expensive, luxury hotels.

Standard room rates: *Twin/double £490 per night*
Neglinnaya Street 4
Moscow 109012
Tel: +7 495 783 1234
Fax: +7 495 783 1235
E-mail: moscow.park@hyatt.com
Website: www.moscow.park.hyatt.com

8

Baltschug Kempinski *****
Just across the river from the Kremlin, the Baltschug Kempinski offers spectacular views of Red Square and St. Basils. Originally built in 1898, the hotel re-opened in its modern incarnation in 1992, becoming then one of only a tiny handful of Moscow hotels providing international standard luxury accommodation.

Standard room rates: *Twin/double £275 per night*
Balchug Street 1
Moscow 115035
Tel: +7 495 287 2000
Fax: +7 495 287 2002
E-mail: info.baltschug@kempinski.com
Website: www.kempinski-moscow.com

Marriott Royal Aurora *****
Situated on one of Moscow's principal historic thoroughfares, the Marriott Royal Aurora is the chain's flagship property in the Russian capital. Services include a personalised butler service for all guest rooms.

Standard room rates: *Twin/double £275 per night*
Petrovka Street 11/20
Moscow 107031
Tel: +7 495 937 1000
Fax: +7 495 937 1001
Website: www.marriott.com

Hotel Metropol *****

The other side of the Bolshoi Theatre from the Hyatt, the Metropol was the luxury hotel of choice for the Party throughout the Soviet period. First opened in 1901, after 1917 it housed the All-Russian Central Executive Committee. The Metropol sits alongside the Baltschug as one of Moscow's oldest top-flight hotels.

Standard room rates: *Twin/double £325 per night*
Teatral'ny Proezd 1/4
Moscow 109012
Tel: +7 499 501 7800
Fax: +7 400 501 78 37
E-mail: metropol@metmos.ru
Website: http://metropol-moscow.ru/en

National Hotel *****

Another major Party hotel (in the specifically Soviet sense), like the Metropol the National offers a glimpse of Russia's imperial past which may be a welcome relief from standard luxury fare. Built in 1903, it was extensively re-fitted in 1995, and is now part of the Royal Meridien group.

Standard room rates: *Twin/double £250 per night*
Mokhovaya Street 15/1 Bld.1
Moscow 125009
Tel: +7 495 258 7000
Fax: +7 495 258 7100
E-mail: sales@national.ru
Website: www.national.ru/english

Ritz Carlton Hotel *****

One of the most recent additions to Moscow's high end hotel market, the Ritz-Carlton opened in 2007 on the site of the old Intourist Hotel, an unloved property which locals dubbed the Rotten Tooth. The Ritz-Carlton is, as you can imagine, light-years away from its predecessor, providing lavish accommodation and located a stone's throw from the Kremlin (don't put this to the test, though).

Standard room rates: *Twin/Double £275 per night*
Tverskaya Street 3
Moscow 125009
Tel: +7 495 225 8888
Fax: +7 495 225 8400
Website: www.ritzcarlton.com/en/Properties/Moscow

Savoy Hotel *****
Much smaller than the other hotels on this list, the Savoy is the only Russian member of the exclusive Small Luxury Hotels of the World association. First opened in 1913, it was known as the Hotel Berlin during the late Soviet period, regaining its original name in 1989. The Savoy reopened after an extensive refit in 2005, and provides opulent accommodation in the very heart of the city.

8

Standard room rates: *Twin/double £325 per night*
Rozhdestvenka Street 3/6
Moscow 109012
Tel: +7 495 620 8555
Fax: +7(495 625 0596
E-mail: infa-hotel@savoy.ru
Website: www.savoy.ru/en

Swissotel Krasnye Holmy *****
At the other end of the scale from the Savoy, both historically and physically, the Swissotel's Moscow flagship is for now one of the capital's tallest buildings. Modern, cutting-edge luxury is the central theme of the hotel, and the view of the city from the 34th floor has to be experienced.

Standard room rates: *Twin/double £240 per night*
Kosmodamianskaya Embankment 52, Bld. 6
Moscow 115054
Tel: +7 495 787 9800
Fax: +7 495 787 9898
E-mail: moscow@swissotel.com
Website: www.swissotel.com

Deluxe hotels

Crowne Plaza Moscow World Trade Centre *****
Formerly named the Mezhdunarodnaya ("International"),
and generally known among foreign travellers as the
Mezh, the Crowne Plaza has undergone a substantial
refit in the past few years and now provides good quality
accommodation and business facilities. Located just
north-west of the centre in one of Moscow's main
business and administrative districts.

Standard room rates: *Twin/double £175 per night*

Golden Apple Hotel ****
Centrally located "boutique" hotel, very stylish and a
nice contrast to your standard business hotel. The
Golden Apple opened in 2004, and is located in a little
enclave of designer shops just behind Tverskaya Street.

Standard room rates: *Twin/double £250 per night*
Malaya Dmitrovka Street 11
Moscow 127006
Tel: +7 495 980 7000
Fax: +7 495 980 7001
E-mail: reservations@goldenapple.ru
Website: www.goldenapple.ru

Golden Ring Hotel *****
The Golden Ring is one of two "twin tower" hotels
built opposite the Ministry of Foreign Affairs, and was
renovated in 1998. The other sibling is the Hotel Belgrade,
which remains pretty much as it was in Soviet times. The
Golden Ring offers relatively good value, and you can
always pop across to the Belgrade to reassure yourself
where the extra money went. Handy for the Arbat.

Standard room rates: *Twin/double £200 per night*
Smolenskaya Street 5
Moscow 119121
Tel: +7 495 725 0100
Fax: +7 495 725 0101
E-mail: info@hotel-goldenring.ru
Website: www.hotel-goldenring.ru/eng

8

Hilton Leningradskaya *****
Opened in 2008, the Hilton Leningradskaya is a
spectacular reinvention of one of the seven Stalin-
conceived *vysotka* buildings that tower over Moscow.
The hotel offers executive-class accommodation and
facilities in the north west part of the city.

Standard room rates: *Twin/double £225 per night*
Kalanchevskaya Street 21/40
Moscow 107078
Tel: +7 495 627 5550
Fax: +7 495 627 5551
Website: www.hilton.com

Marriott Courtyard Hotel ****
Part of the Marriott group's sub-brand of smaller
business hotels, the Courtyard is located in central
Moscow with Tverskaya Street, the Kremlin and Red
Square all within easy reach. Recommended if you
want a break from the larger, more impersonal business
chain hotels.

Standard room rates: *Twin/double £225 per night*
Voznesensky Pereulok 7
Moscow 125009
Tel: +7 495 981 3300
Fax: +7 495 981 3301
Website: www.marriott.com

Marriott Grand Hotel *****
A popular business hotel on Tverskaya, which is
probably the nearest Moscow gets to having a main
street. The Marriott Grand has a large conference centre
downstairs, making it a regular venue for business
forums and events.

Standard room rates: *Twin/double £225 per night*
Tverskaya Street 26/1
Moscow 103050
Tel: +7 495 937 0000
Fax: +7 495 937 0001
Website: www.marriott.com

8

Peter 1st Hotel ****

Another fairly new addition to Moscow's hotel stock, having opened in 2006, the Peter 1st is just up the road from the Ararat Park Hyatt. Relatively small and modern in style, the hotel has good facilities for meetings and conferences.

Standard room rates: *Twin/double £275 per night*
Neglinnaya Street 17/1
Moscow 127051
Tel: +7 495 777 19 38
Website: http://petr-hotel.ru/eng/main (unofficial site)

President Hotel *****

Owned and managed by the presidential administration, the aptly-named President was opened in the mid-1980s to provide accommodation for visiting officials and dignitaries. Perhaps not the most charming of Moscow's hotels, the President nonetheless offers unrivalled conference facilities and a good location across the river from the Kremlin.

Standard room rates: *Twin/double £260 per night*
Bolshaya Yakimanka Street 24
Moscow 103134
Tel: +7 495 239 3800
Fax: +7 495 239 3646
E-mail: reservation@president-hotel.net
Website: www.president-hotel.ru

Radisson SAS Slavyanskaya *****

An enormous business hotel located west-central Moscow, just outside the Garden Ring, the Radisson offers extensive conference facilities and a fully equipped business centre. Serviced offices are available for short-term let in the latter.

Standard room rates: *Twin/double £200 per night*
Europe Square 2
Moscow 121059
Tel: +7 495 941 2080
Fax: +7 495 941 2000
E-mail: reservations.moscow@radissonsas.com
Website: www.radissonsas.com

Renaissance Moscow *****
Originally built for the 1980 Olympics, the Renaissance
is now managed by the Marriott group, and offers
modern facilities just north of Moscow's centre.
Definitely from the "impressive", rather than
"attractive" school of architecture, the Renaissance
is nevertheless a sound choice for a business trip.

Standard room rates: *Twin/double £200 per night*
Olimpiysky Prospekt 18/1
Moscow 129110
Tel: +7 495 931 9000
Fax: +7 495 931 9076
Website: www.marriott.com

Sheraton Palace *****
Built in the late 1990s, further up Tverskaya from the
Marriott Grand, the Sheraton Palace is a good solid
business hotel offering modern accommodation and
excellent facilities. Very handy for transport links to
Sheremetevo airport, especially the express shuttle from
Belorussky Station, which is five minutes walk away.

Standard room rates: *Twin/double £225 per night*
1st Tverskaya Yamskaya Street 19
Moscow 125047
Tel: +7 495 931 9700
Fax: +7 495 931 9704
E-mail: reservations.00137@sheraton.com
Website: www.starwoodhotels.com

Business hotels
Aerostar Hotel ****
Located on the main road to Sheremetevo airport,
roughly 3km from the centre, the Aerostar is a large
modern hotel which was originally planned to be built
for the 1980 Olympics, although it was completed only
in 1991. Good value if you can stand to be away from
the centre.

Standard room rates: *Twin/double £180 per night*
Leningradsky Prospekt 9, Bld.37
Moscow 125993
Tel: +7 495 988 3131
Fax: +7 495 988 3132

8

E-mail: info@aerostar.ru
Website: www.aerostar.ru/en

Aerotel Domodedovo ★★★★
The main hotel of Moscow's second airport, the Aerotel
will never win any prizes for architecture but offers
convenient accommodation if your stop in Moscow is brief.

Standard room rates: *Twin/double £130 per night*
Domodedovo Region
Moscow
Tel: +7 495 506 4842
Fax: +7 495 621 4821
Website: www.aerotelhotel.ru

Akvarel' Hotel ★★★★
A small and oft-overlooked hotel, the Akvarel' has 23
rooms on five floors, and is located a short walk from
Red Square. Well worth a look if you want somewhere
central and not too expensive.

Standard room rates: *Twin/double £200 per night*
Stoleshnikov Pereulok 12, Bld.3
Moscow 107031
Tel: +7 495 502 94 30
E-mail: akvarel@hotelakvarel.ru
Website: www.hotelakvarel.ru

Arbat Hotel ★★★★
As its name suggests, very handy for frequenting old
Moscow's most famous street. The Arbat Hotel is not
the last name in either opulence or modernity, but offers
reasonable accommodation in a gratifyingly quiet part of
town. Government owned and run in the same way as the
President Hotel above.

Standard room rate: *Twin/double £160 per night*
Plotnikov Pereulok 12
Moscow 121002
Tel: +7 499 271 2801
Fax: +7 499 271 2996
E-mail: reservation-arbat@president-hotel.net
Website: www.president-hotel.net/arbat

Art Hotel ****

A small hotel located in parkland north of the centre, the Art Hotel provides a very different setting to what you may be expecting from your stay in Moscow. The hotel provides modest but efficient accommodation and includes an excellent business centre.

Standard room rate: *Twin/double £170 per night*
3rd Peschannaya Street 2
Moscow 125252
Tel: +7 495 540 4640
Website: www.art-hotel.ru

Borodino Hotel ****

A recently-opened business hotel located in the new Borodino Plaza Business Centre in the north of Moscow, the Borodino has 230 rooms and good transport links to the centre. The hotel itself includes a conference centre and extensive business support facilities.

Standard room rate: *Twin/double £240 per night*
Rusakovskaya Street 13/2
Moscow 107140
Tel: +7 495 785 6390
Fax: +7 495 785 6375
E-mail: borodino2000@mail.ru
Website: www.borodino.biz   (group website)

Holiday Inn Moscow Lesnaya ****

Located just north of the centre, not far from the Sheraton Palace, the Holiday Inn Lesnaya offers the kind of efficient, unfussy accommodation for which the group is known. The hotel has a substantial business centre with six separate conference halls.

Standard room rate: *Twin/double £130 per night*
Lesnaya Street 15
Moscow 125047
Tel: +7 495 783 6500
Fax: +7 495 783 6501
E-mail: reservations@hi-mole.ru
Website: www.ichotelsgroup.com

8

Holiday Inn Moscow Sokolniki ****

Situated to the north of the centre on the same street as the Borodino, the Holiday Inn Sokolniki is a large business hotel, sharing the benefits of the former in a good location on the Garden Ring.

Standard room rate: Twin/double room £130 per night
Rusakovskaya Street 24
Moscow 107014
Tel: +7 495 783 7373
Fax: +7 495 783 7374
E-mail: sokolniki.reservations@ihg.com
Website: www.ichotelsgroup.com

Holiday Inn Moscow Suschevsky ****

A large business-oriented hotel, also located to the north of the city, the Holiday Inn Suschevsky provides all the facilities you would expect from the group. Nothing very exciting, but a sound choice if you are on a budget and do not need to be right in the centre.

Standard room rate: Twin/double room £130 per night
Suschevsky Val Street 74
Moscow 129272
Tel: +7 495 225 8282
Fax: +7 495 225 8283
E-mail: reservations@hi-moscow-lesnaya.ru
Website: www.ichotelsgroup.com

Holiday Inn Moscow Vinogradovo ****

Built on the outskirts of Moscow to service Sheremetevo airport, the Holiday Inn Vinogradovo is a 150-room business hotel set in a fairly green part of the city. The hotel has 12 conference rooms and can accommodate events of up to 400 people.

Standard room rate: Twin/double room £120 per night
Dmitrovskoye Shosse 171
Moscow 127204
Tel: +7 495 937 0670
Fax: +7 495 937 0672
E-mail: reservations@himv.ru
Website: www.ichotelsgroup.com

Iris Congress Hotel ****

Also located close to Sheremetevo airport in the far north of the city, the Iris Congress opened in 1991 as a large business-oriented hotel in a suburban setting, with around 200 guest rooms and extensive conference facilities.

Standard room rate: Twin/double room £120 per night
Korovinskoye Shosse 10
Moscow 127486
Tel: +7 495 933 0533
Fax: +7 495 937 8700
E-mail: reservation@soft-proekt.ru
Website: www.iris-hotel.ru

Katerina City Hotel ****

A smart, modern hotel located south east of the centre, not far from the Swissotel Krasnye Holmy. The Katerina is medium-sized, clean and efficient, as you would expect given its Swedish management.

Standard room rate: Twin/double room £220 per night
Shlyuzovaya Embankment 6/1
Moscow 113114
Tel: +7 495 933 0401
Fax: +7 495 795 2443
E-mail: reservation@umaco.org
Website: www.katerinahotels.com/moscow

Kebur Palace Hotel ****

A very smart new hotel just south east of the centre, on one of Moscow's oldest streets. With only 79 rooms, the Kebur Palace is at the smaller end of the scale but may be all the better for that if you can make your booking early.

Standard room rate: Twin/double room £150 per night
Ostozhenka Street 32
Moscow 119034
Tel: +7 495 733 9070
Fax: +7 495 733 9054
E-mail: hotel@tiflis.ru
Website: www.keburpalace.ru

8

Marco Polo Presnja Hotel ****

A small business hotel set in the quiet central Moscow enclave of the Patriarchs' Ponds, a short walk north from the Kremlin. The hotel was once a club popular with high-ranking Communist Party officials, and reopened in its present form in 2000. Rack rates are spectacularly expensive though, so try to get a discount through an agent.

Standard room rate: *Twin/double £350 per night*
Spiridonievsky Pereulok 9
Moscow 103104
Tel: +7 495 244 3631
Fax: +7 495 626 5402
E-mail: marcopolo@presnja.ru
Website: www.presnja.ru

Marriott Tverskaya Hotel ****

In the same general area as the Sheraton Palace, near the Belorussky Station, the Marriott Tverskaya is generally a little less expensive than its other siblings by virtue of its location further from the centre.

Standard room rate: *Twin/double £200 per night*
1st Tverskaya-Yamskaya Street 34
Moscow 125047
Tel: +7 495 258 3000
Fax: +7 495 258 3099
Website: www.marriott.com

Medea Hotel ****

A recently opened business hotel in Moscow's historical centre, the Medea is located in a four storey 19th century mansion. There are just 21 rooms and suites, so you will most likely have to book well in advance whatever the time of year.

Standard room rate: *Twin/double £150 per night*
Pyatnicky Pereulok 4/1
Moscow 115184
Tel: +7 495 232 4898
Fax: +7 495 232 4892
E-mail: reservation@hotel-medea.ru
Website: www.hotel-medea.ru

Novotel Moscow Centre ****
Not strictly speaking in the centre of the city, but just to
the north, the 18-storey Novotel Centre was completed
in 2002, offering the kind of slick, slightly funky
business hotel surroundings that you expect from the
Accor group's sub-brand.

Standard room rate: *Twin/double £275 per night*
Novoslobodskaya Street 23
Moscow 121099
Tel: +7 495 780 4000
Fax: +7 495 780 4003
E-mail: reservations@novotelmoscow.ru
Website: www.novotel.com

Novotel Moscow Sheremetevo ****
A monolithic airport hotel, the Novotel's six storeys
house 488 rooms, a substantial business and conference
centre and all the things you need to help you forget you
are staying next door to an airport. The hotel also offers
a free shuttle bus into the centre.

Standard room rate: *Twin/double £185 per night*
Sheremetevo-2, Bld. 3
Khimky Region
Moscow 141400
Tel: +7 495 626 5900
Fax: +7 495 626 5903
E-mail: novotel.reservations@co.ru
Website: www.novotel.com

Park Inn Sadu ****
Opened in 2008, the Sadu is the Park Inn chain's first
property in the Russian capital, offering international
standard business accommodation and facilities in a
fairly central location, just north east of Red Square
and the Kremlin.

Standard room rate: *Twin/double £150 per night*
Bolshaya Polyanka 17
Moscow 119180
Tel: +7 495 644 4844
Fax: +7 495 644 4944
E-mail: info.sadu-moscow@rezidorparkinn.com
Website: www.rezidorparkinn.com

8

8

Hotel Sovietsky ****

Built on the orders of Stalin in 1951, and sharing its gothic styling with the Hilton Leningradskaya, the Sovietsky provides a fascinating combination of imperial elegance and 1950s pomp for fairly reasonable rates, at least by Moscow standards.

Standard room rate: *Twin/double £120 per night*
Leningradsky Prospekt 32/2
Moscow 125040
Tel: +7 495 960 2000
Fax: +7 495 250 8003
E-mail: reception@sovietsky.ru
Website: www.sovietsky.ru

Hotel Sretenskaya ****

A small friendly hotel in central Moscow, the Sretenskaya was opened in 2000. The hotel has 38 rooms, and while it is not overburdened with business facilities, offers good value considering it is only a twenty minute walk from the Kremlin.

Standard room rate: *Twin/double £200 per night*
Sretenka Street 15
Moscow 107045
Tel: +7 495 933 5544
Fax: +7 495 933 5545
E-mail: info@hotel-sretenskaya.ru
Website: www.hotel-sretenskaya.ru

Hotel Tatiana ****

A modern, comfortable business hotel in south east Moscow, not far from Paveletsky Station, destination of the Domodedovo Express from Moscow's second airport. The Tatiana was built in 2002 and has 72 rooms, along with a conference centre for up to 100 people.

Standard room rate: *Twin/double £250 per night*
Stremyanny Pereulok 11
Moscow 115054
Tel: +7 495 721 2500
Fax: +7 495 721 2521
E-mail: reservation@hotel-tatiana.ru
Website: www.hotel-tatiana.ru

Restaurants
Café Pushkin
Centrally located, and if you're not careful what you order, vastly expensive, Café Pushkin is a slice of old Russia and considered perhaps the country's finest restaurant. Staff are trained to offer olde worlde subservience, which you will find either charming or nauseating.

Tverskoy Boulevard 26A
Moscow 125009
Tel: +7 495 787 4087

1 Red Square
Located inside the State Historical Museum, the restaurant with the best address in Moscow offers a heady mix of traditional Russian cuisine and roving balalaika players. Great for a kitsch-Russian evening followed by an unsteady walk around the square gawping at the sights.

Krasnaya Ploshchad' 1
Moscow 109012
Tel: +7 495 692 1196

Petrovich
A world apart from the two restaurants above, Petrovich is a café/jazz venue tucked away in a quiet corner of central Moscow. The café is devoted to one of Russia's (indeed, the Soviet Union's) best-loved cartoon characters. You wouldn't come here for a lavish night out, but in the opinion of this author, the real Moscow is here.

Myasnitskaya Street 24, Bld.3
Moscow 101000
Tel: +7 495 623 0082

Yar'
Located in the same building as the Sovietsky hotel, Yar' is a gloriously over-the-top restaurant-and-floor-show experience, with excellent food and service in surroundings that are far too opulent to really remain in good taste. Just make sure you avoid the eye of the acts when they come around the tables looking for volunteers or, like me, you may end up on a unicycle.

8

Leningradsky Prospekt 32/2
Moscow 125040
Tel: +7 495 960 2004

Praga
Situated at the eastern end of the Arbat, the Praga is
one of Moscow's oldest surviving restaurants. Serving a
wide variety of cuisines, from South American to Central
Asian, in its luxurious interior, it is well worth a visit.
Rivals the Café Pushkin for having the most annoying
website.

Arbat 2/1
Moscow 119019
Tel: +7 495 290 6171

Tiflis
Attached to the Kebur Palace hotel, the Tiflis is a superb,
authentic Georgian restaurant suited equally well for
an intimate dinner for two as for a corporate meal.
Decorated to conjure up some of the feel of the old part
of Georgia's capital (Tiflis is the old name for Tbilisi),
the atmosphere is relaxed and hospitable.

Ostozhenka Street 32
Moscow 119034
Tel: +7 495 290 2897

Khodzha Nasreddin in Khiva
Should the Caucasus not be sufficiently exotic, you can
always come to this place for a taste of Central Asia in
surroundings modelled (we are told) on the harem of
Muhamad Rakhim Khan. The sensation of stepping
from a busy Moscow street into Uzbekistan is a little
disorienting, but not unpleasant. Just read the menu
carefully, or you could end up eating a part of a sheep's
anatomy which you always thought they threw away.

Pokrovka Street 10/2
Moscow 101000
Tel: +7 495 917 0444

Moscow attractions

The Armoury Chamber

If you have a spare afternoon during your trip, this sumptuous collection of imperial Russia's treasures is well worth a visit. Made up of nine rooms containing everything from ancient artworks from Byzantium to 19th century European silver, the Armoury Chamber is an extraordinary record of the wealth accrued by Russia throughout its turbulent history. Highlights include the throne of Ivan the Terrible, the ceremonial carriage given to Boris Godunov by James I, and the gold and sable Crown of Monomakh, which was a gift, according to somewhat disputed legend, to the father of Moscow's founder from Byzantium's Constantin IX, and which conferred divine authority on all Russia's rulers until the reign of Peter the Great. If you have a taste for cold steel, hall 4 has all the chainmail, close-combat battle weapons and unwieldable-looking broadswords you could possibly wish for. The Armoury is located in a section of the Grand Kremlin Palace.

The Bolshoi Theatre

Arguably as much a symbol of Moscow as St. Basil's or the Kremlin itself, the Bolshoi Theatre was completed in 1825 to host the Bolshoi Ballet and Bolshoi Opera companies, themselves founded almost half a century earlier. The Bolshoi has seen numerous premieres, including that of Tchaikovsky's Swan Lake in 1877, and its programme of both opera and ballet performances continued throughout the Soviet period. In 2005 the theatre was closed for an immensely expensive restoration, and is due to re-open in late 2009. During the work, a "New Bolshoi" built alongside the original building has filled in – if you have to see a performance here, don't feel too regretful, the performance is still world-class, and if the original building had not been restored when it was, it may have become structurally unsound and been lost forever.

Novodevichi Convent

Lying to the south west of Moscow's centre, Novodevichi is a time tunnel back to medieval Russia in the same way that the Tower of London offers a still-vivid glimpse of Plantagenet and Tudor England. The convent was founded in the early 16th century in

8

celebration of the liberation of Smolensk from Polish occupation, and its early occupants included the wives of Ivan the Terrible's sons Dmitry and Fyodor. Peter the Great banished his sister Sophia here at the end of the 17th century for her part in inciting the Streltsy Rebellion. To underline his point, as part of the reprisals Peter had 300 rebels hanged on gallows set up around the walls of the convent. In 1812, the convent was one of the Moscow landmarks which the desperate Napoleon determined to destroy before making the long march home to Paris but, like the Kremlin, it defied the concerted attempts of the Grande Armee to destroy it. In 1922, the few remaining nuns living at the convent were expelled and it was reinvented as a Museum of Women's Liberation, before becoming a museum of old Russian architecture four years later. In 1932, Stalin's first wife Nadezhda Allilueva was buried here following her suicide. Other famous occupants of the adjacent cemetery include Nikita Khrushchev, the composers Sergei Prokofiev and Dmitry Shostakovich, and the writers Mikhail Bulgakov, Anton Chekhov and Nikolai Gogol. The convent and monastery were declared a UNESCO World Heritage Site in 2004.

The Sandunovsky Baths

Just as in the West it is said that the most important business deals are made on the golf course, in Russia the bath house is where people go to talk turkey in confidence. If you are staying in one of Moscow's more opulent hotels, you may be able to go for an invigorating steam there, but you should in any case consider visiting a public *banya* as part of your cultural programme. The Sandunovsky Baths on Neglinnaya Street in the centre of Moscow are without doubt the city's most famous, and since their restoration in 1992 are far more presentable than when your author first visited them. The bath house itself dates back to the end of the 18th century, when the piece of ground on which it stands was bought by Sila Sandunov, on the proceeds of jewellery presented to his wife by the Empress Elizabeth. You can opt for the full massage/plunge-bath/beating-with-birch-besoms programme, alternatively just buy a standard ticket with a few companions and spend an afternoon having a few beers punctuated by trips to the parilka, or steam room. If you haven't been before, the main thing is not to overdo it – the air temperature is insanely hot, and every time water is added to the hot stones in the corner of the steam room it will become ever more oppressive. Do not sit too high up at first (there is a stepped bench on which everyone sits – the top step is the hottest, of course), as there will invariably be the odd enthusiast who will walk in, say something like "it's a bit chilly in here, lads" and whirl a towel round his head: at this point, just as you have grown accustomed to static air approaching 100°C, you will be hit with a gusting wind at the same temperature. You do, however, emerge back onto the street after your ordeal knowing the true meaning of re-birth.

8

St Petersburg

9

9 st petersburg

A brief history of Russia's second
city, with an overview of
St Petersburg today and its prospects
for the future. The chapter also
includes a history of the city's hotels
and a sampling of restaurants

History

Russia's Northern Capital, as it is sometimes called, developed at a very different rate from its older sister to the south east. It is arguable that for the first 300 years of its history, Moscow did little more than to go from being a small town with a wooden fortress in the middle to a slightly larger town with a stone one. Over a similar period, St Petersburg was constructed from scratch, became the imperial capital and one of the cultural centres of Europe, witnessed a series of uprisings culminating in the Bolshevik revolution, lost its status as capital, endured one of history's longest and most destructive sieges, and became the centre of one of the most ambitious urban regeneration projects of modern times. The city also changed its name three times, was largely destroyed by fire in 1737, and flooded over *300* times. Although no longer the national capital, St Petersburg today is still the third most populous city in Europe after Moscow and London, with around 4.5m inhabitants, or slightly less than the total population of Norway.

9

For many centuries, Russia had struggled to establish and maintain a sea-route to the markets of the west, and found its ambitions towards the Baltic continually thwarted by Sweden. In 1700, Peter the Great declared war on Charles XII as part of a tripartite coalition with Denmark and Saxony, and three years later he established a small fortress in the territory of Ingria, one of the few pieces of land he had managed to capture in the early part of the war. The fortress was named Sankt-Peter-Burgh, in honour of the Tsar's patron saint, and was located on a small island in the delta of the river Neva where it entered the Gulf of Finland. History had shown that Russia's foothold in the Baltic was precarious, so the priority was to reinforce this territorial gain as quickly as possible. Brick factories were built in this swampy outpost of Russian territory, and stonemasonry elsewhere in the empire was outlawed by decree: all resources were to be diverted to constructing the tsar's new city. Europe's ambassadors were informed that Russia now had a port on the Baltic, and rewards of gold were offered to the first three foreign ships to arrive. In 1709, the same year that Peter's troops inflicted a crushing defeat on the Swedes at Poltava in modern-day

The foundation of St Petersburg

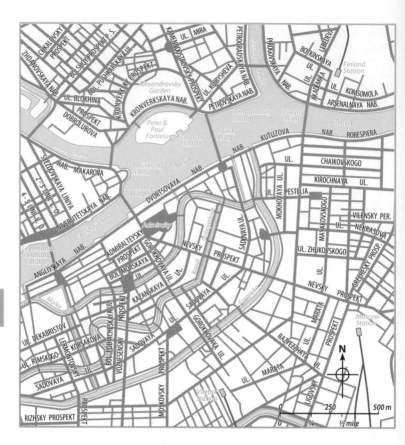

St Petersburg

Ukraine, the city was declared Russia's new capital. Peter's choice of location was not the best: low-lying, marshy, and desperately prone to flooding, the land on which St Petersburg stands would never naturally have supported a medium-sized settlement, let alone a city. By the time he took up residence in 1712, an estimated 100,000 labourers had died in the initial construction of the city.

The Peter and Paul Cathedral

Peter was determined, following his travels around the continent in his youth, to create a modern European capital, a world away from the Byzantium-esque

Moscow with which he had always associated the worst kind of Russian backwardness and reaction. St Petersburg would be a renaissance city, a clean break with the past, a new Amsterdam, and in 1712 the tsar brought in the Italian-Swiss architect Domenico Trezzini to turn his vision into reality. Trezzini rebuilt the original fortress with its centrepiece, the intentionally un-Russian Peter and Paul Cathedral, and drew up the first master-plan for the city, centred on Vassilievsky Island. The island itself was to incorporate a rectangular grid of canals, and although these waterways were never built, Trezzini's idea can still be seen in the series of east-west avenues and north-south "lines" which criss-cross the island today. Peter's determination to use the city to make Russia a naval power cannot be overstated – for some time he personally gave compulsory sailing lessons on the Neva to the local gentry, and woe betide anyone who failed to turn up for instruction. Trezzini, incidentally, is also credited with the Twelve Collegia, now the main building of St Petersburg State University, along with many of the early fortifications of the naval garrison on the island of Kronstadt in the Gulf of Finland, which is now linked to the mainland by a wharf road.

9

Following Peter's death in 1725, the city's development shifted to its southern, mainland side, and it is here that you will see the most spectacular architecture today. Directly across the river from the Peter and Paul Fortress, and under the protection of its guns (before 1917, at least), is perhaps the most instantly recognisable of the city's buildings, the Winter Palace. Completed in 1762 for the Empress Elizabeth (who also died that year), the green, white and gold baroque masterpiece that we see today is the fifth palace to occupy the spot, and the second one built by the Italian master Bartolomeo Rastrelli. The Winter Palace now houses the State Hermitage Museum, one of the largest collections of art in the world, although not all the three million exhibits are ever on display at the same time. If they were, it has been calculated that it would take a visitor around three years to look at them all. The Hermitage forms one side of Palace Square, which is enclosed on its southern flank by a stately neo-classical semicircle built to house the General Staff and the Ministry of Foreign Affairs. The

The Winter Palace

two ministries were arranged either side of a triumphal arch, built to commemorate the defeat of Napoleon in 1812, and crowned by a winged statue of Victory driving a chariot drawn by six horses. The bronze sculpture is so heavy that many thought the arch would collapse under its weight, but the architect Carlo Rossi demonstrated his (as it turned out, well-placed) faith in his design by standing beneath the arch as it was installed. In the centre of the square stands the Alexander Column, erected in celebration of the same victory, albeit twenty-odd years later, and also no featherweight. Topped by an angel with the face of Alexander I, the granite obelisk weighs 600 tonnes, and is held in place by nothing other than its own mass. Even the sustained German bombardment of 1941-43 did not shift it.

The most famous symbol of St Petersburg is, of course, the Bronze Horseman, the memorial to the city's founder which took its name from Pushkin's epic poem, considered one of the most important single works of the Russian literary canon. Unveiled two decades after the completion of the Winter Palace, the statue sits atop the Thunder Stone, a chunk of granite which is claimed to be the heaviest stone ever moved by man. Throughout the year you will see a procession of wedding parties lined up along the Neva embankment waiting for their turn to be photographed in front of it, before moving on to the Rostral Columns across the river for the second photo-session. The columns themselves date back to the beginning of the 19th century, and were originally used as beacons to guide shipping bound for the Baltic around Vassilievsky island. Today they are still lit on ceremonial occasions.

Although the canals of Vassilievsky island never materialised, the mainland side of the flood-prone city is drained by a series of waterways, the most prominent of which are the Fontanka, the Moika and the Canal Griboedova. You are never far from a bridge in St Petersburg: today there are just over five hundred, in fact if you find yourself on the southern side of St Isaac's Square you are standing on a bridge over the Moika without necessarily even knowing it. The bridges across the Neva, as mentioned elsewhere, all open at night during the summer, which can catch you out if you find yourself on the wrong side. The bridges open in sequence

Palace Square

9

The Bronze Horseman

The city of canals

to a strict timetable, so be aware if you are out and about at night, and you will save yourself from a lengthy detour to St Petersburg's only suspension bridge at its eastern end. If you do end up stranded, you will at least be able to pass the time watching the stately procession of shipping making its way from the open sea towards Lake Ladoga, Europe's largest body of fresh water.

Lake Ladoga played a prominent role in one of the darkest periods of the city's history, the Siege of Leningrad, which began in September 1941 and lasted for almost 900 days. Capturing the city, as the Soviet Union's former capital and base of the Baltic Fleet, was a key element of Operation Barbarossa, as encapsulated by Hitler's order: "Leningrad first, Donetsk Basin second, Moscow third". Of the three, the Donbass and Moscow were to be preserved for their strategic importance, but Leningrad, more opulent and spectacular even than Berlin, was to be obliterated even in the event of capitulation. In a directive headed "On the future of the City of St Petersburg", it was noted that "After the defeat of Soviet Russia there will be not the slightest reason for the future existence of this large city." So confident was the Wehrmacht of taking Leningrad that invitations had been printed to a victory celebration at the Hotel Astoria on August 9th, 1942. In the event, on that very evening the half-starved remnants of the Leningrad Radio Orchestra performed Shostakovich's seventh symphony, "Leningrad", through a huge array of loudspeakers that could be heard by the German lines, an act of defiance that was seen by many, not least the inhabitants of the city itself, as the turning point of the siege. During the winter months of the blockade, the vast frozen lake to the east became the city's only link with the rest of Russia, and the Road of Life laid across it was used to bring in food, fuel and ammunition, and to evacuate the young, sick and elderly.

At the end of the war, Leningrad was made one of the Hero Cities of the Soviet Union, along with Moscow, Stalingrad, Kiev, Smolensk and seven others. It is estimated that the city lost over 1.1m people during the siege. Some of the damaged facades along Nevsky Prospekt have been preserved, complete with bullet-holes, to this day, and towards the avenue's eastern end

Lake Ladoga

9

The Siege of Leningrad

The Road of Life

you can still see the placards on the sides of the buildings advising the citizenry on which side of the street to shelter in the event of an aerial bombardment.

St Petersburg today

Where Moscow is a fascinating, jumbled mixture of ancient and ultra-modern, St Petersburg presents a much more cohesive aspect to the visitor. You are immediately aware that the city has been constructed to a plan, with the three avenues of Nevsky Prospekt, Voznesensky Prospekt and Gorokhovaya Ulitsa (the third thoroughfare's former real and imagined habitants include Rasputin and Dostoevsky's Raskolnikov) converging on the Admiralty with geometric precision. The entire centre is currently undergoing a rolling programme of reconstruction which will last many years yet, as some of the city's ornate facades conceal buildings fit for little other than demolition. The future skyline of St Petersburg will be dominated by the Okhta Centre, formerly called Gazprom City, a 400m high business centre which will stand over three times as high as the spire of the Peter and Paul Cathedral, one of the centre's oldest buildings and, for now, still the tallest.

The announcement of the tower in 2006 provoked uproar in a city much more anxious to preserve its heritage than the more pragmatic Moscow. Indeed, if you come to do business in St Petersburg, you will quickly become aware of a very different commercial culture there from that in the capital. It is difficult to put your finger on, but if it can be summed up in one phrase, it would have to be that everything happens a good deal more slowly. Moscow is your classic, mercantile (some might say mercenary) centre, while Russia's second city, in spite of its stated aim to be Russia's window on the west, has always been more introspective. It can be frustrating at first, no doubt, but working here is an object lesson in the importance of respecting your market. The rivalry between Russia's two main cities is, of course, legendary, and is best encapsulated by what each says of the other: Petersburgers call Moscow the biggest village in the world, while Muscovites call the city on the Neva the world's biggest museum.

The Okhta Centre

9

It is true that the city's post-1991 has been overshadowed by that of Moscow, but more recently the growth of St Petersburg and the surrounding region has accelerated strongly, posting an annual increase in GRP of just under 10% in 2007. Europe's third largest city is rapidly becoming the centre of attention for foreign manufacturers, particularly in the automotive sector, with the result that it now likes to call itself Russia's Detroit (a sobriquet previously applied to Nizhniy Novgorod).

Key to the city's economic development has undoubtedly been the fact that since 2000 key posts in the Russian government have been occupied by its favoured sons. Besides Vladimir Putin, Russia's new president Dmitry Medvedev, deputy Prime Minister Sergey Ivanov, and Finance Minister Alexey Kudrin all hail from St Petersburg. With Medvedev's election as president in 2008, and Putin's move to the White House (the Moscow one...), it seems fair to expect that St Petersburg will be able to count on the support of friends in high places for some time yet. It is even regaining some degree of federal clout, as the Russian Constitutional Court has now been relocated there from Moscow.

If, and it is still 'if', the money keeps flowing for St Petersburg's ambitious development programme, the city could still see yet another renaissance over the next decade.

Hotels and restaurants

The hotel sector in St Petersburg is expanding at a similarly headlong rate as everywhere else in Russia. It is estimated that the city currently has around half the hotel accommodation it needs, and it is reasonable to expect that the pace of construction will not abate for a while yet, rendering a list such as the one below obsolete within months. St Petersburg differs from Moscow in that it has a large number of small bed and breakfast hotels in the centre, which offer a good alternative if you are on a budget and if location is more important to you than opulence. There are a number of agencies which can arrange bookings in these smaller hotels, one of the most

9

user-friendly is Nevsky Hotels Group (hyyp://hon.ru/en), where you can also book serviced apartments for short-term let.

Restaurants and cafés have long been an intrinsic part of St Petersburg's culture, and you will not be short of choice for an evening out, whether you intend to ravage your expense account at the Palkin or grab something simpler in the Socialist Realist confines of the Propaganda café.

Luxury hotels

Grand Hotel Europe *****

Looming over Nevsky Prospekt, the Grand Hotel Europe is probably the city's grandest luxury hotel. The hotel was bought by Orient Express group a few years ago, in what was at the time the biggest international real estate transaction in Russian history. The Grand Hotel Europe was opened in 1875, and its famous guests include Pyotr Tchaikovsky (who spent his honeymoon here) and George Bernard Shaw. Excellent conference space on the top floor for business events and functions.

Standard room rates: Twin/double £260 per night
Mikhailovskaya Street 1/7
St Petersburg 191011
Tel: +7 812 329 6000
Fax: +7 812 329 6001
E-mail: res@grandhoteleurope.com
Website: www.grandhoteleurope.com

Hotel Astoria *****

The Astoria is the reason that the Grand Hotel Europe is only "probably" the grandest accommodation in the city. Sitting on the corner of St. Isaac's Square, the Astoria has one of the best locations in the city, which is some claim given where we're talking about. A few years ago Sir Rocco Forte added it to his prestigious collection, and in 2007 it was nominated by Forbes' magazine as one of the world's most romantic hotels.

Standard room rates: Twin/double £210 per night
Bolshaya Morskaya Street 39
St Petersburg 190000
Tel: +7 812 494 5757

9

Fax: +7 812 494 5059
E-mail: reservations.astoria@roccofortecollection.com
Website: Website: www.roccofortecollection.com

Kempinski Moika 22 *****
A spring chicken compared with the two hotels above,
the Kempinski opened its doors on the banks of the
Moika canal only in 2005. The hotel offers just under
200 beautifully decorated rooms, opulent décor and
one of the best views of the city from its 9th floor bar
and restaurant.

Standard room rates: Twin/double £220 per night
Moika Embankment 22
St Petersburg 191186
Tel: +7 812 335 9111
Fax: +7 812 335 9190
E-mail: reservations.moika@kempinski.com
Website: www.kempinski.com

Radisson SAS Royal *****
On the corner of Nevsky and Vladimirsky Prospekts, the
Radisson SAS Royal occupies the 18th century mansion
of a wealthy (presumably fabulously wealthy) merchant.
The interior was completely reconstructed in 2001,
retaining many of the façade's original features. The
hotel is popular for its central location and excellent
business and meeting facilities.

Standard room rates: Twin/double £215 per night
Nevsky Prospekt 49
St Petersburg 191025
Tel: +7 812 322 5000
Fax: +7 812 322 5001
E-mail: reservations.led@radissonsas.com
Website: www.radissonsas.com

Corinthia Nevsky Palace *****
Just along Nevsky Prospekt from the Radisson, the
Corinthia Nevsky Palace provides a more modern take
on the luxury hotel theme. The front of the hotel has
recently been remodelled, and the interior includes spacious
guest rooms and excellent conference facilities. Not perhaps
as opulent and luxurious as the Astoria or the Grand, the
Nevsky Palace is nonetheless an excellent place to stay.

9

Standard room rates: *Twin/double £190 per night*
Nevsky Prospekt 57
St Petersburg 191025
Tel: +7 812 380 2001
Fax: +7 812 380 1937
E-mail: reservation@corinthia.ru
Website: www.corinthia.com

Grand Hotel Emerald *****

One of the newest additions to the St Petersburg luxury
hotel market, the Emerald was confirmed as a five star
hotel only in late 2008. Slightly away from the centre
when compared to the others in this list, it remains a
short walk from many of the city's attractions, and you
may find the quieter setting very welcome. Excellent
event space, particularly for receptions.

Standard room rates: *Twin/double £185 per night*
Souvorovsky Prospekt 18
St Petersburg 191036
Tel: +7 812 740 5000
Fax: +7 812 740 5001
E-mail: info@grandhotelemerald.com
Website: www.grandhotelemerald.com

Deluxe hotels

Hotel Angleterre ****

The slightly more modest twin and neighbour of the
Astoria, the Angleterre is also one of St Petersburg's
oldest hotels. A very popular destination for business
travellers, the Angleterre offers a good mix of location,
price and standards, and has a very versatile events space
for conferences and meetings.

Standard room rates: *Twin/double £165 per night*
Bolshaya Morskaya Street 39
St Petersburg 190000
Tel: +7 812 494 5666
Fax: +7 812 313 5125
E-mail: reservations.spb@angleterrehotel.com
Website: www.angleterrehotel.com

Hotel Ambassador ****

A modern, more business-oriented hotel in one of the
older parts of St Petersburg, the Ambassador offers 255

9

rooms and an excellent range of business and leisure facilities.

Standard room rates: *Twin/double £125 per night*
Rimsky-Korsakov Street 5-7
St Petersburg 190068
Tel: +7 812 331 8844
Fax: +7 812 331 9300
E-mail: info@ambassador-hotel.ru
Website: www.ambassador-hotel.ru

Hotel Arbat Nord ****
A smaller hotel, recently appeared on the scene in St Petersburg, the Arbat Nord offers 33 rooms and a pleasant, comfortable feel. The hotel is close by the Fontanka canal, north of Nevsky Prospekt.

Standard room rates: *Twin/double £100 per night*
Artilleriyskaya Street 4
St Petersburg 191104
Tel: +7 812 703 1899
Fax: +7 812 703 1898
E-mail: info@arbat-nord.ru
Website: www.arbat-nord.ru

Casa Leto ****
An excellent boutique hotel in the centre, which you can walk straight past if you don't know it's there. Walk through the ordinary looking door and you are confronted with a sweeping staircase leading up to a tastefully decorated interior with each room having its own character. Casa Leto is also a very good business hotel, with all the facilities you would expect from a more modern-looking establishment. Highly recommended.

Standard room rates: *From £110 per night*
Bolshaya Morskaya Street 34
St Petersburg 190000
Tel: +7 812 600 1096
Fax: +7 812 314 66396
E-mail: info@casaleto.com
Website: www.casaleto.com

9

Golden Garden Hotel ****

A five minute walk south from Nevsky Prospekt, the Golden Garden is a luxurious if slightly gaudy hotel with a good location and excellent facilities. If you want to arrive in style, they have a Bentley on hand which will whisk you in from the airport for a fee.

Standard room rates: *Twin/double £150 per night*
Vladimirsky Prospekt 9
St Petersburg 191025
Tel: +7 812 329 2656
Website: www.golden-garden-petersburg-hotel.ru

Helvetia Hotel ****

Located just south of Nevsky Prospekt, the Helvetia is a pleasant, smaller hotel with a relaxed atmosphere and its own internal courtyard. Until recently the building housed the Swiss consulate.

Standard room rates: *Twin/double £110 per night*
Marata Street 11
St Petersburg 191025
Tel: +7 812 326 5353
Fax: +7 812 326 2009
E-mail: info@helvetia-suites.ru
Website: http://en.helvetia-suites.ru

Holiday Club St Petersburg *****

Another recent offering in the city, the Holiday Club is located on Vassilievsky Island, and combines the facilities of an upper-end business hotel and spa. Again, it isn't right in the centre of things, but the island has a separate atmosphere all its own which you may prefer.

Standard room rates: *Twin/double £185 per night*
V.O. Birzhevoy Pereulok 2-4
St Petersburg 199004
Tel: +7 812 335 2200
E-mail: sales@shotels.ru
Website: www.holidayclubhotels.ru

Marco Polo Hotel ****

Located on Vassilievsky Island, the Marco Polo's building dates from the 1870s, and was completely refurbished in

2004. A good choice if you want to be away from the bustle of the centre.

Standard room rates: Twin/double £100 per night
V.O. 12th Line 27
St Petersburg 199178
Tel: +7 812 449 8877
Fax: +7 812 323 1867
E-mail: info@mpolo-spb.ru
Website: www.mpolo-spb.ru/english

Novotel St Petersburg Centre ****
Much more "central" than its Moscow sibling, the Novotel St Petersburg Centre is just off Nevsky Prospekt, a 10 minute walk from Moscow Station. A modern hotel very much in the group's idiom, it offers excellent business and conference facilities.

Standard room rates: Twin/double £140 per night
Mayakovskogo Street 3a
St Petersburg 191025
Tel: +7 812 335 1188
Fax: +7 812 335 1180
E-mail: h5679@accor.com
Website: www.novotel.com

Park Inn Pribaltiyskaya Hotel ****
A very big, very ugly hotel on the western side of Vassilievsky Island, the Pribaltiyskaya is better to look out of than to look at, offering fabulous views of the Gulf of Finland. With 1200 rooms and a 1000 seat congress hall, one of the city's largest hotel properties has undergone an extensive refit in that past few years.

Standard room rates: Twin/double £115 per night
Korablestroiteley Street 14
St Petersburg 199226
Tel: +7 812 329 2626
Fax: +7 812 356 6094
E-mail: info.pribaltiyskaya@rezidorparkinn.com
Website: www.pribaltiyskaya.parkinn.com.ru

Park Inn Pulkovskaya Hotel ****
Located roughly half way between the centre and Pulkovo airport, the Pulkovskaya is another Park Inn

9

giant, with 840 rooms and congress facilities to host up to 600 people. Not the most visually prepossessing building in St Petersburg, it is nonetheless considerably redeemed by having its own German-managed micro-brewery.

Standard room rates: *Twin/Double £110 per night*
Pobedy Square 1
St Petersburg 196240
Tel: +7 812 740 3900
Fax: +7 812 740 3913
E-mail: reservations.ledpd@rezidorparkinn.com
Website: www.pulkovskaya.parkinn.com.ru

Petro Palace Hotel **
Centrally located, the Petro Palace combines a good mix of good location, comfort and price, with a little under 200 rooms and seven separate meeting spaces. A good solid business hotel.

Standard room rates: *Twin/double £120 per night*
Malaya Morskaya Street 14
St Petersburg 190000
Tel: +7 812 571 2880
Fax: +7 812 571 2704
E-mail: info@petropalacehotel.com
Website: www.petropalacehotel.com

Rossi Hotel **
A newly opened, small luxury hotel on the Fontanka Canal, the Rossi is ideal if you can survive without the last word in business facilities and want to stay somewhere more redolent of historic St Petersburg.

Standard room rates: *not known*
Fontanka Embankment 55
St Petersburg 191011
Tel: +7 812 635 6333
Fax: +7 812 571 8587

Restaurants
Palkin
Probably the finest restaurant in town, certainly one of the most expensive, St Petersburg's answer to the Café Pushkin will fill your belly and empty your wallet with

9

style. On Nevsky (where else?) right next to the Radisson
SAS Royal.

Nevsky Prospekt 47
St Petersburg 191025
Tel: +7 812 703 5371

Hermitage
Tucked beneath one of the main arches looking onto
Palace Square, the Hermitage has several different
rooms, all tastefully decorated. Excellent cuisine, and
whenever I've been there, fairly quiet.
Palace Square 6/8
Arch of the General Staff
St Petersburg 191055
Tel: +7 812 314 4772

Pushka Inn
On the Moika embankment, the Pushka is a good, solid
café with (hopefully this is still the case) free wi-fi access.
A great place to duck into, grab something to eat and
check your emails.
Moika Embankment 14
St Petersburg 191186
Tel: +7 812 312 0957

Propaganda
A couple of canals up from the Pushka, the Propaganda
is an entertaining Socialist-Realist themed restaurant
with excellent, reasonably priced food and a memorable
interior. Well worth a visit.
Fontanka Embankment 40
St Petersburg
Tel: +7 812 275 3558

Udachny Vystrel
Another memorable venue, the name of this restaurant
translates as "The Lucky Shot" which should give you
an idea of its theme. If you don't want to be confronted
by a stuffed bear as you walk in from the street, don't
come here. Otherwise, you will find hearty fare in a
rustic setting.
Gorokhovaya Street 3
St Petersburg 19000
Tel: +7 812 571 6949

9

St Petersburg attractions
The Peter and Paul Fortress

St Petersburg's first building remains the centrepiece of the city and its historical lodestone. It has survived outwardly intact since its rebuilding as a stone fortress in 1740, although Catherine the Great ordered that the side of the fortress facing the Winter Palace across the river be faced with granite, as its original walls appeared to her blood red when reflected in the Neva's waters. The fortress itself has seen plenty of violence – Peter the Great's son Alexei was secretly executed here, and it became the site of the Secret Chancery established by the city's founder to investigate anti-governmental activities. The Decembrists were also tried here, and you can still visit the cell where the writer Maxim Gorky was briefly incarcerated. The Peter and Paul Cathedral in the centre of the complex was the final resting place for nearly all Russia's leaders from Peter the Great to Nicholas II – the latter was finally moved here with the rest of the imperial family in 1998. Only the tomb of Alexander I is allegedly empty, as according to legend he ended his days as a wandering hermit in Siberia, haunted by guilt at the death of his father and his inability to cure Russia's ills (see Chapter 1).

Petrodvorets

During the construction of St Petersburg in the early 18th century, and the city's outer garrison on the island of Kronstadt, Peter the Great ordered a small residence to be built on the mainland side so that he could have somewhere to stay while he was observing the construction work. The building became known as Peterhof, or Peter's house, a name which was subsequently de-Germanicised to Petrodvorets. The new term, literally meaning Peter's palace, reflected the complex's transformation over the years from a modest country house to an enormous and spectacular collection of palaces, gardens, statuary and fountains as successive rulers added their own mark to the place. Almost destroyed during the Siege of Leningrad (it was occupied by the German forces), Petrodvorets was painstakingly restored to its former grandeur in the years following the war, and now it once again makes Versailles look relatively ordinary. The palace and grounds are accessible by road from the city, but much better to arrive as Peter the Great would have wanted you to, from the sea. Hydrofoils depart for Petrodvorets from a quay in front of the Winter Palace, and the trip takes around 45 minutes each way.

9

Russia's regional cities

Russia's regional cities

For readers interested in venturing
beyond Moscow and St Petersburg,
this section gives a birds-eye view of
some of Russia's key regional cities

There is a saying that "Moscow is not Russia, and Russia is not Moscow", and it is tempting to consider the Russian Federation's capital as a market in itself, ignoring the rest of the country's vast interior. But it is only Russia's size that makes the centres described below seem so small and unimportant compared to the mother of Russian cities. As mentioned earlier, Moscow's retail trade in 2007 was greater than that of all the million-plus cities combined (including St Petersburg), and there are more people in Russia's two largest cities than in the next twelve put together. Consider this, though: even the most sparsely peopled city in this chapter has more people than Brussels, or Stockholm, or, for that matter, Washington DC. More compellingly for the business traveller, many of them have recorded annual economic growth in excess of 15% over the past few years, and the rate of expansion of their local economies is, if anything, increasing. Of the cities below, some are younger than St Petersburg, one is even older than Moscow, and all are major industrial and commercial centres. Even if they do not figure in your initial plans in Russia, you should be at least aware of their existence and potential.

10

Chelyabinsk

Located at the southern end of the Ural mountains, Chelyabinsk was founded in 1736 as a military staging fort on the river Miass. Little more than a Cossack garrison town for the first century and a half of its existence, the city began to develop more rapidly when the railway line from Moscow reached it in 1892. More important still for Chelyabinsk was the completion of a rail link with the regional capital Ekaterinburg four years later, which led to an exponential increase in its population. Chelyabinsk became a major centre of engineering and production during the mass industrialisation of Soviet Union during the 1920s and 1930s, and was key to the war effort against Germany, producing the Katyusha artillery rockets and the legendary T-34 tank which were to prove so decisive on the eastern front.

Today the major industries in Chelyabinsk are mining (principally ferrous metals and coal) and engineering, and the area is also rich in nickel, gold and bauxite.

The city centre itself is relatively compact, surrounded as you might expect by high-rise apartment blocks. In 1992, work commenced on an underground metro system for the city, although the first 4 stations are not due to open until 2012.

Both Aeroflot and S7 Siberian Airlines operate several daily flights between Moscow and Chelyabinsk, the flight time is just over two hours. The city's population in 2007 was 1.1m.

Hotels

ParkCity Business Hotel
Lesoparkovaya Street 6, Chelyabinsk 454080
Tel: +7 351 265 44 55
Fax: +7 351 731 22 22
Website: www.parkcityhotel.ru/eng

Hotel Slavyanka
Prospekt Lenina 20, Chelyabinsk 454007
Tel: +7 351 775 29 50
Fax: +7 351 775 29 50
Website: www.slavyanka74.ru/en

Berezka Hotel Complex
Chapaeva Street 118, Smolino, nr. Chelyabinsk
Tel: +7 351 267 30 30
Fax: +7 351 271 55 55
Website: www.berezka74.ru

Hotel Victoria
Mologvardeytsev Street 34, Chelyabinsk
Tel: +7 351 798 98 20
Fax: +7 351 798 98 21
Website: http://victoria.ru/en

Ekaterinburg

Around 200km north of Chelyabinsk, Ekaterinburg was founded in 1723, and named in honour of Catherine I (not Catherine the Great as is sometimes thought – she took the throne some forty years after the city was founded). Over the course of the 18th century the city slowly became the administrative centre for the southern Urals region, before gaining national importance as a

10

major producer of Imperial Russia's currency, minting up to 80% of the country's bronze coinage in the 19th century. Parallel with this, the city became a centre of gold-smelting, using material mined in western Siberia. In 1878, the first railway line in the Urals was built using private funds to link Ekaterinburg with Perm'. Over the next few decades the city became a local transport hub, with lines built to Tyumen' and Omsk in 1885, and Chelyabinsk in 1896, although direct links to St Petersburg and Moscow would not be established until 1909 and 1920 respectively. Immediately following the October Revolution, Ekaterinburg became the official administrative centre for the Urals Oblast', and the exiled Imperial family were held here until their execution in July 1918. Just over a week later the Red Army was driven out of the city, and for almost exactly a year Ekaterinburg was held by the White forces under General Kolchak. In 1923 the city became the capital of the extended Urals Oblast', and a year later it was renamed Sverdlovsk in honour of the leading Bolshevik, Yakov Sverdlov.

10

In the 1920s, the heavy machinery plant Uralmash was built in the city, at the time the largest factory of its kind in Europe. Sverdlovsk was also a major industrial centre during the war years, and many of the factories relocated there from Moscow remained after the end of hostilities, contributing to its economic recovery in the '50s and '60s. In 1979 over 100 people in the city were killed by an outbreak of anthrax, which was subsequently attributed by international investigators to a leak from the Sverdlovsk-19 chemical weapons research facility, although this was denied by the local authorities.

Ekaterinburg regained its original name in December 1991, a few months after the former regional governor, Boris Yeltsin, became president of the newly created Russian Federation. It remains the main industrial, administrative and cultural centre in the Southern Urals, as well as its largest population centre, with just over 1.3m people. The principal economic sectors are heavy engineering and metallurgy, but the city's industrial foundation is broad-based, including everything from aero-engine production to railway locomotive repair. The city centre boasts over 600 historical and cultural monuments, along with the consulates of the US, the UK, Germany, France, Italy and Spain among others.

Ekaterinburg's main airport, Kol'tsovo, is served by Aeroflot and a number of regional carriers, as well as Austrian, bmi, Malev and Lufthansa.

Hotels

Atrium Palace Hotel
Kuibysheva Street 44, Ekaterinburg 620026
Tel: +7 343 359 60 00
Fax: +7 343 359 60 01
Website: www.aph-ural.ru/eng

Aleksandrovsky Park Hotel
Shchorsa Street 24, Ekaterinburg 620142
Tel: +7 343 257 54 54
Fax: +7 343 257 27 77
Website: http://parkhotel-ural.ru

Park Inn Ekaterinburg
Mamina-Sibiryaka St. 98, Ekaterinburg 620075
Tel: +7 343 216 60 00
Fax: +7 343 216 60 06
Website: www.rezidor.com

Voznesensky Hotel
Mamina-Sibiryaka St. 52, Chelyabinsk 620075
Tel: +7 343 379 35 35
Fax: +7 343 379 45 45
Website: http://v-hotel/ru

Kazan'

One of the largest cities on the Volga, Kazan' is also one of Russia's oldest. Controversy persists over whether the city was founded by the Tatars themselves in the mid-fifteenth century, or by the Volga Bulgars several centuries earlier. The official version of events is the latter, supported by archaeological finds made on the site of the ancient kremlin. Whatever its historical context, Kazan's geographical location meant that from the beginning it was an important trading centre, linking the markets of Europe to the Caspian and thence to Persia

10

and beyond. Becoming capital of the Kazan' Khanate in 1438, the city remained one of the key assets of the Tatar-Mongol empire until it fell to Ivan the Terrible's forces in 1552. The kremlin as you see it today was built in this period, although the fortress walls were rebuilt at the beginning of the 18th century.

In 1767, Catherine the Great visited the Kazan' and gave her blessing for the building of its first stone mosque, the Al Marjani, which was the only Muslim temple to survive the Soviet period. Less than a decade after Catherine's visit, the city was taken by Pugachev's troops, and largely destroyed in the ensuing battle with the Imperial Russian army. Kazan's recovery as a trading centre continued through the 19th century, and by 1900 it had become Russia's fifth largest city, having more than doubled its population to 130,000 people in less than fifty years. Today the city has around 1.2m inhabitants.

Sometimes nicknamed "Little Moscow", Kazan' today sits at the centre of a vibrant and broad-based local economy. The region produces around 9% of Russia's oil, and the chemical and engineering sectors are also highly developed. There are two major aerospace manufacturers in the city, producing both fixed wing aircraft and helicopters, and Tatarstan as a whole is a key agricultural centre, as well as being home to the truck-maker Kamaz. Like Moscow, the centre of the city blends ancient and modern with varying success, and also boasts a small metro system of five stations completed in 2005.

Kazan' airport has several daily flights to Moscow, a daily flight to St Petersburg, and less frequent services to Russia's other cities. Lufthansa also operates a daily service from Frankfurt.

Hotels

Hotel Mirage
Moskovskaya Street 1a, Kazan' 420951
Tel: +7 843 278 05 05
Fax: +7 843 278 92 70
Website: www.mirage-hotel.ru

10

Kortson Hotel and Mall
N. Ershova Street 1a, Kazan' 420061
Tel: +7 843 279 33 66
Fax: +7 843 279 33 77
Website: www.kzn.korston.ru/en

Shalyapin Palace Hotel
Universitetskaya St. 7, Kazan' 420111
Tel: +7 843 238 28 00
Fax: +7 843 231 10 22
Website: www.shalyapin-hotel.ru/en

Hotel Gulfstream
2ns Azinskaya St. 1G, Kazan' 420088
Tel: +7 843 279 11 40
Fax: +7 843 279 11 41
Website: www.g-hotel.ru/eng

Krasnodar

Not strictly a million-plus city, Krasnodar is nonetheless the administrative centre of one of Russia's largest agro-industrial areas, with a regional population of over 5m people. Officially home to just under 800,000 people, Krasnodar is one of the few Russian cities showing a net population increase, and is expected to officially become a "*millionnik*" in 2012.

The modern city was founded as a military garrison in 1793, named Ekaterinodar (Catherine's Gift) in honour of Catherine the Great, although evidence of previous settlement of the area goes back as far as the 6th century BC. Ekaterinodar officially became a town in 1867, and with the coming of the railway over the following decades it became a centre of trade and industry in the region. The city was given its modern name in 1920.

Krasnodar is now a major investment destination in Russia, as a result of its agricultural potential and the region's rich natural resources. Increased international attention has been focused on the region as a whole in advance of the 2014 Winter Olympics, which will be held in Sochi on the Black Sea coast.

10

Krasnodar's main airport, Pashkovsky-2, is served by daily flights from Moscow, and less frequent services from Russia's other cities.

Hotels

Hotel Europa
Severnaya Street 319, Krasnodar 350015
Tel: +7 861 251 75 27
Fax: +7 861 251 75 61
Website: www.europe.su/hotel

Hotel Luxe-Platan
Rashpilevskaya Street 4/1, Krasnodar 350063
Tel: +7 861 262 86 84
Fax: +7 861 262 86 90
Website: www.platanhotel.ru/en

Premier Hotel
Vasnetsova Street 14, Krasnodar 350059
Tel: +7 861 274 11 55
Fax: +7 861 274 55 95
Website: www.hotelpremimier.ru/eng

Red Royal Hotel
Krasnykh Partizan Street 238, Krasnodar 350020
Tel: +7 861 215 01 01
Fax: +7 861 215 50 50
Website: www.redroyalhotel.com

Krasnoyarsk

Eastern Siberia's largest city was founded as a military fortress in 1628, and was originally named Krasny Yar (Beautiful Hill), before gaining both its current name and civil town status in 1690. Located at the confluence of the Yenisei and the smaller river Kacha, its economic growth began in earnest in the 1730s with the arrival of the *trakt*, the first permanent road to be built across the Siberian plain. Much of the city was destroyed by a fire in 1773, with only 30 buildings left intact, and Krasnoyarsk was subsequently rebuilt to a modern grid-plan scheme. In 1822, it became capital of the newly-created Yenisei province.

10

Krasnoyarsk saw its first railway locomotive in 1895, and the city has developed ever since as an important transport hub, located at the conjunction of the Trans-Siberian Railway, one of Siberia's strategic highways, and of course the mighty Yenisei itself. The Krasnoyarsk Territory, Russia's second largest, is rich in oil and gas, as well as possessing substantial deposits of coal and non-ferrous metals. The city is a major centre of metallurgy and heavy engineering, and has a highly developed forestry, pulp and paper industry.

The city is just under 4,000km from Moscow, and is served by multiple daily flights from the capital on both Aeroflot and S7 Siberian Airlines. Flight time is a little under five hours.

Hotels

Hotel Krasnoyarsk
Uritskogo Street 94, Krasnoyarsk 660049
Tel: +7 391 274 94 03
Fax: +7 391 274 94 16
Website: www.hotelkrs.ru

Hotel Yahont
Telmana Street 44a, Krasnoyarsk 660073
Tel: +7 391 256 67 67
Fax: +7 391 256 67 01
Website: http://yahont.ru

Hotel Metelitsa
Prospekt Mira 14, Krasnoyarsk 660049
Tel: +7 391 227 60 60
Fax: +7 391 227 61 61
Website: www.hotelpremimier.ru/eng

Hotel Oktyabrskaya
Prospekt Mira 15, Krasnoyarsk 660049
Tel: +7 391 227 37 80
Fax: +7 391 227 05 81
Website: www.hoteloctober.ru

Nizhny Novgorod
Founded in 1221 by Yuri Vsevolodovich of Vladimir as a defensive bastion against the Volga Bulgars and,

10

subsequently, the Tatars, Nizhny Novgorod's strategic position overlooking two of Russia's greatest rivers would forever determine its future history and development. Situated at the confluence of the Volga and Oka, the young city (the name literally means "Lower New Town") was taken by the Golden Horde in 1238, but was spared the fate of more established settlements on account of its relative insignificance, a piece of good fortune which it shared with the equally unremarkable Moscow. Novgorod quickly recovered after the Mongol invasion, and vied for supremacy over the Vladimir-Suzdal province with Moscow, Tver and others during the Tatar-Mongol Yoke. In 1350, the city's importance was augmented still further when it became the seat of power of the Suzdal Principality. Nizhniy Novgorod did not entirely escape the attentions of the Mongols, and came under siege on two separate occasions in the early 16th century, but by this time its fortifications were strong enough to withstand the assault. The city was incorporated into the state of Muscovy in 1592, and during the Time of Troubles became a centre of Russian resistance against the Polish intervention. It was from here that in 1612 Kuzma Minin and Dmitry Pozharsky led the national militia which eventually expelled the Polish troops from Moscow, and in 2005 an exact copy of the 1818 monument to the two men on Red Square was unveiled, on the very spot where they issued the call to arms.

Nizhny Novgorod's status as a centre of trade on the Volga had become increasingly important with the Russian victories over the Tatars at Kazan' and Astrakhan, and the city came to be the major point of trans-shipment of oriental goods from the Caspian onto smaller vessels for the journey to western Russia along the Upper Volga and Oka. Nizhny Novgorod continued to flourish throughout the 17th and 18th centuries, and received a further boost in 1816 when the Makariev Monastery, 90km south along the Volga, burned down and its annual fair was transferred to the city. The relocation proved advantageous to both sides, with millions of visitors coming to the city every July. By the mid-19th century, Nizhny Novgorod was firmly established as Russia's third city, and its trade capital.

10

In the Soviet period, the first bridges over Nizhny Novgorod's two rivers were built, and in 1932 it was renamed in honour of the writer Maxim Gorky, born Alexey Peshkov in the city some sixty years previously. The same year, the Gorky Automotive Works (GAZ), still one of Russia's biggest, was opened, initially producing lorries and later cars and light vans. If you've ever travelled in a Volga taxi, it came from here. Today a city if 1.37m people, Nizhny Novgorod remains one of Russia's most developed, with the leading industries being engineering and machine- and ship-building, metal fabrication, chemical and petrochemical processing, forestry, pulp and paper. It is worth a visit in its own right as one of Russia's historic centres, not least for a chance to see the magnificent Kremlin at its heart.

Moscow is only 400km away, so getting to Nizhny Novgorod from the capital is not challenging. Flights are plentiful and regular, and an express train service has operated since 2002, taking around five hours. Lufthansa and Austrian airlines also both operate a daily service from their Frankfurt and Vienna hubs.

Hotels

Hotel Volna
Prospekt Lenina 98, Nizhny Novgorod 603004
Tel: +7 831 295 19 00
Fax: +7 831 295 14 14
Website: www.volnahotel.ru/en

Alexandrovsky Garden
Georgievsky S'ezd 3, Nizhny Novgorod 603005
Tel: +7 831 277 81 41
Fax: +7 831 277 81 51
Website: www.achotel.ru/eng

Hotel Nizhegorodskaya
Zalomova Street 2, Nizhny Novgorod 603109
Tel: +7 831 430 53 87
Fax: +7 831 430 50 42
Website: www.hotel-nn.ru

Hotel Jouk Jaque
Bolshaya Pokrovskaya St. 57, Nizhny Novgorod 603000
Tel: +7 831 433 04 62

Fax: +7 831 433 37 43
Website: www.jak-hotel.ru

Novosibirsk

The youngest of all Russia's major cities, the administrative capital of Siberia has only recently celebrated its first anniversary. In 1893, work commenced on a bridge to carry the Trans Siberian railway across the river Ob, and a small community spontaneously sprang up around the construction site. The new village was called Alexandrovsk, and had its name changed to Novonikolaevsk in 1896, allowing a discreet two year delay following the sudden death of Alexander III. With a population of just under 8,000 people by the time the bridge opened, Novonikolaevsk began its remarkable rise, and by 1907 it had already achieved the status of a town. By the time of the Bolshevik Revolution a decade later, the population had risen to over 100,000 people and Novonikolaevsk was firmly established as a trade and industrial centre. In 1925 it became the administrative centre of Siberia, gaining its current name the following year, and during the industrialisation drive of the next decade Novosibirsk rapidly turned into one of the country's largest industrial centres. By the time that the original bridge across the Ob was replaced in 1955, the population of the city was nudging 300,000 people. Two years later, a branch of the Soviet Academy of Sciences was established on the outskirts of the city, 30km from the centre, which became known as Akademgorodok. Novosibirsk's expansion accelerated still further, and in 1962 it became the youngest city in the world to have over 1m inhabitants.

Today the city is Russia's largest east of the Urals, with a population of 1.7m people. Aside from being the country's principal centre of scientific and academic research, the local economy is devoted to machine-building, heavy industry and power generation, and the region is also a major agricultural centre. With technological innovation declared as a priority by the federal government in recent years, Novosibirsk and Akademgorodok will undoubtedly attract further investment and attention over the coming decades.

10

The city is served by Tolmachevo airport, which has regular flights from Moscow (flight time approximately 4 hours). A number of international carriers also fly to Novosibirsk, and there are direct services from the city to Delhi, Beijing and Dubai.

Hotels

Hotel Zhemchuzhina
Zhukovskogo Street 8, Novosibirsk 630123
Tel: +7 383 200 11 10
Fax: +7 383 200 13 33
Website: www.jemchuzhina.ru

Hotel Deluxe
Lenina Street 11, Novosibirsk 630004
Tel: +7 383 218 77 90
Fax: +7 383 218 76 58
Website: www.hoteldeluxe.ru

Hotel Sibir
Lenina Street 21, Novosibirsk 630004
Tel: +7 383 223 12 15
Fax: +7 383 223 87 66
Website: www.hotel-sibir.ru

Garden Apple Hotel
Vostochny Poselok Str. 9a, Novosibirsk
Tel: +7 383 291 32 21
Fax: +7 383 291 32 21
Website: www.garden-apple.ru

Omsk

Just down the road from Novosibirsk, in Siberian terms at least, Omsk was for many years the de facto capital of Western Siberia, and remains a powerful industrial centre and home to Russia's largest oil refinery complex. The city was founded as a military stronghold in 1716, at the height of Peter the Great's concerted push to open up Siberia. In 1782 the garrison gained full town status, and with the administrative division of Siberia into Western and Eastern provinces forty years later, Omsk became the principle city of the former, in preference to its older neighbours Tyumen', Tomsk and Tobolsk. As the Russian Empire pushed ever eastward, Omsk's significance as a frontier town receded and it settled into becoming a commercial and administrative centre. Dostoevsky was exiled here following his participation in the abortive Decembrists' Revolt, along with many other intellectuals – it was joked at the time that in Omsk, they sold ink by the bucket. With the arrival of the Trans-Siberian towards the end of the 19th century, the city experienced a renewed boom as the junction of the new railway and the river Irtysh. Irkutsk on the shores of lake Baikal is sometimes called the Paris of Siberia, but Omsk was its Chicago, at least in the early 1900s. After 1917 the city became one of the strongholds of the White Russians, and it was temporarily declared the capital of Russia – the imperial gold reserves were even stored here before the Whites were forced to flee eastwards.

Omsk's status as provisional capital returned during World War II, when it was decided that should Moscow fall to the Germans, the Soviet government would retreat here. As with many of the other cities east of the Urals, Omsk retained many of the military factories that were transferred to the city during the war, and became a key pillar of the USSR's military industrial complex. During the Soviet period, it lost many of its administrative importance to Novosibirsk, engendering a rivalry between the cities that persists to this day.

Omsk had to draw on all its mercantile instincts to re-establish itself following the collapse of the Soviet Union and subsequent drastic cuts in military spending, and today 30% of its economy is based on private commerce. With a population of just over 1.1m people, its principal industries apart from oil refining are machine-building and engineering, forestry and metallurgy. The historical centre of Omsk is very attractive, and has a very different aspect from the modernity of Novosibirsk, something to which your attention will be drawn almost instantly should you announce to a local that you have just arrived from the latter.

The city is served by multiple daily Aeroflot and S7 flights to Moscow, and a single daily flight to Kaliningrad on KD Avia airlines.

10

Hotel Lermontov
Lermontova Street 77, Omsk 644070
Tel: +7 381 237 22 11
Fax: +7 381 237 22 11
Website: www.lermontov-hotel.ru

Hotel Irtysh
Krasny Put' Street 155/1, Omsk 644033
Tel: +7 381 223 27 02
Fax: +7 381 222 95 20
Website: www.hotel-irtysh.ru

Hotel Voskhod
3rd Ostrovskaya Street 4, Omsk 644011
Tel: +7 381 231 17 87
Fax: +7 381 231 45 41
Website: www.hotel-sibir.ru

Hotel Tourist
Broz Tito Strreet 2, Omsk 644024
Tel: +7 381 231 64 19
Fax: +7 381 231 64 14
Website: http://eng.tourist-omsk.ru

10

Perm'

Situated just west of the Urals, Russia's third largest city
by area was founded in 1723 by Vassily Tatishchev (who
also founded Ekaterinburg) as a settlement to house
workers of a major copper-smelting plant. The area
around Perm' shows signs of human habitation going
back a great deal further, to 15,000 BC in fact. The Perm'
region was a famously rich source of both furs and salt in
the medieval period, and both Nizhny Novgorod and
Moscow coveted its wealth leading to bitter rivalry
between the principalities. In the event, Moscow won
the battle in 1472.

The city is situated at the confluence of the Kama river
and its tributary, the Yegoshikha. The Kama itself is
Europe's fifth largest river, and the main tributary of the
Volga, draining an area the size of Spain as it flows first
north, then east, then south west to meet the great
waterway south of Kazan'. In the 19th century it rose to

prominence as a trade and industrial centre, as well as a major producer of munitions. This latter fact made the city a major prize for both the Red and White armies during the Civil War, and it was on the outskirts of Perm' that the Tsar's younger brother, Grand Duke Mikhail, was executed in 1918. The military importance of Perm' increased still further during the Second World War, as factories were moved east out of reach of the German invaders. In 1940 the city was renamed in honour of Vyacheslav Molotov, the Soviet politician and diplomat, but it reverted to its original name in 1957 when Molotov was expelled from the Party for his part in a plot to oust Nikita Khrushchev.

Perm's military importance meant that it was closed to foreigners until 1989, and with the fall of the Soviet Union it faced the same challenge to reinvent itself as did Omsk. The two share many of the same advantages both in terms of geographical location at the hub of major rail, river and road routes, and a diversified, prosperous local economy. Perm', now a city of around 1m people, is a major centre of shipbuilding and aero-engine production, and the region is rich in far more than just salt and fur. The oil and gas sector is highly developed here, and Perm' exports fuel oil, fertilizers, paper and cardboard products to Europe and the US. Metallurgy, both ferrous and non-ferrous, is an important area of the economy, as is agriculture, with around 2m hectares devoted to growing crops. The centre of Perm' is a mixture of modern construction and well-preserved examples of the cultural heritage of this part of Siberia.

The city's main airport is served by scheduled daily services to Moscow and other Russian cities, and Lufthansa operates a weekly direct service from Frankfurt.

Hotels
Hotel Eurotel
Kommunisticheskaya St 55, Perm' 614000
Tel: +7 342 220 63 40
Fax: +7 342 220 63 07
Website: www.eurotel-hotel.ru

Amaks Premier Hotel
Ordzhonikidze Street 43, Perm' 614000
Tel: +7 342 220 60 60
Fax: +7 342 212 23 23
Website: www.amaks-hotels.ru

Hotel Gabriel
Kirova Street 78A, Perm' 614000
Tel: +7 342 210 12 30
Fax: +7 342 212 16 90
Website: www.gabrielhotel.ru

New Star Hotel
Gazeta Zvezda Street 38B, Perm' 614000
Tel: +7 342 220 68 01
Fax: +7 342 220 68 08
Website: www.newstar-hotel.ru/en

Rostov-on-Don

Now the administrative capital of Russia's Southern Federal District, Rostov-on-Don was founded in 1749 as a fortress to help secure the south western edge of the empire. Named in honour of St. Dmitry of Rostov, in 1796 its title was extended to prevent confusion with Golden Ring city of Rostov the Great, from where the newly canonised archbishop originally hailed. Located 65km from the mouth of the river Don, where it drains into the Sea of Azov, the city rapidly developed as a centre of trade, industry and transport, and at the time of its first centenary it was home to 15,000 people. By the end of the 19th century, Rostov-on-Don's population had risen to 110,000. A truly international port city, at the time it was estimated that a third of its factories were foreign-owned. As an important strategic asset, Rostov-on-Don suffered heavily in both the Civil and Great Patriotic Wars, with German forces occupying it on two separate occasions. By the time they were driven out the second time, they had left just six of the city's 270 factories intact.

After the war, the city was substantially rebuilt, and today it sits at the centre of one of the most economically developed regions of Russia. The power, fuel, engineering and food processing sectors account for 75% of the gross regional product, and the region is the second largest producer of high quality hard coal, as well as a major centre of helicopter production. Through the Rostsel'mash conglomerate, first established in 1926, the city is Russia's second largest producer of agricultural machinery, and if you ever take a train in Russia, you can be 100% sure that the locomotive at the front came from Rostov-on-Don, because they don't make them anywhere else. The city population is 1.1m people.

Rostov-on-Don is served by frequent scheduled flights to all the major cities of Russia and the CIS, and both Lufthansa and Austrian operate direct services from Frankfurt and Vienna.

Hotels

Avrora Park Hotel
Martovitskogo Street 89, Rostov-on-Don 344000
Tel: +7 863 231 09 05
Fax: +7 863 231 09 15
Website: www.avroraparkhotel.ru

Congress Hotel Don-Plaza
Bolshaya Sadovaya Str. 115, Rostov-on-Don 344021
Tel: +7 863 263 90 40
Fax: +7 863 263 50 49
Website: www.don-plaza.ru/en

Hotel Parus
Taganrogskaya Street 205, Rostov-on-Don 344000
Tel: +7 863 206 02 81
Fax: +7 863 296 02 80
Website: http://parus-rostov.ru

Hotel Europa
Voroshilovsky Prospekt 41, Rostov-on-Don 344002
Tel: +7 863 200 80 01
Fax: +7 863 200 80 08
Website: http://europahotel.ru

10

Samara

Another of the great Volga cities, Samara officially came into being in 1586, during the brief reign of Ivan the Terrible's son, Fyodor I, although earlier maps of the region show it as a harbour at the confluence of the Volga and Samara rivers. The fortress at Samara was built to secure the south eastern territories from the Tatars, who had only recently been forced out of their strongholds further downriver at Kazan' and Astrakhan. In an example of diplomacy rare for the period, Fyodor diffused the threat of the Nogai people, Turkic nomads who had already attempted to burn down the new city, by promoting Samara to them as a defensive bastion against the Volga Cossacks. He even went as far as to execute a Cossack ataman at the fortress to underline his point. The Nogai nonetheless made two attempts to storm Samara in 1615 and 1622 (the Kalmyks also had a go in 1639) but the legendary 14th century prediction by Metropolitan Alexi that a city built on this spot "would never be taken by anyone" held true.

As the threat of the hordes receded, Samara slowly changed from being a garrison town to a centre of trade. In 1688, Peter the Great granted Samara town status, and throughout the 18th and 19th centuries it continued to flourish. The city benefits from its location on a major transport artery and in the heart of south-eastern Russia's arable heartland. When Russian gained access to the trade routes of the Black Sea towards the end of the 18th century, Samara wheat became a major source of export income for the Russian empire, and by 1900 it was a city of more than 100,000 people. In 1935 the city was renamed Kuybyshev in honour of the revolutionary leader, and from 1941-43 the headquarters of both the Party and government, along with many foreign diplomatic missions, were evacuated here as the German forces closed in on Moscow. After the war, Kuybyshev's origins as a military stronghold returned, and as the centre of the Soviet Union's missile shield, it was closed to foreigners. Yuri Gagarin blasted off on his historic mission from here in 1961.

Three decades on, the city reverted to its original name, and today Samara is a city of over 1.1m people. The principal sectors of the local economy are engineering and metallurgy, and Samara has retained its place as one of the centres of Russia's aeronautical and space industry. Agribusiness is also a major source of income for the city and region, as are the chemical and petrochemical industries, and the automotive sector (AvtoVaz, Russia's largest car maker, is based in Togliatti, less than 100km from Samara). The city's historical centre is well-preserved and includes many examples of 18th and 19th century architecture, not least because the prediction of Metropolitan Alexi held throughout the Second World War.

Samara is served with regular flights by Aeroflot and many of Russia's regional carriers. Flight time to Moscow is around an hour and a half. There is also a daily Lufthansa flight from Frankfurt.

Hotels

Holiday Inn Samara
Alexeya Tolstogo Street 99, Samara 443099
Tel: +7 846 372 70 00
Fax: +7 846 372 70 01
Website: www.ichotelsgroup.com

Renaissance Samara Hotel
Novo-Sadovaya Street 162B, Samara 443011
Tel: +7 846 277 83 40
Fax: +7 846 277 83 50
Website: www.renaissancesamara.ru

Domik v Samare
Zhukovskogo Street 4, Samara 443068
Tel: +7 846 372 80 03
Fax: +7 846 334 86 26
Website: www.domik-v-samare.ru

Hotel Zarech'e
Groznenskaya Street 20, Samara 443004
Tel: +7 846 377 31 80
Fax: +7 846 377 36 76
Website: www.zarechie.com

10

Ufa

The capital of the republic of Bashkortostan in the southern Urals, Ufa is just a few years older than Samara, although evidence of human settlement of the area goes back as far as 5,000 BC. The Bashkirs are an ethnically Turkic people, and their elders clearly had a good view which way the wind was blowing when they approached Ivan the Terrible with a request to become part of Muscovy soon after the fall of the Kazan' khanate in the 16th century. The Bashkirs are still a major ethnic group in Russia today, numbering just over 1.6m people. Ufa itself was founded in 1574, officially gaining town status twelve years later.

Ufa's growth over the decades and centuries has been inexorable, but relatively without incident. The city's location along one of the main routes between European Russia and Siberia soon made it a powerful trade, commercial and administrative centre. From the second half of the 19th century, metal-processing and agriculture became key sources of regional income, and with the arrival of the railway in 1890 the local economy flourished still further. Both sectors remain important to Ufa and Bashkortostan today, but oil is now the major driver of the region's economy. Bashkortostan as a whole is currently Russia's third largest producer of oil.

The city of Ufa today is a major historical and cultural centre of over 1.1m people, and its architecture reflects its diverse Russian and Bashkir heritage. It is also the birthplace of one of Russia's most famous ballet dancers, Rudolph Nureyev.

Ufa airport is served by regular scheduled flights from Moscow (flight time around two hours) and most major regional cities.

Hotels

Hotel Bashkortostan
Lenina Street 25/29, Ufa 450025
Tel: +7 347 279 00 00
Fax: +7 347 279 00 09
Website: www.gkbashkortostan.ru

Hotel Kleopatra
Communisticheskaya St. 53, Ufa 450000
Tel: +7 347 273 41 00
Fax: +7 347 272 84 70
Website: www.kleopatra-ufa.ru

President Hotel
Avrory Street 2, Ufa 450092
Tel: +7 347 279 80 08
Fax: +7 347 254 94 75
Website: http://presidenthotel.ru

Hotel Ufa Astoria
Karl Marx Street 25, Ufa 450077
Tel: +7 347 273 35 51
Fax: +7 347 272 73 87
Website: http://hotel-ufa.ru

Vladivostok

Like Krasnodar, Vladivostok is not a true million-plus city, but is included here by virtue of its economic importance past, present and future. More than six times closer to Tokyo than it is to Moscow, Russia's largest port city on the Pacific seaboard is the country's gateway to east and south east Asia. Should you go there, you will notice almost immediately that most of the cars are not only Japanese, but also right hand drive. Vladivostok has hoovered up second hand cars from its neighbour just across the Sea of Japan ever since the collapse of communism, and, for the lucky few, since well before then.

Vladivostok is only a few decades older, officially at least, than Novosibirsk. It was founded as a naval fortress in 1860 to secure Russia's new eastern territories (its name means "Ruler of the East"), becoming a town two decades later. The Trans Siberian railway reached its eastern terminus in the city in 1903, by which time Vladivostok was home to around 30,000 people. Within twenty years this number had almost trebled as the new capital of the Primorsky Krai flourished as a transport hub, fishing port, centre of trade, and base of the Soviet Union's mighty pacific fleet. Like some of the other cities in this chapter, owing to its strategic importance

10

Vladivostok was a closed city for much of the second half of the last century, opening its doors again only in 1991. The modern city's 600,000 strong population represents many nationalities, with a particularly strong contingent of Korean immigrants (Seoul is just 750km away, Pyongyang is closer still). In July 2005 Russia formally applied to join the East Asia Summit, an annual economic and trade forum held by 16 countries in the region, including China, Japan, India, Australia and Indonesia, prompting alarm in the US at the thought of a powerful new trade bloc forming. Vladivostok today is a prosperous port city, exporting timber, fish, and metals, and importing pharmaceutical products, clothing and consumer goods. The local economy is diverse, with highly developed agriculture, metals and mining, forestry and shipbuilding.

The city is relatively well-preserved, with many of its historical buildings still intact, including the first hotel in the table below. If you cannot spare the week that it takes to get here from Moscow by train, the airport is served by regular flights from Moscow (nine hours), Seoul, Anchorage, Seattle and Bangkok.

10

Hotels

Hotel Versailles
Svetlanskaya Street 10, Vladivostok 69000
Tel: +7 423 226 42 01
Fax: +7 423 226 51 24
Website: http://versailles.da.ru

Hotel Meridian
Ochakovskaya Street 5, Vladivostok 690012
Tel: +7 423 265 04 44
Fax: +7 423 227 41 00
Website: http://meridian-vl.ru

Hotel Gavan
Krygina Street 3, Vladivostok 690065
Tel: +7 423 249 53 63
Fax: +7 423 249 53 64
Website: http://gavan.ru

Hotel Amursky Zaliv
Naberezhnaya Street 9, Vladivostok 690091

Tel: +7 423 246 20 46
Fax: +7 423 246 20 90
Website: http://azimuthotels.ru

Volgograd

Russia's "Southern gateway" was founded in 1589,
although there is unconfirmed evidence of a settlement
here since the middle of the 16th century. The fortress
town was originally called Tsaritsyn, although this
was not in honour of the ruling monarch, rather a
Russification of the Tatar Sary Su, meaning "Yellow
River". The city's importance as a strategic asset has
always placed it at the centre of Russian history,
particularly during periods of conflict. During the Time
of Troubles, Tsaritsyn was seized by the Volga Cossacks,
although they abandoned their plan to march on
Moscow following the death of the first false Dmitry
(see Chapter 1). The city was also a principal centre of
the Stenka Razin rebellion in the second half of the 17th
century, and fell to the Don Cossacks in 1708, although
it was soon recaptured by the government forces. Twenty
years later the entire central part of Tsaritsyn burned to
the ground, with only a very few buildings left standing.
In 1774 the rebel leader Pugachev laid siege to the city
on two separate occasions, but without success.

Tsaritsyn developed rapidly as a centre of trade,
commerce, oil refining and ship building during the
relatively peaceful years of the 19th century. The city
was the scene of heavy fighting during the Civil War,
but this turned out to be a mere prelude to the carnage
unleashed during the Second World War. The battle of
Stalingrad (as the city had been renamed in 1925) is
estimated to have been the single bloodiest battle in
human history. Between August 1942 and February
1943, between 1.7 and 2 million soldiers and civilians
were killed, wounded or captured. The ultimate defeat of
Germany's 6th Army at Stalingrad is seen as one of the
pivotal moments of the war, not least because it denied
Nazi Germany access to the oil fields south east of the
city in the Caucasus and Caspian regions.

The shattered city was entirely rebuilt in the decades
following the war, and was renamed Volgograd in 1961,

10

following Khrushchev's denunciation of Stalin. In 1967 a monument was erected to commemorate the battle of Stalingrad. Named 'The Motherland Calls', at the time it was the tallest sculpture in the world, larger than New York's Statue of Liberty by some measure. Volgograd today is a city of just over 1m inhabitants, and remains a key industrial and transport centre. Major sectors of the local economy include shipbuilding, oil refining, metallurgy and heavy engineering, and the city stands at the eastern end
of the Volga-Don canal, completed in 1951.

Volgograd is served by daily scheduled flights to Moscow, and less frequent services to St Petersburg and Kaliningrad. Scheduled services also operate to the Armenian capital Yerevan and Aktau in Kazakhstan.

Hotels

Hotel Volgograd
Mira Street 12, Volgograd 400131
Tel: +7 844 240 80 30
Fax: +7 844 238 84 28
Website: www.hotelvolgograd.ru/en

Hotel Intourist
Mira Street 14, Volgograd 400131
Tel: +7 844 230 23 02
Fax: +7 844 230 23 00
Website: www.volgograd-intourist.ru

Hotel Yuzhnaya
Raboche-Krestyanskaya 18, Volgograd 400074
Tel: +7 844 290 11 11
Fax: +7 844 297 54 40
Website: www.hotelug.ru

Hotel Stalingrad
Mamaev Kurgan, Volgograd 400000
Tel: +7 844 250 22 25
Fax: +7 844 250 22 25
Website: www.volgograd-hotel.ru

appendix one

A1

appendix one

Russian embassies, consulates and trade representations

UK

Embassy of the Russian Federation in the United Kingdom
7 Kensington Palace Gardens
London W8 4QP
Tel: +44 (0) 20 7229 6412
           +44 (0) 20 7229 7281
Fax: +44 (0) 20 7727 8625
E-mail: office@rusemblon.org
Website: www.great-britain.mid.ru

Consular Division
5 Kensington Palace Gardens
London W8 4QS
Tel: +44 (0) 20 3051 1199
           0845 868 1199 (*From the UK*)
Fax: +44 (0) 20 7229 3215
E-mail: info@rusemblon.org
Website: www.rusemblon.org

Consulate General of the Russian Federation in Edinburgh
58 Melville Street
Edinburgh EH3 7HL
Tel: +44 (0) 131 225 7098
Fax: +44 (0) 131 225 9587
E-mail: visa@edconsul.co.uk

Trade Delegation of the Russian Federation in the United Kingdom
32-33 Highgate West Hill
London N6 6NL
Tel: +44 (0) 20 8340 1907
           +44 (0) 20 8340 4491
           +44 (0) 20 8340 3272
Fax: +44 (0) 20 8348 0112
E-mail: info@rustradeuk.org
Website: www.rustradeuk.org

US

Embassy of the Russian Federation in the United States of America
2650 Wisconsin Avenue NW
Washington DC 20007
Tel: +1 (202) 298 5700/01/04
Fax: +1 (202) 298 5735
Website: www.russianembassy.org

A1

Consular Division
2641 Tunlaw Road, N.W.
Washington DC 20007
Tel.:   +1 (202) 939 8907
Fax: +1 (202) 483 7579

**Consulate General of the Russian Federation
in New York**
9 East 91st Street
New York
NY 10128
Tel: +1 (212) 348 0926
Fax: +1 (212) 831 9162

**Consulate General of the Russian Federation
in San Francisco**
2790 Green Street
San-Francisco
CA 94123
Tel: +1 (415) 928 6878
Fax: +1 (415) 929 0306

Consulate General of the Russian Federation in Seattle
2323 Westin Building
2001 6th Ave.
Seattle WA 98121
Tel: +1 (206) 728 1910
Fax: +1 (206) 728 1871

Consulate General of the Russian Federation in Houston
1333 West Loop South, Ste.1300
Houston
TX 77027
Tel: +1 (713) 337 3300
Fax: +1 (713) 337 3305

**Trade Representation of the Russian Federation
in the United States of America**
2001 Connecticut Avenue NW
Washington DC 20007
Tel: +1 (202) 232 5988
          +1 (202) 234 7170
          +1 (202) 232 0975
Fax: +1 (202) 232 2917
E-mail: rustrade@verizon.net

A1

Trade and Economic Council of the Russian Federation in the USA, New York
400 Madison Ave., Suite 901
New York
NY 10017
Tel: +1 (212) 682 8592
Fax: +1 (212) 682-8605
E-mail: info@russiantradeny.com

Trade and Economic Council of the Russian Federation in the USA, San Francisco
2790 Green Street
San Francisco
CA 94123
Tel: +1 (415) 474 5605
Fax: +1 (415) 682 8605

Canada

Embassy of the Russian Federation in Canada
285 Charlotte Street
Ottawa
Ontario K1N 8L5
Tel: +1 (613) 235 4341
Fax: +1 (613) 236 6342
E-mail: rusemb@rogers.com
Website: www.rusembcanada.mid.ru

Consular Division
52 Range Road
Ottawa
Ontario K1N 8L5
Tel: +1 (613) 236 7220
Fax: +1 (613) 238 6158
E-mail: ruscons@rogers.com

Consulate General of the Russian Federation in Toronto
175 Bloor Street East
South Tower, Suite 801
Toronto
ON M4W 3R8
Tel: +1 (416) 962 9911
Fax: +1 (416) 962 6611
E-mail: rusconsul@bellnet.ca
Website: www.toronto.mid.ru

A.1

Consulate General of the Russian Federation in Montreal
3685 Avenue du Musee
Montreal
Quebec H3G 2E1
Tel: +1 (514) 843 5901
Fax: +1 (514) 842 2012
E-mail: consulat_mtl@bellnet.ca
Website: www.montreal.mid.ru

Trade mission of the Russian Federation in Canada
95 Wurtemburg Street
Ottawa
Ontario K1N 8Z7
Tel: +1 (613) 789 1222
            +1 (613) 789 1066
Fax: +1 (613) 789 2951

Australia

Embassy of the Russian Federation in Australia
78 Canberra Avenue
Griffith
ACT 2603
Tel: +61 (02) 6295 9033
Fax: +61 (02) 6295 1847
E-mail: rusembassy.australia@rambler.ru
Website: www.australia.mid.ru

Consular Division
Tel: +61 (02) 6295 9474
Fax: +61 (02) 6295 1001
E-mail: rusconsul@lightningpl.net.au
Commercial Office
5 Arkana Street
Yarralumla
ACT 2600
Tel: +61 (02) 6281 2716
Fax: +61 (02) 6285 2396

Consulate General of the Russian Federation in Sydney
7-9 Fullerton Street
Woollahra
NSW 2025
Tel: +61 (02) 9326 1188
Fax: +61 (02) 9327-5065
E-mail: ruscon@bigpond.com
Website: www.sydneyrussianconsulate.com

A1

Russian embassies in Europe

Austria

Reisnerstrasse 45-47
1030 Vienna
Tel: +43 1 712 1229
Fax: +43 1 712 3388
E-mail: rusemb@chello.at
           info@rusemb.at
Website: www.austria.mid.ru
           www.rusemb.at

Consular Division

Tel: +43 1 712 3233
Fax: +43 1 714 7612
Email: info@rusemb.at
Website: www.rusemb.at

Belgium

66 Avenue de Fré
1180 Brussels
Tel: +32 2 374 3400
Fax: +32 2 374 2613
E-mail: amrusbel@skynet.be
Website: www.belgium.mid.ru

Consular Division

Tel: +32 2 375 9121
Fax: +32 2 375 9415

Denmark

Kristianiagade 5
2100 Copenhagen
Tel: +45 35 42 5585
Fax: +45 35 42 3741
Email: embrus@mail.dk
Website: www.denmark.mid.ru

Consular Division

Tel: +45 35 38 2370
Fax: +45 35 42 0287
Email: ruscons@mail.dk

France

40-50 Boulevard Lannes
75116 Paris
Tel: +33 1 4504 0550
Fax: +33 1 4504 1765
E-mail: ambrus@wanadoo.fr
Website: www.france.mid.ru

A1

Consular Division
Tel: +33 1 4504 0501
Fax: +33 1 4504 4409
E-mail: conru@wanadoo.fr

Germany
Unter den Linden 63-65
10117 Berlin
Tel: +49 30 229 1110
Fax: +49 30 229 9397
E-mail: info@russische-botschaft.de
Website: www.russische-botschaft.de

Consular Division
Tel: +49 30 226 51184
Fax: +49 30 226 51999
E-mail: infokonsulat@russische-botschaft.de

Greece
28 Nikiforou Litra St.
Pfleo Psikhiko
Athens 15452
Tel: +30 210 672 6130
Fax: +30 210 674 97 08
E-mail: embraf@otenet.gr
Website: www.greece.mid.ru

Consular Division
Tel: +30 210 674 2949
Fax: +30 210 672 5235
E-mail: consafl@athens.compulink.gr

Ireland
184-186 Orwell Road
Rathgar
Dublin 14
Tel: +353 1 492 2048
Fax: +353 1 492 3525
E-mail: russiane@indigo.ie
Website: www.ireland.mid.ru

Consular Division
Tel: +353 1 492 3492
Fax: +353 1 492 6938
E-mail: duconsul@indigo.ie

A1

Italy
Via Gaeta, 5
00185 Rome
Tel: +39 06 494 1680
Fax: +39 06 491 031
E-mail: ambrus@ambrussia.it
Website: www.ambrussia.com

Consular Division
Tel: +39 06 442 34149
Fax: +39 06 442 34031
E-mail: kdrome@libero.it

The Netherlands
Andries Bickerweg 2
2517 JP The Hague
Tel: +31 70 345 1300
Fax: +31 70 361 7960
E-mail: ambrusnl@euronet.nl
Website: www.netherlands.mid.ru

Consular Division
Tel: +31 70 364 6473
Fax: +31 70 365 8634
Email: ambrucon@ambru.nl

Portugal
Rua Visconde de Santarem 59
1000-286 Lisbon
Tel: +351 21 846 2423
Fax: +351 21 846 3008
E-mail: mail@embaixadarussia.pt
Website: www.portugal.mid.ru

Consular Division
Tel: +351 21 846 4476
Fax: +351 21 847 9327
Email: liconsul@mail.ptprime.pt

Spain
C/Velazquez 155
Madrid 28002
Tel: +34 91 562 2264
Fax: +34 91 562 9712
E-mail: embrues@infonegocio.com
Website: www.spain.mid.ru

A1

Consular Division
Tel: +34 91 564 2049
Fax: +34 91 562 7830

Sweden
Gjorwellsgatan 31
11260 Stockholm
Tel: +46 8 130 441
Fax: +46 8 618 2703
Email: rusembassy@telia.com
Website: www.ryssland.se

Consular Division
Tel: +46 8 656 6792
Fax: +46 8 656 4485
E-mail: info.consrust@telia.com
visa.consrust@telia.com

Switzerland
Brunnadernrain 37
3006 Bern
Tel: +41 31 352 0566
Fax: +41 31 352 5595
E-mail: rusbotschaft@bluewin.ch
Website: www.switzerland.mid.ru

Consular Division
Tel.:   +41 31 352 0567
Fax: +41 31 352 6460

Ministries and other government agencies

UK

UK Trade and Investment
Kingsgate House
66-74 Victoria Street
London SW1E 6SW
Tel: +44 (0) 20 7215 8000
Website: www.uktradeinvest.gov.uk

Scottish Development International
Atlantic Quay
150 Broomielaw
Glasgow G2 8LU
Tel: +44 (0) 141 228 2828
Fax: +44 (0) 141 228 2089
Website: www.sdi.co.uk

A1

International Business Wales
Trafalgar House
5 Fitzalan Place
Cardiff CF24 0ED
Tel: +44 (0) 1443 845500
E-mail: ibw@wales.gsi.gov.uk
Website: www.ibwales.com

Invest Northern Ireland
Bedford Square
Bedford Street
Belfast BT2 7ES
Tel: +44 (0) 28 9023 9090
Fax: +44 (0) 28 9043 6536
E-mail: eo@investni.com
Website: www.investni.com

UK Trade Support Agencies in Russia
UKTI Moscow
British Embassy
Smolenskaya Embankment 10
Moscow 121099
Tel: +7 495 956 7200
Fax: +7 495 956 7201
Website: www.ukinrussia.fco.gov.uk

UKTI St Petersburg
British Consulate General
Proletarskoy Diktatury Square 5
St Petersburg 191124
Tel: +7 812 320 3200
Fax: +7 812 320 3222

UKTI Ekaterinburg
British Consulate General
Gogol Street 15a
Ekaterinburg 620075
Tel: +7 343 379 4931
Fax: +7 343 359 2901

US

US and Foreign Commercial Service
International Trade Administration
U.S. Department of Commerce
1401 Constitution Ave., NW
ITC Reagan
Washington DC 20230

A1

Tel: +1 202 482 6220
Fax: +1 202 482 2526
Website: www.buyusa.gov

US Commercial Service offices in Russia

US Commercial Service Moscow
US Embassy Moscow
23/38 Bolshaya Molchanovka
Building 2
Moscow 121069
Tel: +7 495 737 5030
Fax: +7 495 737 5033
E-mail: moscow.office.box@mail.doc.gov
Website: www.buyusa.gov/russia/en

US Commercial Service St Petersburg
US Consulate General
25 Nevsky Prospect
St Petersburg 191186
Tel: +7 812 326 2560
Fax: +7 812 326 2561
E-mail: stpetersburg.office.box@mail.doc.gov

US Commercial Service Ekaterinburg
US Consulate General
15 Gogol Street
Yekaterinburg 626450
Tel: +7 495 737 5030 (Moscow)
Fax: +7 495 737 5033 (Moscow)
E-mail: moscow.office.box@mail.doc.gov

US Commercial Service Vladivostok
US Consulate General
32 Pushkinskaya Street
Vladivostok 690001
Tel: +7 4232 499 381
Fax: +7 4232 300 092
E-mail: vladivostok.office.box@mail.doc.gov

Canada

Foreign Affairs and International Trade Canada
125 Sussex Drive
Ottawa
Ontario K1A 0G2
Tel: +1 613 944 4000
Fax: +1 613 996 9709
Website: www.international.gc.ca

A1

Foreign Affairs and International Trade Canada
Embassy of Canada Moscow
23 Starokonyushenny Pereulok
Moscow 119002
Tel: +7 495 105 6000
Fax: +7 495 105 6004
E-mail: moscow@international.gc.ca
Website: www.russia.gc.ca

Australia

Austrade
Minter Ellison Building, 2nd Floor
25 National Circuit
Forrest ACT 2603
Tel: 13 28 78   (*Australia only*)
E-mail: info@austrade.gov.au
Website: www.austrade.gov.au

Austrade Russia/CIS
Australian Embassy
10A/2 Podkolokolny pereulok
Moscow 109028
Tel: +7 495 232 3257
Fax: +7 495 232 3298
Website: www.austrade.gov.au

The European Union

European Commission Enterprise and Industry DG
Communication and Information Unit/R4
BREY 13/ 092
B - 1049 Brussels
Belgium
Tel: 0800 6 7 8 9 10 11 (*Europe Direct*)
Website: http://ec.europa.eu/enterprise

United Kingdom Permanent Representation to the European Union
10 Avenue d'Auderghem
1040 Brussels
Belgium
Tel: +32 2 287 8211
Website: www.ukrep.be

A1

Credit Guarantees

Export Credit Guarantees Department
PO Box 2200
2 Exchange Tower
Harbour Exchange Square
London E14 9GS
Tel: +44 (0)20 7512 7000
Fax: +44 (0)20 7512 7649
E-mail: help@ecgd.gsi.gov.uk
Website: www.ecgd.gov.uk

Russian Federation Chambers of Commerce and Industry

RFCCI Head Office
Ilyinka Street 6
Moscow 109012
Tel: +7 495 620 0009
Fax: +7 495 620 0360
E-mail: tpprf@tpprf.ru
Website: http://eng.tpprf.ru

Below is a list of the regional chambers covering the cities
described in chapters 8-10 of this guide.

Moscow Chamber of Commerce and Industry
22 Akademika Pilyugina St.
Moscow 117393
Tel: +7 495 132 7510
Fax: +7 495 132 0547
E-mail: mtpp@mtpp.org
Website: www.mostpp.ru/eng

Moscow Region Chamber of Commerce and Industry
8/1 Sretenka St., 5th floor
Moscow 107045
Tel: +7 495 223 4125
Fax: +7 495 223 4125
E-mail: info@tppmo.ru
Website: www.tppmo.ru (*Russian only*)

St Petersburg Chamber of Commerce and Industry
46-48 Chaikovskogo ul.
St Petersburg 191123
Tel: +7 812 719 6644
Fax: +7 812 272 9713

A1

E-mail: spbcci@spbcci.ru
Website: www.spbcci.ru/english

Leningrad Region Chamber of Commerce & Industry
Konnogvardeisky Blvd. 3
St Petersburg 190000
Tel: +7 812 571 12 22
Fax: +7 812 312 31 00
E-mail: international@lotpp.ru
Website: http://english.lotpp.ru

Southern Urals Chamber of Commerce and Industry
(Chelyabinsk and region)
56 Soni Krivoy Street
Chelyabinsk 454000
Tel: +7 351 266 1816
Fax: +7 351 247 9028
E-mail: mail@uralreg.ru
Website: www.uralreg.ru

Urals Chamber of Commerce and Industry (*Ekaterinburg and region*)
6 Vostochnaya St.
Yekaterinburg 620027
Tel: +7 343 353 0449
Fax: +7 343 353 5863
E-mail: ucci@ucci.ur.ru
Website: www.ucci.ur.ru   (*Russian only*)

Chamber of Commerce of the Republic of Tatarstan
(*Kazan' and region*)
18 Pushkin Street
Kazan 420111
Tel: +7 843 264 6207
Fax: +7 843 236 0966
E-mail: tpprt@tpprt.ru
Website: www.tpprt.ru

Krasnodar Chamber of Commerce and Industry
(*Krasnodar and region*)
8 Kommunarov St.
Krasnodar 350063
Tel: +7 861 268 2213
Fax: +7 861 268 2213

A1

E-mail: tppkk@tppkuban.ru
Website: www.tppkuban.ru

Central Siberian Chamber of Commerce and Industry
(*Krasnoyarsk and region*)
6 Kirov Street
Krasnoyarsk 660049
Tel: +7 391 223 9613
Fax: +7 391 223 9683
E-mail: cstp@krasmail.ru
Website: www.cstpp.ru

Chamber of Commerce and Industry of the Nizhny Novgorod Region
1 October Square
Nizhny Novgorod 603005
Tel: +7 831 419 4210
Fax: +7 831 419 4009
E-mail: tpp@tpp.nnov.ru
Website: www.tpp.nnov.ru

Novosibirsk City Chamber of Commerce and Industry
220/10 Krasny Prospekt
Novosibirsk 630049
Tel: +7 383 227 6791
Fax: +7 383 222 50052
E-mail: info@ngtpp.ru
Website: http://eng.ngtpp.ru

Novosibirsk Region Chamber of Commerce and Industry
1 Prospekt Marksa
Novosibirsk 630064
Tel: +7 383 346 4150
Fax: +7 383 346 3047
E-mail: org@ntpp.ru
Website: www.ntpp.ru

Omsk Chamber of Commerce and Industry
51-53 Hertzen St.
Omsk 644007
Tel: +7 381 225 4350
Fax: +7 381 223 4580
E-mail: omtpp@omsknet.ru
Website: www.omsktpp.ru

Perm' Chamber of Commerce and Industry
24B Sovetskaya Street
Perm 614000

A1

Tel: +7 342 212 2811
Fax: +7 342 212 4112
E-mail: permtpp@permtpp.ru
Website: www.permtpp.ru

Rostov Region Chamber of Commerce and Industry
40A Kirovsky Prospekt
Rostov-on-Don 344022
Tel: +7 863 268 7601
Fax: +7 863 268 7601
E-mail: tpp@rostel.ru
Website: www.tppro.ru   (*Russian only*)

Samara Chamber of Commerce and Industry
6 Aleksey Tolstoi Street
Samara 443099
Tel: +7 846 332 1159
Fax: +7 846 332 7662
E-mail: ccisr@transit.samara.ru
Website: www.cci.samara.ru

Chamber of Commerce and Industry of the Republic of Baskortostan (*Ufa and region*)
22 Mira Street
Ufa 450064
Tel: +7 347 279 9797
Fax: +7 347 279 9711
E-mail: office@tpprb.ru
Website: www.tpprb.ru

Chamber of Commerce and Industry of the Primorsk Territory (*Vladivostok and region*)
13A Okeansky Prospekt
Vladivostok 690600
Tel: +7 423 226 9630
Fax: +7 423 222 7226
E-mail: palata@online.vladivostok.ru
Website: www.ptpp.ru

Volgograd Chamber of Commerce and Industry
2 7-Gvardeyskaya Street
Volgograd 400005
Tel: +7 844 224 2262
Fax: +7 844 223 4426
E-mail: cci@volgorgradcci.ru
Website: www.volgogradcci.ru

A1

Business support organisations/International Chambers of Commerce

Russo-British Chamber of Commerce (RBCC)
Head Office
Willcox House
42 Southwark Street
London SE1 1UN
Tel: +44 (0) 20 7403 1706
Fax: +44 (0) 20 7403 1245
E-mail: infolondon@rbcc.com
Website: www.rbcc.com

Moscow Office
Galereya Aktyor Business Centre
Tverskaya Street 16/2
Moscow 125009
Tel: +7 495 961 2160
Fax: +7 495 961 2161
E-mail: infomoscow@rbcc.com

St Petersburg Office
Ovental History Business Centre
Sotsialisticheskaya Street 14
St Petersburg 191119
Tel: +7 812 448 8464
Fax: +7 812 448 8459
E-mail: infospb@rbcc.com

The American Chamber of Commerce in Russia (AmCham)

Moscow Office
Dolgorukovskaya Ul. 7, 14th Floor
Moscow 127006
Tel: +7 (495) 961 2141
Fax: +7 (495) 961 2142
Website: www.amcham.ru

St Petersburg Office
Na Novo-Isaakievskoy Business Centre
Yakubovicha Street 24, 3rd Floor
St Petersburg 190000
E-mail: reception@spb.amcham.ru
Website: www.amcham.ru/spb

A1

The Association of European Business (AEB)

Krasnoproletarskaya Street 16 bld. 3
(4th floor)
Moscow 127473
Tel: +7 (495) 967 9765
Fax: +7 (495) 967 9779
E-mail: info@aebrus.ru
Website: www.aebrus.ru

The Canada Eurasia Russia Business Association (CERBA)

CERBA-Moscow
c/o Ronald A. Chisholm Intl.
Bolshoi Strochenovski, 15a
Moscow 113054
Tel: +7 (495) 937 4760
Fax: +7 (495) 937 4763
Website: www.cerbanet.org

The US-Russia Business Council

1110 Vermont Avenue, NW
Suite 350
Washington, DC 20005
Tel: +1 202 739 9180
Fax: +1 202 659 5920
Website: www.usrbc.org

Moscow Office
Bolshaya Nikitskaya Street 21/18
Building 1, Office 201
Moscow 125009
Tel: +7 (495) 291 2105
Fax: +7 (495) 291 2152

The St Petersburg International Business Association (SPIBA)

36 Shpalernaya Street
St Petersburg 191123
Tel: +7 (812) 325 9091
Fax: +7 (812) 279 9789
Website: www.spiba.ru

A1

Exhibition and conference organisers

Euromoney Conferences
Nestor House, Playhouse Yard
London EC4V 5EX
Tel: +44 (0) 20 7779 8700
Fax: +44 (0) 20 7779 8795
E-mail: conferences@euromoneyplc.com
Website: www.euromoneyconferences.com

Adam Smith Conferences
6th Floor, 29 Bressenden Place
London SW1E 5DR
Tel: +44 (0) 20 7490 3774
Fax: +44 (0) 20 7505 0079
E-mail: info@adamsmithconferences.com
Website: www.adamsmithconferences.com

Marcus Evans
11 Connaught Place
London W2 2ET
Tel: +44 (0) 20 3002 3002
Fax: +44 (0) 20 3002 3003
Website: www.marcusevans.com

ITE Group
105 Salusbury Road
London NW6 6RG
Tel: +44 (0) 20 7596 5000
Fax: +44 (0) 20 7596 5111
E-mail: enquiry@ite-exhibitions.com
Website: www.ite-exhibitions.com

C5
Albert House, First Floor, 1-4 Singer Street
London EC2A 4BQ
Tel: +44 (0) 20 7878 6886
E-mail: enquiries@c5-online.com
Website: www.c5-online.com

Restec Exhibition Company
12 Petrozavodskaya Street
St Petersburg 197110
Tel: +7 812 320 6363
Fax: +7 812 320 8090
E-mail: main@restec.ru
Website: www.restec.ru

A1

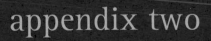

appendix two

A2

appendix two

Russian Language

Russian belongs to the East Slavonic group of languages, together with Ukrainian and Belarusian (or Belorussian). It has a reputation for being a difficult language to learn, chiefly due to its use of the Cyrillic alphabet and an extensive case system for nouns and adjectives. The verbs conjugate as well, something which can come as a shock if you were never "lucky" enough to study Latin at school. Also unnerving at first is the absence of definite and indefinite articles ("the" and "a/an" in English), and the almost total lack of the verb "to be" in the present tense. If you want to know where the station is, in Russian the phrase is literally "Where station?".

Pronunciation in Russian should hold few surprises to speakers of either English or most European languages, although the language's range of "hush" sybillants (sh, sch, shch) is wider than most. There is one particular vowel sound, "ы", normally transliterated as a "y", which you will struggle to find in any other language – probably the closest way it can be expressed in words is as a normal short "i"(as in "kitchen"), but pronounce it with your tongue towards the back of your mouth, rather than the front. The Russian alphabet also includes two qualifying symbols, a soft sign "ь" and rarely seen hard sign "ъ" which both affect the pronunciation of the consonant which immediately precedes them. You will not see the hard sign in the samples below, but where there is a soft sign it will be expressed as an apostrophe in line with convention.

Stress is important in Russian, something made more annoying by the fact that it can move about on the same word depending on its form (case, number, person). In the examples below, the stressed syllable is shown in bold. Whether a syllable is stressed or not affects both the sound of the vowel and the meaning of the word, so keep it in mind. Also bear in mind that, in common with some other languages, such as French and German, Russian uses the plural second person "you" form in formal conversation or to convey respect.

If you want to learn Russian properly – by all means go for it. It is a beautiful, melodic and expressive language. Bear in mind, however, that it will require both commitment and time, the latter of which you may not have if you are in business. I suggest that you at least try

A2

to master the alphabet – it looks a bit strange at first, but believe me you will become accustomed to it more quickly that you expect. Above all, try to use at least some of the words and phrases below – Russians are very generous and encouraging with anyone attempting the language, and a few choice phrases will always go down well. Try and remember at all times that Russian is a soft sounding language, whatever may be your preconceptions of it. Keep the consonants gentle and un-aspirated and the rest of it will follow.

The Cyrillic alphabet

Cyrillic is a synthesis of Latin and Greek character-sets, with a few more thrown in to express particular sounds. Apart from Russian, Cyrillic is used in a number of other Slavonic (eg. Ukrainian, Bulgarian, Serbo-Croat) and non-Slavonic (eg. Kazakh, Uzbek, Mongolian) languages. Below is a pronunciation guide – all vowel-sounds are for the vowel in stressed positions. Some of the pronunciation examples may look strange, but they are the closest available to the actual sounds in Russian.

A2

Letter	Transliteration	Pronunciation
а	a	cut
б	b	big
в	v	very
г	g	golf
д	d	dog
е	ye	yet
ё	yo	yonder
ж	zh	montage
з	z	zoo
и	i	sheep
й	y	young
к	k	cable
л	l	love
м	m	mast
н	n	number
о	o	short
п	p	pull

р	r	roll
с	s	small
т	t	tower
у	u	boot
ф	f	foot
х	kh	archive
ц	ts	mints
ч	ch	cheese
ш	sh	shuffle
щ	shch	horse-chestnut
ъ	–	–
ы	y	green (see above)
ь	–	–
э	e	tent
ю	yu	future
я	ya	young

Basics

Yes	Da
No	Nyet
Hello	Zdravstvuytye
Goodbye	Do svidanya
Please	Pozhaluysta
Thank you	Spasibo
Thank you very much	Spasibo bol'shoye
Good morning	Dobroye utro
Good afternoon	Dobry dyen'
Good evening	Dobry vyechyer
Good night	Spokoynoy nochi

A2

Making conversation

My name is Chris	Menya zovut Chris
What is your name?	Kak vas zovut?
Nice to meet you	Ochen' priyatno
How are you?	Kak dela?
Fine, thanks	Normal'no, spasibo
Very well, thanks	Ochen' khorosho, spasibo

Do you speak English?	Vy govoritye po angliyski?
I don't speak Russian	Ya ne govoryu po **russki**
I speak a little Russian	Ya nemnozhko govor**yu** po **russki**
This is my first time in Russia	Eto moy **pyer**vy raz v Rossii
I am from the United Kingdom	Ya iz **V**yelikobritanii
I am from the United States	Ya iz Soyedinyonnykh Sh**tat**ov
I am from Australia	Ya iz Avstralii
I am from Canada	Ya iz Ka**na**dy
I am from Germany	Ya iz **G**ermanii
I am from France	Ya iz **F**rantsii
Excuse me	Izvinitye
After you	Pro**shu** vas
That's alright	**Nye** za chto

Numbers

One	Odin
Two	Dva
Three	Tri
Four	Che**tyr**ye
Five	Pyat'
Six	Shest'
Seven	Syem'
Eight	**V**osem'
Nine	**D**yevyat'
Ten	**D**yesyat'
Eleven	Odinnadtsat'
Twelve	Dvye**na**dtsat'
Thirteen	Trinadtsat'
Fourteen	Che**tyr**nadtsat'
Fifteen	Pyat**na**dtsat'
Sixteen	Shest**na**dtsat'
Seventeen	Syem**na**dtsat'
Eighteen	Vosyem**na**dtsat'
Nineteen	Devyat**na**dtsat'

A2

Twenty	Dvadtsat'
Thirty	Tridtsat'
Forty	Sorok
Fifty	Pyatdyesyat
Sixty	Shest'dyesyat
Seventy	Syem'dyesyat
Eighty	Vosyem'dyesyat
Ninety	Dyevyanosto
Hundred	Sto
Two hundred	Dvyesti
Three hundred	Trista
Four hundred	Chetyresta
Five hundred	Pyat'sot
Six hundred	Shest'sot
Seven hundred	Syem'sot
Eight hundred	Vosyem'sot
Nine hundred	Dyevyat'sot
Thousand	Tysyacha
Million	Million
Billion	Milliard
Once	(Odin) raz
Twice	Dva raza
Five times	Pyat' raz
First	Pyervy
Second	Vtoroy
Third	Tryetiy
Last	Poslyedniy

Questions

Why...?	Pochemu...?
How...?	Kak...?
How much/many...?	Skol'ko...?
Can...?	Mozhno...?

Time

When...?	Kogda...?
Now	Seychas
Then	Togda

A2

Soon	Skoro
Sometime	Kogda-to
Anytime	Kogda-nibud'
Always	Vsegda
Never	Nikogda
Today	Syevodnya
Yesterday	Vchera
Tomorrow	Zavtra
Day	Dyen'
Hour	Chas
Minute	Minuta
Second	Syekunda
What time is it?	Skol'ko vryemyeni?
It is two o'clock	Dva chasa
It is half past two	Poltryet'evo
It is ten to three	Byez desyati tri

Days

What day is it?	Syevodnya kakoy dyen'?
Monday	Ponyedyel'nik
Tuesday	Vtornik
Wednesday	Sryeda
Thursday	Chetvyerg
Friday	Pyatnitsa
Saturday	Subbota
Sunday	Voskryesyen'ye

Place

Where...?	Gdye...?
Here	Zdyes'
There	Tam
Somewhere	Gdye-to
Anywhere	Gdye-nibud'
Everywhere	Vezdye
Nowhere	Nigdye
Near	Blizko
Far	Daleko
(To the) right	(Na-)pravo
(To the) left	(Na-)lyevo

A2

Entrance	Vkhod
Exit	Vykhod

Useful places

Shop	Magazin
Station	Vokzal
Airport	Aeroport
Hotel	Gostinitsa
Museum	Muzyey
Office	Ofis
Restaurant	Restoran
Hospital	Bol'nitsa
Post Office	Pochtamt
Chemist	Aptyeka
Police	Militsiya

Common adjectives

Large	Bol'shoy
Small	Malenkiy
Wide	Shirokiy
Narrow	Uzkiy
Long	Dlinny
Short	Korotkiy
High	Vysokiy
Low	Nizkiy
Fast	Bystry
Slow	Myedlyenny

Instructions

Look	Smotritye
Give me	Daytye
Take this	Voz'mitye
Come here	Iditye syuda
Go away	Ukhoditye
Hurry up	Bystryeye
Stop	Stop

A2

Useful phrases

How much to get to the centre?	Do tsentra skol'ko?
Where is the station?	Gdye vokzal?
Where is the check-in desk?	Gdye registratsiya?
I have a reservation	U menya bron'
Do you have a room?	U vas nomer yest'?
I need the room for two days	Mnye nuzhen nomer na dvye nochi
Do you have a quieter room?	U vas yest' nomer po-tishche?
Where can I change money?	Gdye mozhno dyen'gi pomyenyat'?
Do you have a menu in English?	U vas yest' myenyu na angliyskom?
Can I have the bill?	Mozhno schyot pozhaluysta
Do you have Wi-Fi here?	U vas yest' Wi-Fi zdyes'?
Where can I charge my phone?	Gdye mozhno telefon zaryadit'?

A2